A Special Issue of
The Quarterly Journal of
Experimental Psychology: Section A
Human Experimental Psychology

Cognitive Gerontology:
Cognitive Change in Old Age

Edited by

Patrick Rabbitt
University of Oxford, UK

Ψ **Psychology Press**
Taylor & Francis Group

HOVE AND NEW YORK

Published in 2005 by Psychology Press Ltd
27 Church Road, Hove, East Sussex, BN3 2FA

www.psypress.co.uk

Simultaneously published in the USA and Canada
by Psychology Press
270 Madison Avenue, New York, NY 10016

Psychology Press is a part of the Taylor & Francis Group

British Library Cataloguing in Publication Data
A catalogue record for this book is available from the British Library

ISBN   1–84169–981–0
ISSN   0272–4987

This publication has been produced with paper manufactured to strict
environmental standards and with pulp derived from sustainable forests.

Cover design by Hybert Design, Waltham St Lawrence, Berkshire, UK
Typeset by Techset Composition Limited, Salisbury, Wiltshire, UK
Printed by Hobbs The Printer, Totton, Hampshire, UK
Bound by TJ International, Padstow, Cornwall, UK

Contents*

*This book is also a special issue of *The Quarterly Journal of Experimental Psychology:
Section A: Human Experimental Psychology*, and forms issue 1 of Volume 58A (2005).

THE QUARTERLY JOURNAL OF EXPERIMENTAL PSYCHOLOGY
2005, 58A (1), 1–4

Ψ Psychology Press
Taylor & Francis Group

Introduction

Patrick M. A. Rabbitt

Department of Experimental Psychology, University of Oxford, UK

A striking weakness of models in contemporary experimental cognitive psychology is that they only describe functional systems that cannot occur in nature because they do not alter with practice, or during childhood development and age-related decline, and are identical in all individuals. Cognitive gerontologists are deprived of such convenient fictions because their hope is to explain how we gradually become less competent at things that we once did extraordinarily well. They encounter another quite different, and salutary, difficulty that calendar time, the dimension in terms of which old and young people are conventionally differentiated, only indicates the maximum period within which an enormous range of disparate changes can have occurred. These changes certainly include poorly understood processes of "normal" or "usual" ageing, but also the cumulative effects of pathologies and biological life events that, to varying degrees, affect our brains so also our cognition. Thus we cannot assume that differences in calendar years are reliable indices of the relative amounts of change that people have experienced, nor that all individuals change at the same rates over time, nor, indeed, that they all experience the same sequences or patterns of changes. Anstey's impressive body of previous work, and, most explicitly, the results of the massive study that Anstey and colleagues report in this issue, illustrate that it is nevertheless possible to evaluate markers of age-related changes in global physiology as indices of neurophysiological integrity and, consequently, also of cognitive efficiency in later life.

Anstey, Dear, Christensen, and Jorm's results, and those of many other investigators such as Baltes and Lindenberger (1994; Lindenberger & Baltes, 1997), illustrate that age-related changes in sensory acuity not only entail obvious losses of peripheral functions; they can also be strong markers for central changes in the brain that affect cognitive processes.

Relationships between sensory acuity and cognition are more complex still. McCoy, Tun, Cox, Colangelo, Stewart, and Wingfield extend earlier findings by Murphy, Craik, Li, and Schneider (2000), Rabbitt (1968, 1991), and Dickenson and Rabbitt (1991) to show that age-related sensory degradation of auditory and visual input imposes extra demands on language processing and consumes resources that might otherwise be used to improve comprehension and memory for what is heard or read. All losses in working-memory efficiency, whether imposed by the increased demands of decoding degraded language or by age-related attenuation of central resources, can affect the management of language in everyday life.

Correspondence should be addressed to Patrick M. A. Rabbitt, University of Oxford, Department of Experimental Psychology, South Parks Road, Oxford OX1 3UD, UK. Email: rabbitt@psy.man.ac.uk

http://www.tandf.co.uk/journals/pp/02724987.html   DOI:10.1080/0272498044300421

Haarman, Ashling, Davelaar, and Usher elegantly show how reduced cognitive resources affect the ability of older people to maintain and use context.

It is noteworthy that Haarman and colleagues interpret age-related changes in the cognitive behaviour of older people in terms of current models of working memory that were originally developed to explore how changes in task demands affect the efficiency of young adults. If taken only at this level of description, Rendell, Castel, and Craik's paper is a useful addition to demonstrations that older people experience relatively more difficulty than do the young at remembering proper names. It might then be misread as yet another example of a general rule that anything that is difficult in youth becomes even harder in old age. Other papers in this issue also run the same risk of incomplete interpretation. For example, Whiting, Madden, Pierce, and Allen's demonstration of declines in efficiency of top-down guidance of visual search might be caricatured in this way. We shall see further on that this would miss its actual theoretical importance.

The use in age comparisons of paradigms originally developed to study the effects of changing task demands on the performance of young adults can be defended on many grounds. In practical terms this can reveal some of the particular difficulties that older people encounter in managing their everyday lives. In theoretical terms such comparisons often provide useful insights into the limitations of the models that these paradigms have been developed to test. However such endeavours can disable theory when they result in descriptions of the elderly as less able, slower, or more error-prone younger adults.

An illustration of how this may happen comes from widely replicated findings that most or all of the age-associated variance in competence on many cognitive tasks can be accounted for if individual differences in information processing speed (Salthouse, 1985, 1991, 1996) or in intelligence test scores (Rabbitt & Anderson, in press) are also taken into account. The resulting tacit assumption that, for most practical purposes, older adults can be regarded simply as slower and less efficient certainly provides a powerful and reliable rule of thumb for applied psychologists and human engineers, but it is also a powerful and reliable intellectual irritation to all who hope for a better understanding of how ageing of the brain brings about changes in cognition.

The discovery of strong relationships between age, speed, and general fluid mental ability (gf) does not invalidate more detailed explorations of age differences on tasks. For example, we still have to explain just how global slowing, or declines in gf, actually affect performance in particular situations. An excellent illustration is Ward and Maylor's demonstration that older people make more errors in immediate recall largely because their slower information-processing rates reduce their maximum rehearsal speeds. However, these strong relationships have encouraged the much more radical view that all mental abilities must decline at similar rates because they are all driven by declines in some single "master" performance characteristic such as speed or gf. This has, aptly, been described by Perfect and Maylor (2000) as "the dull hypothesis" of cognitive ageing. We need to preserve a vigilant agnosticism as to whether individual differences associated with the passage of calendar years, or with levels of biological markers of global physiological efficiency, are functionally indistinguishable from those associated with individual differences in overall cognitive competence.

There are at least two good reasons for this, sometimes uncomfortable, posture. First, older people have had a great deal of time to discover the most effective ways of dealing with the demands that their lives make of them. They are not just less able or slower than young persons but also much better educated in techniques of life management and knowledge of the world. The successful maintenance of this "crystallized intelligence" into old age provides seniors with useful cognitive toolkits of techniques for handling information and of knowledge of the world (Horn, 1982, 1987). We have noted that a striking limitation of mainstream cognitive psychology has been neglect of the point that prolonged practice does not simply improve the speed and accuracy with which people can carry out particular sequences of operations to reach a particular end. It also allows development of new and more efficient ways of achieving the same ends, and even discovery of new and more rewarding attainable end-states. Kim and Hasher's paper neatly illustrates how increasing age can alter the technique as well as the efficiency of problem solving. How well older people can do things depends on their levels of speed or intellectual power but also, and perhaps equally, on their discoveries of efficient ways to do them.

A second, and more radical way to bypass the "dull hypothesis" is to analyse tasks in sufficient detail to test whether advancing age affects some functional systems, and so putatively some brain systems, earlier and more severely than others. Many anatomical and neurophysiological studies concur that age-related degenerative changes occur earlier in frontal and prefrontal cortex than in other parts of the brain. This evidence has encouraged search for behavioural indices that may reveal correspondingly local and circumscribed cognitive changes. Comparisons on tasks that have been regarded as especially sensitive diagnostic indices of failures of frontal and executive function have been discouraging for this aspiration. For example, meta-analyses of published age-related declines in performance on the Stroop test and on tasks putatively diagnostic of frontal and executive changes, variance between age-groups can be completely accounted for by global changes in speed (Verhaeghen & Cerella, 2002; Verhaeghen & De-Meersman, 1998a, 1998b). Specific comparisons have found that age differences on the Stroop and on other purportedly frontal tasks can be accounted for by differences in gf (Lowe, 1998). In this context of null and dull results it is refreshing to have Whiting, Madden, Pierce, and Allen's new study. This suggests specific and robust deficits in top-down, or executively managed, visual search. An equally encouraging study is Verhaeghen and Basak's excellent new contribution to our understanding of task switching. They show how the models developed in mainstream cognitive psychology by Nelson Cowan and others can not only be applied, but adapted and extended to show that age-related differences in selective attention cannot entirely be explained in terms of declines in information processing speed. Such excellent work may, at last, move us beyond the dull hypothesis to much more interesting and well-articulated scenarios of description for cognitive changes in old age.

REFERENCES

Baltes, P. B., & Lindenberger, U. (1997). Emergence of a powerful connection between sensory and cognitive functions across the lifespan: A new window to the study of cognitive aging? *Psychology and Aging, 12,* 12–21.

Dickenson, C. M., & Rabbitt, P. M. A. (1991). Simulated visual impairment: Effects on text comprehension and reading speed. *Clinical Vision Sciences, 6,* 301–308.

Horn, J. (1982). The theory of fluid and crystallised intelligence in relation to concepts of cognitive psychology and aging in adulthood. In F. I. M. Craik & S. Trehub (Eds.), *Aging and cognitive processes* (pp. 237–278). New York: Plenum Press.

Horn, J. L. (1987). A context for understanding information processing studies of human abilities. In P. A. Vernon (Ed.), *Speed of information processing and intelligence* (pp. 201–238) Norwood, NJ: Ablex.

Lindenberger, U., & Baltes, P. (1994). Sensory functioning and intelligence in old age: A strong connection. *Psychology and Aging, 9*, 339–355.

Lowe, C. (1998). Cognitive models of aging and frontal lobe deficits. In P. M. A. Rabbitt (Ed.), *Methodology of frontal and executive function*. Hove, UK: Psychology Press.

Murphy, D. R., Craik, F. I. M., Li, K. Z., & Schneider, B. A. (2000). Comparing the effects of aging and background noise on short-term memory performance. *Psychology and Aging, 15*, 323–334.

Perfect, T. J., & Maylor, E. A. (2000). Rejecting the dull hypothesis: The relation between method and theory in cognitive aging research. In T. J. Perfect & E. A. Maylor (Eds.), *Models of cognitive aging*. Oxford, UK: Oxford University Press.

Rabbitt, P. M. A. (1968). Channel capacity, intelligibility and immediate memory. *Quarterly Journal of Experimental Psychology, 20*, 241–248.

Rabbitt, P. M. A. (1991). Mild hearing loss can cause apparent memory failures which increase with age and reduce with IQ. *Acta Otolaryngologica, Supplimentum, 476*, 167–176.

Rabbitt, P. M. A., & Anderson, M. (in press). The lacunae of loss? Aging and the differentiation of human abilities. In E. Bialystok & F. I. M. Craik (Eds.), *Lifespan cognition: Mechanisms of change*. New York: Oxford University Press.

Salthouse, T. A. (1985). *A theory of cognitive aging*. Amsterdam: Elsevier.

Salthouse, T. A. (1991). *Theoretical perspectives in cognitive aging*. Hillsdale, NJ: Lawrence Erlbaum Associates, Inc.

Salthouse, T. A. (1996). The processing speed theory of adult age differences in cognition. *Psychological Review, 103*, 403–428.

Verhaeghen, P., & Cerella, J. (2002). Aging, executive control and attention: A review of meta-analyses. *Neuroscience and Behavioural Reviews, 26*, 849–857.

Verhaeghen, P., & De-Meersman, L. (1998a). Aging and the Stroop-effect: A meta-analysis. *Psychology and Aging, 13*, 120–126.

Verhaeghen, P., & De-Meersman, L. (1998b). Aging and negative priming: A meta-analysis. *Psychology and Aging, 13*, 435–444.

THE QUARTERLY JOURNAL OF EXPERIMENTAL PSYCHOLOGY
2005, 58A (1), 5–21

Ψ Psychology Press
Taylor & Francis Group

Biomarkers, health, lifestyle, and demographic variables as correlates of reaction time performance in early, middle, and late adulthood

Kaarin J. Anstey, Keith Dear, Helen Christensen, and Anthony F. Jorm

Australian National University, Canberra, Australia

We aimed to identify demographic, health, and biomarker correlates of reaction time perfor-mance and to determine whether biomarkers explained age differences in reaction time perfor-mance. The sample comprised three representative cohorts aged 20–24, 40–44, and 60–64 years, including a total of 7,485 participants. Reaction time measures of intraindividual variability and latency were used. The measure of intraindividual variability used was independent of mean reaction time. Older adults were more variable than younger adults in choice reaction time per-formance but not simple reaction time performance. The most important correlates of reaction time performance after gender and education were biological markers such as forced expiratory volume at one second, grip strength, and vision. Few measures of physical or mental health or lifestyle were associated with poorer performance on reaction time measures. Biomarkers explained the majority of age-related variance in simple reaction time and a large proportion of variance in choice reaction time. We conclude that for the ages studied, biomarkers are more important than health factors for explaining age differences in reaction time performance.

Two of the key findings in cognitive ageing research are observed in reaction time (RT) tasks. These are the ubiquitous slowing of behaviour in old age (Birren, 1965; Salthouse, 1996) and the increasing variability in performance (Anstey, 1999; Christensen et al., 1994; Hultsch, MacDonald, & Dixon, 2002; Morse, 1993; Rabbitt, Osman, Moore, & Stollery, 2001). Although cognitive slowing has been proposed as the factor underlying more general cognitive decline in old age (Salthouse, 1996), age-related increase in variability has been noted in the literature for some time (Christensen et al., 1994, 1999; Morse, 1993). However, there has recently been a renewed emphasis on variability in test performance as a means of

Correspondence should be addressed to Kaarin Anstey, Centre for Mental Health Research, Australian National University, Canberra, ACT, 0200, Australia. Email: kaarin.anstey@anu.edu.au

This research was funded by a NHMRC Program Grant to the Centre for Mental Health Research. We grate-fully acknowledge the men and women who participated in this study, Ruth Parslow, Patricia Jacomb, Ms Karen Maxwell, and PATH interviewers for their assistance.

http://www.tandf.co.uk/journals/pp/02724987.html   DOI:10.1080/02724980443000232

investigating the neural basis of cognitive decline (Hultsch & MacDonald, 2004; Hultsch et al., 2002; Li, Aggen, Nesselroade, & Baltes, 2001; Rabbitt et al., 2001). Hultsch in particular has recently proposed that variability in performance may provide a window to view cognitive change and frame key research questions in this field. This proposal follows studies showing that patient groups with neurological conditions show increased variability in performance on reaction time tasks (Hultsch, MacDonald, Hunter, Levey-Bencheton, & Strauss, 2000) and studies showing that interindividual variability is strongly related to intraindividual variability both within and between occasions (Rabbitt et al., 2001).

There are several types of variability identified in the literature but the main subtypes involve either interindividual differences or intraindividual differences in cognitive test performance. Research by Rabbitt et al. (2001) and Hultsch et al. (2002) suggests that intraindividual differences in RT are fundamental to explaining between group differences in RT and other aspects of cognitive performance. Of particular importance are within-occasion intraindividual differences that have been described as "inconsistency" measures by Hultsch et al. (2001). It is assumed that inconsistency is a function of neurological integrity (Hultsch & McDonald, 2004; Li & Lindenberger, 1999). Other authors have argued that increased variability in RT performance is due to lapses of attention caused by frontal lobe deficits (Theodore & Mirsky, 1999). Li and Lindenberger propose that deterioration in neurotransmitter systems may be at the heart of cognitive ageing and increased variability in performance. For example, in Parkinson's disease, slowing of RT (not movement time) has been observed after administration of levodopa (Mueller, Benz, & Boernke, 2001). If this were the case, we would expect that correlates of consistency would more probably be direct indicators of neurological efficiency or impairment.

Most psychological research on RT has been conducted on convenience samples within strictly controlled experimental designs, or on clinical samples. Experimental studies have the advantage of permitting longer testing sessions with manipulation of test parameters (e.g., Rabbitt & Banerji, 1989). Clinical studies allow for the neuropsychological import of experimentally derived effects to be evaluated between patient samples and controls (e.g., Hultsch et al., 2000). Population-based research has yet another contribution to make to this field. With the advantage of large sample sizes and the collection of data on a range of health, lifestyle, and functional variables, population-based studies allow for the examination of effect sizes at the population level and for the identification of individual differences variables associated with cognitive phenomena. In ageing, individual differences in physical function and health become increasingly important for explaining age differences in cognitive test performance (e.g., Luszcz, Bryan, & Kent, 1997). Therefore, a substantial body of cognitive ageing research involves taking cognitive phenomena established in the laboratory into larger studies where they can be examined in the context of health, physical function, and demographic factors (e.g., Bryan & Luszcz, 2000; Christensen et al., 2000).

Although population-based studies and large community-based volunteer studies are less tightly controlled than experiments (testing is usually conducted in participants' homes, and testing batteries cover a wide range of material), they provide the opportunity to evaluate a unique and important set of questions relating to cognitive ageing that are not available with smaller scale studies. They also have the potential to link cognitive phenomena that have been well described in an experimental setting with genetic indicators and observations based on neuroimaging such as cortical atrophy or white matter changes (e.g., Deary et al., 2003). In the field of cognitive ageing, the cross-fertilization of ideas between experimental cognitive psychology and population-based studies has led to several important theoretical advances. For example, the reporting of the association between sensorimotor and cognitive function in community samples has led to further experimental work on vision, hearing, and cognition (e.g., Lindenberger, Sherer, & Baltes, 2001) suggesting some common factors may underlie a proportion of sensory and cognitive ageing. Hybrid individual differences and experimental designs have also become a feature of much cognitive ageing work (e.g., Bryan & Luszcz, 2000; Salthouse, 1994).

To date few studies have evaluated the association of variables used as biomarkers of ageing (e.g., vision, hearing, grip strength, and lung function) and health and other contextual variables with reaction time performance. Likewise few studies have focused on relating RT performance to contextual factors in young and middle-aged adults. The studies that have linked biomarkers and health with reaction time have been restricted to samples of older adults. For example, Anstey (1999) showed that biomarkers of ageing explained all the chronological age-related variance in both visual and auditory reaction time tasks in women aged 60 to 90 years, and Christensen et al. (2000) report the lack of relationship of reaction time to change in memory performance in a longitudinal study of 425 very old adults. The only population-based study of RT in middle-aged adults obtains population-based estimates of reaction time but does not link RT data to health and biological variables (Deary, Der, & Ford, 2001).

Rationale for the present study

The specific aim of the present study was to identify the effects of demographic variables, biomarkers, and health and lifestyle factors on RT test performance in young, middle, and older aged adults. We also sought to determine whether there were age differences in the importance of these effects. The approach taken in the present study therefore follows from a tradition in cognitive ageing, where questions developed in experimental psychology laboratories are taken up in the context of large epidemiological studies. Previous research has shown that biological markers of ageing, such as forced expiratory volume, grip strength, and vision, explain virtually all age-related variance in cognitive test performance and often additional variance (Anstey, 1999; Christensen, Mackinnon, Korten, & Jorm, 2001). Biomarkers have also emerged as the most important set of variables when compared with physical and mental health, personality, and education within samples of older adults (Anstey & Smith, 1999). Therefore, the present study also sought to determine whether biomarkers as a group were the most important set of variables for explaining differences in RT performance between cohorts aged 20–24, 40–44 and 60–64 years.

In the present study covariates of RT performance were drawn from domains measuring demographics, biological age, physical health, and mental health. Education was included in all analyses as a control variable because of the well-documented association between education and cognitive test performance (Anstey & Christensen, 2000). Gender was also included as a demographic variable because of gender differences observed in cognitive test performance in the sample used for this study (Jorm, Anstey, Christensen, & Rodgers, 2004) and gender differences observed in RT and cognitive test performance performance (Deary et al., 2001; Rabbitt, Donlan, Watson, McInnes, & Bent, 1995). Medical conditions (heart disease, epilepsy, stroke, asthma, and head injury) that potentially affect neuropsychological test performance and biological markers (grip, forced expiratory volume at one second, vision, and systolic blood pressure) that have been shown to correlate with cognitive performance and RT were included (Anstey, 1999; Anstey, Lord, & Williams, 1997; Anstey & Smith, 1999; Christensen et al., 2001). Lifestyle and mental health variables (smoking, alcohol, physical activity, depression, anxiety) were included because there is evidence of associations of these factors with cognitive test performance in previous studies (Anstey & Christensen, 2000; Dustman, Emmerson, & Shearer, 1994; Hill, 1989; Luszcz et al., 1997; Parsons & Nixon, 1998; Rabbitt et al., 1995). These last variables also provide a base for comparison with the physical health and biomarker variables in terms of strength of association with RT measures.

On the basis of previous research (e.g., Anstey & Smith, 1999; Christensen et al., 2000) we hypothesized that biomarkers would be most strongly associated with variability and slowing, followed by diseases known to affect neurological function, and that measures of mental health will have the weakest associations with RT performance. One reason that biomarkers do correlate with cognitive performance is that they reflect not only individual differences in neurological integrity but also the impact of disease. For example, a disease such as diabetes, or neurological insult such as a stroke, may affect vision, muscle strength, and sensation. A battery of sensorimotor tests may measure the impact of the disease on function, and this may be more sensitive to the effects of disease than a simple questionnaire measure of medical conditions. In this sense biomarkers may operationalize the effects of ageing, disease, and insult to the brain (Anstey, Lord, & Smith, 1996).

Measure of intraindividual variability

Given the recent theoretical importance of intraindividual variability for explaining cognitive ageing and cognitive impairment (Martin & Hofer, 2004; Nesselroade, 2004), an aim of the present study was to evaluate whether there were specific correlates of intraindividual variability at the population level. One feature of some commonly used available measures of intraindividual variability in RT, such as the standard deviation and the coefficient of variation, is that they correlate with mean RT. This means that the unique contribution of intraindividual variability to cognitive ageing cannot be estimated and that associations between measures of intraindividual variability and other predictors may in fact be confounded by associations with mean RT. Concern about the problem of intraindividual variability measures being confounded by mean performance led to the development of a measure of intraindividual variability that was independent of the mean RT (see also Christensen et al., 2004).

Method

The sample came from the PATH Through Life Project, a large community survey concerned with the health and well being of people aged 20 to 24, 40 to 44, and 60 to 64 years who live in Canberra or the neighbouring town of Queanbeyan. Each cohort is to be followed up every 4 years over a total period of 20 years. Results presented here concern the first-wave interviews with 20- to 24-year-olds, which were conducted in 1999 and early 2000, with 40- to 44-year-olds, which were conducted in 2000 or early 2001, and with 60- to 64-year-olds, conducted in 2001 and early 2002. Participants had to be in their respective age group on the 1st January 1999 (for 20- to 24-year-olds), 2000 (for 40- to 44-year-olds), or 2001 (for 60- to 64-year-olds). The sampling frames were the electoral rolls for Canberra and

Queanbeyan, Australia. Registration on the electoral roll is compulsory for Australian citizens. Because the Australian Electoral Commission would only release decade age ranges for research purposes, we wrote to 12,414 persons recorded as aged 20–29 years on the electoral roll and asked for participation of those aged 20 to 24 years. Out of these, 5,058 were found to be out of the required age range, 1,061 were known to have moved out of the area, 2,190 could not be found, 1,701 refused or had poor English language skills, and 2,404 were interviewed. The participation rate of those who were found and who were in the required age range was 58.6%. Similarly, for the 40- to 44-year-olds, 9,033 persons were sent letters, 4,222 were out of the required age range, 280 had moved, 612 could not be found, 1,389 refused or had poor English, and 2,530 were interviewed (64.6% of those found and in age range). For the 60- to 64-year-olds, there was a change to the law allowing the Australian Electoral Commission to release more specific age group information. Letters were sent to 4,832 persons, 34 were out of the required age range, 182 had moved, 28 were dead, 209 could not be found, 1,827 refused or their English was too poor to allow an interview, and 2,551 were interviewed (58.3% of those found and in age range). The gender breakdown of the sample was 1,163 males and 1,241 females at age 20 to 24 years, 1,193 males and 1,337 females at age 40 to 44 years, and 1,319 males and 1,232 females at age 60 to 64 years.

Procedure

Participants were asked to complete a questionnaire on hand-held computers, which covered socio-demographic characteristics, anxiety and depression, substance abuse, cognitive function, well-being, physical health, health habits, use of health services, personality, coping, early life psychosocial risk factors, current psychosocial risk factors, and nutrition. This was done under the supervision of a professional interviewer. Some basic physical tests were also carried out (e.g., blood pressure, grip strength, visual acuity, lung functioning), and the participants were asked to provide a cheek swab from which DNA could be extracted. Most of the interview was self-completed on a Hewlett-Packard 620LX palmtop personal computer using the Surveycraft software for computer-assisted personal interviewing. However, testing by the interviewer was required for the physical tests, some of the cognitive tests, and the cheek swab.

Demographic variables and height

Participants were asked a series of questions about educational activities, and these were used to calculate years of education (*Education*). *Gender* was coded 0 = male, 1 = female. Participants were asked to report their height in either feet and inches or centimetres.

Health variables

Self-reported history of heart problems, diabetes, asthma, epilepsy, and head injury were coded 1 = yes, 2 = no. General physical health was assessed using the short-form SF-12 Physical Health Summary Scale. This scale consists of a 12-item subset of the SF-36 (Ware et al., 1996) with higher scores indicating better health.

Biomarker variables

Forced expiratory volume at one second (FEV_1) was measured in litres using a Micro Medical "Micro" spirometer (Micro Medical Limited, Rochester, Kent, UK), which is a hand-held microprocessor–based unit. The participant was given the following instruction: " Breathe in until your lungs are completely full, now seal your lips around the mouthpiece and blow out as hard and as fast as possible until you cannot push any more air out." Participants completed the procedure three times, and the average of the second and third trials was used. *Grip strength* was taken using the Smedley hand dynamometer (Model No PE7, Stoelting Co., Wood Dale, Illinois), which measures the force exerted in kilograms. Four trials were given for each hand, and the mean of the average score of left and right hands was the measure used in this study. Participants were first shown how to grip the hand and began with their dominant hand (the hand they wrote with). The interviewer said: "Now squeeze your fingers and thumb together. Good. Hold the grip meter like this down by your side. Squeeze as hard as you can." Participants swapped hand after two trials and then repeated the procedure. Across the eight trials at Wave 1, Cronbach's alpha was .82 based on 838 individuals. FEV_1 and grip strength are known to correlate with gender and height so adjustments for these variables were made in the multiple regression analyses. *Corrected visual acuity* was measured using a 3-m Snellen Chart. It contained seven lines that subtend 1 min of arc at distances of 60, 36, 24, 16, 9, 6, and 5 m. A participant's score was the total number of letters readable, and scores ranged from 0 to 28. Blood pressure was measured twice during the interview using an Omron M4 blood pressure monitor, and values for diastolic and systolic pressure were averaged.

Measures of mental health

Anxiety and *depression* symptoms in the past month were assessed by the Goldberg anxiety and depression scales (Goldberg, Bridges, Duncan-Jones, & Grayson, 1988), which give scores of 0 to 9 for number of symptoms of anxiety and of depression.

Lifestyle variables

Current smoking status was assessed with a single item ("yes" or "no"; *Smoking*). Items used in the UK Whitehall II study (Marmot et al., 1991) were used to produce a physical activity variable (*phys act*). Participants were asked to rate the frequency with which they engaged in mildly energetic (e.g., walking, weeding), moderately energetic (e.g., dancing, cycling), or vigorous (e.g., running, squash) activity, and to also report the average number of hours and minutes per week that they spent in mild, moderate, or vigorous activity (Marmot et al., 1991). Combined responses to the items were then used to classify participants into three activity levels: mild or no activity, moderate activity, and vigorous activity.

Alcohol use was assessed using the Alcohol Use Disorders Identification Test (AUDIT; Saunders, Aasland, Babor, De La Fuente, & Grant, 1993). Categorical estimates of weekly consumption were derived from the quantity and frequency items of the AUDIT as described previously (Caldwell et al., 2002). Participants were defined as hazardous/harmful drinkers based on the definitions of the National Health and Medical Research Council (2001), namely, more than 28 standard drinks per week for men and more than 14 for women. Abstainers/occasional drinkers were defined as consuming less than 8 standard drinks per week for men and less than 4 for women. For the present study, a dichotomous variable was created: coded hazardous/harmful drinker (1), not hazardous/harmful drinker (0).

Measures of reaction time

Mean level.   RT was tested using a small box held with both hands, with left and right buttons at the top to be depressed by the index fingers. The front of the box had three lights: two red stimulus lights under the left and right buttons, respectively, and a green get-ready light in the middle beneath these. There were four blocks of 20 trials measuring simple reaction time (SRT), followed by two blocks of 20 trials measuring choice reaction time (CRT). For SRT everyone used their right hand regardless of dominance. The interval between the "get-ready" light and the first light of the trial was 2.3 for both SRT and CRT.

Means were calculated after removing outliers. This was done by first eliminating any values over 2,000 ms for the younger age groups and over 6,000 ms for the 60–64 age group. Next, means and standard deviations were calculated for each individual for each block, and values were eliminated that lay outside three standard deviations for each individual. A number of very slow individuals still retained RT scores greater than 1,000 ms. In a final step, these values were dropped before the final means per block were calculated for each participant.

Calculation of measures of intraindividual variability in RT.   Figure 1 shows all the data points for one participant about a summary function for each of the RTs over the 80 trials. Mean absolute residuals (in ms; MAR) were calculated for each individual by averaging the deviations from quadratic models for the reaction time in each of the simple and complex RT series (Blocks 1–4 inclusive were SRT, and Blocks 5–6 were CRT blocks). These models were designed to remove both intra-block practice effects and the effect of the short rest periods between blocks, leaving residuals that measure only random variation. The distribution of MAR across subjects showed the expected pattern of increasing mean and variance with age. For example 92% of the 20–24 age group, but only 76% of the 40–44 and 54% of the 60–64 age groups, had MAR under 50 ms (Figure 2).

Also as expected, the between-subject variance of absolute residuals for the sample was found to increase as subjects' mean RT increased, reflecting the association between intraindividual variability and reaction time. To develop a measure of intra-individual variability that was independent of mean RT, the size of the associations between the MAR and mean RT needed to be estimated. Then a function had to be developed that adjusted for this association to achieve a measure of mean independent variation. To do this, the log of MAR was calculated and plotted against speed (-1/mean RT). The linear slope of this function was calculated for simple (b = 0.55) and choice times (b = 0.35) using the 40 CRTs and 80 SRTs. The slope indicates the degree of association between log MAR and speed. To adjust for speed, deviations from the line of best fit were calculated using the formula log MIV = log MAR $-$ b(-1/RT), where MIV is the individual mean independent variability (i.e., the mean absolute residual adjusted for speed). Two scores of intraindividual variability adjusted for speed were computed for each individual. These were the MIV for SRTs (MIVS) and the MIV for CRTs (MIVC). For example, for the simple reaction times the corrected variation was given by:

$$MIVS = MAR.exp(0.55/Mean)$$

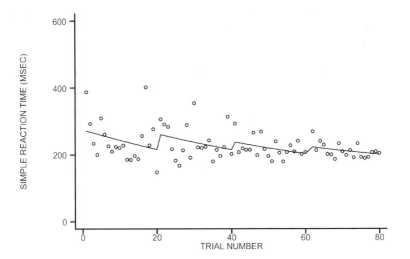

Figure 1.   An example of one individual's raw SRTs showing how the residuals are corrected both for trend over the whole series and for steps between blocks.

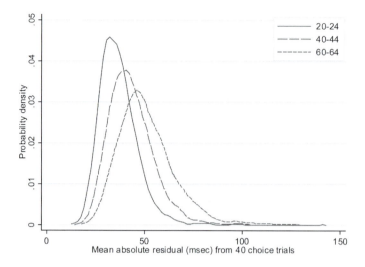

Figure 2.   Kernel density estimates (smoothed histograms) of mean absolute residuals from choice trials, by age group.

Here "Mean" is mean RT in seconds, and the coefficient 0.55 is the regression slope described above (the regression intercept is ignored). The effect of this is that the variance is adjusted upwards more in subjects with fast reaction times, to achieve a measure of variation independent of speed.

Statistical analyses

Hierarchical regression analyses of correlates of reaction time measures.   A hierarchical regression model was tested to allow for the evaluation of groups of predictors of SRT, CRT, MIVS, and MIVC. Demographic variables were entered first, followed by physical health variables, biomarkers, lifestyle variables, and measures of mental health. Age group was entered as a demographic variable in the initial hierarchical regression analyses. Analyses were conducted to evaluate whether there were any significant interactions between predictor variables and age (where age was a significant predictor). A block of interactions between age and the independent variables was entered on a final block in the hierarchical model that had been developed. If inclusion of this block led to a significant increment in the R square, then the individual beta weights were viewed to determine which interaction was significant. Independent variables were centred by conversion to z-scores.

Age differences were evaluated by examining interactions of significant predictors with age group; p values less than or equal to .01 were treated as statistically significant.

Treatment of missing data.   Missing data were imputed with the EM algorithm in SPSS using all the variables in the present study (Shafer & Graham, 2002). Missing data frequencies before imputation were less than 2% for most variables and less than 5% for all variables except MIVC (5.3%) and moderate hours of physical activity (7.7%).

Evaluation of biomarkers versus age in explaining individual differences in cognitive test performance.   The relative importance of biomarkers versus age for explaining individual differences in RT performance was evaluated using hierarchical multiple regression models. In both models gender and height were entered at Step 1 to control for the effect of these on FEV_1 and grip strength. In Model 1, age was entered at Step 2, and the biomarkers were entered at Step 3. In Model 2, the bio-markers were entered at Step 2, and age was entered at Step 3. The proportion of age-related variance explained by biomarkers was calculated using the formula $1 - (q/p)$ where q = the variance explained by age after controlling for biomarkers and height and gender, p = the variance explained by age after controlling for height and gender (as described in Anstey et al., 1997).

Results

Descriptive data on the reaction time and consistency measures

Table 1 shows the descriptive statistics for the RT performance parameters for each age group. There were significant differences between age groups on the SRT task, $F(2, 7482) = 372.26$, $p < .01$, with post hoc tests showing that the 40–44-year-old age group was slower on the SRT than was the 20–24-year-old age group, and the 60–64-year old age group was slower than the 40–44-year-old age group ($p < .01$). Likewise, there were significant differences on the CRT task, $F(2, 7482) = 971.64$, $p < .01$, with post hoc tests showing that the 40–44-year-olds were slower than the 20–24-year-olds, and the 60–64-year-olds were slower than the 40–44-year-olds ($p < .01$). Significant group differences were found for the MIVS, $F(2, 7482) = 7.19$, $p < .01$, with post hoc tests revealing no significant difference in consistency between the 20–24-year-olds and the 40–44-year-olds on the SRT task, and a very small yet significant difference between the 60–64-year-olds and the 40–44-year-olds ($p < .01$). Significant group differences were also found for the MIVC, $F(2, 7483) = 116.90$, $p < .01$, with post hoc tests showing that the 40–44-year-olds were less consistent than the 20–24-year-olds ($p < .01$), and the 60–64-year-olds were less consistent that the 40–44-year-olds ($p < .01$).

TABLE 1

Descriptive statistics for RT measures for each age group based on the imputed dataset and (effect sizes) for group differences

| | Age group[a] | | | | | | | | |
| | 20–24 | | 40–44 | | | 60–64 | | |
RT measure	M	SD	M	SD	ES1	M	SD	ES2
SRT	.22	.03	.23**	.04	.33	.25**	.06	1.00
CRT	.27	.02	.29**	.04	1.00	.32**	.04	2.50
MIVS	.26	.07	.26	.07	.01	.26**	.08	.01
MIVC	.14	.03	.15**	.03	.33	.16**	.05	.67

Note: ES1 = Effect size comparing 40–44-year-olds with 20–24-year-olds; ES2 = Effect size comparing 60–64-year-olds with 40–44-year-olds. Effect sizes calculated on values to 3 decimal places, using standard deviation of 20–24-year-old age group but values for MIVS appear the same due to rounding to 2 decimal places. RT = reaction time. SRT = simple reaction time. CRT = choice reaction time. MIVS = mean independent variability on SRT task. MIVC = mean independent variability on CRT task.

[a] In years.

**$p < .01$.

TABLE 2
Intercorrelations among RT measures

	SRT	*CRT*	*MIVS*	*MIVC*	*MARS*
SRT					
CRT	.67*				
MIVS	.07*	.03			
MIVC	.00	.10	.29*		
MARS	.80*	.34*	.60*	.21*	
MARC	.52*	.59*	.19*	.86*	.39*

Note: RT = reaction time; SRT = simple reaction time; CRT = choice reaction time; MIVS = mean independent variability on SRT task; MIVC = mean independent variability on CRT task; MARS = mean absolute residuals of the SRT task; MARC = mean absolute residuals of the CRT task.
  *$p < .01$.

Intercorrelations among the reaction time measures are shown in Table 2. Here the difference between MIV and MAR in their correlations with mean RTs is illustrated. Very small associations were observed between RT and consistency measures, with the largest (MIVC and CRT) sharing 1% of variance. In contrast, moderate to large associations were observed between the MAR of the SRT and CRT tasks, and the mean SRT and mean CRT. This illustrates that the MIVS and MIVC measures were successful in measuring relatively independent intraindividual variability. A large correlation was observed between SRT and CRT($r = .67$), and a moderate-sized correlation was observed between MIVC and MIVS ($r = .29$). Moderate to large associations are shown between the MAR for SRT and CRT, and mean RTs.

Demographic, physical health, biomarker, lifestyle, and mental health correlates of mean reaction times and intraindividual variability in reaction times

Table 3 shows the standardized beta weights and *p values* for each predictor in the hierarchical regression equations of SRT, CRT, MIVS, and MIVC. Age group was the strongest predictor of SRT, CRT, and MIVC, but was not associated with MIVS. Gender was a significant predictor of all RT measures except MIVC, with men showing faster performance but women showing less intraindividual variability on MIVS. Education was associated with performance on SRT only. Of the medical conditions, diabetes was the only condition associated with SRT, and diabetes and head injury approached a significant association with CRT. None of the medical conditions were associated with MIVS or MIVC. After the demographic variables, the biomarkers had the strongest and most frequent associations with the RT performance measures, explaining between 1 and 4% of the variance after controlling for demographics. Specifically, after controlling for demographic and health variables, grip, FEV_1, and vision were associated with SRT and CRT. FEV_1 was also associated with MIVS and MIVC.

The association of physical activity with MIVS approached significance ($p = .01$) but no other lifestyle variables were associated with RT performance. Depression was associated

TABLE 3
Standardized beta weights and p values for correlates of RT parameters in hierarchical multiple regression analyses

Step	Variables	SRT Beta	SRT p	SRT Incr R²	CRT Beta	CRT p	CRT Incr R²	MIVS Beta	MIVS p	MIVS Incr R²	MIVC Beta	MIVC p	MIVC Incr R²
1	Age group	.20	.00		.39	.00		.01	.74		.17	.00	
	Gender	-.13	.00		-.09	.00		-.13	.00		-.03	.16	
	Education	.06	.00		-.01	.24		-.02	.11		-.01	.32	
	Height	.03	.09	.11	.05	.00	.22	-.01	.55	.01	.01	.62	.03
2	SF-12 PH	.01	.37		-.01	.35		-.01	.73		-.01	.37	
	Heart	-.01	.50		.00	.12		.01	.29		.02	.16	
	Diabetes	-.06	.00		-.03	.01		.01	.50		.02	.05	
	Asthma	-.01	.61		.00	.81		-.02	.09		-.01	.15	
	Epilepsy	.01	.56		.00	.86		-.02	.13		.00	.89	
	Head inj	.02	.13		.03	.01		-.02	.16		.01	.63	
	Stroke	.01	.95	.12	.00	.95	.22	-.01	.26	.01	-.04	.00	.03
3	Grip	.27	.00		-.18	.00		-.01	.82		.03	.12	
	Sysbp	-.01	.29		-.03	.02		-.03	.05		-.02	.10	
	FEV₁	-.09	.00		-.07	.00		-.10	.00		-.06	.00	
	Vision	-.06	.00	.16	-.04	.00	.24	-.02	.05	.02	-.02	.17	.04
4	Smoking	.01	.28		.01	.33		-.03	.02		-.03	.03	
	Phys act	-.02	.09		-.03	.02		-.03	.01		.00	.97	
	Alcohol	.00	.78	.16	.00	.98	.24	-.02	.19	.02	.01	.77	.04
5	Depress	.01	.73		.04	.00		.03	.03		.01	.53	
	Anxiety	.03	.04	.16	.00	.28	.24	.00	.95	.02	.01	.51	.04

Note: RT = reaction time; SRT = simple reaction time; CRT = choice reaction time; MIVS = mean independent variation of simple reaction time; MIVC = mean independent variation of choice reaction time; Incr = incremental; Head inj = head injury; Sysbp = systolic blood pressure; Phys act = physical activity; Depress = depression.

15

with CRT. Altogether the predictors explained 16% of the variance in SRT, $F(25, 7459) = 55.59$, $p < .01$, 24% of the variance in CRT, $F(25, 7459) = 92.31$, $p < .01$, 2% of the variance in MIVS, $F(25, 7459) = 7.36$, $p < .01$, and 4% of the variance in MIVC, $F(25, 7459) = 11.92$, $p < .01$. After adjusting for demographic variables, medical conditions explained 1% of the variance in SRT and less than 1% in all the other measures.

Interactions of potential covariates with age group were evaluated for significance in a final step of a set of further regression models. For SRT, entry of the interaction terms led to a significant increment in R^2, $F_{Change}(6, 7481) = 15.37$, $p = .000$, which explained an additional 1% of variance in mean SRT. Significant interactions occurred between age group and education, beta $= -.192$, $p < .01$, age group and grip strength, beta $= -.495$, $p < .01$, and age group and gender, beta $= -.205$, $p < .01$. The interaction between age group and education occurred because higher education was associated with faster SRTs in the 20–24-year-olds and the 60–64-year-olds, but there was no association between education and SRT in the 40–44-year-old age group. The interaction between age group and grip strength occurred because higher scores on grip strength were associated with faster SRTs in the 20–24-year-olds and 40–44-year-olds but not in the 60–64-year-olds.

For CRT and MIVS, inclusion of interactions did not lead to an increase in the variance explained. For MIVC, interactions explained an additional 0.01% of variance, $F(2, 7448) = 4.71$, $p < .01$, and the age group by FEV_1 beta weight was significant, beta $= -.300$, $p < .01$; however, the effect size was deemed too small to interpret.

Comparison of biomarkers with age group in explaining individual differences in reaction time performance

To evaluate how much age-related variance was explained by the biomarkers, a series of hierarchical regressions was conducted. Summary results from these are shown in Table 4. In all cases blocks of biomarkers and age made a statistically significant contribution to explaining variance in RT performance, even where the size of this effect was extremely small. Biomarkers explained more total variance in mean SRT than did age, but this pattern was reversed for the CRT measures. Together, the biomarkers explained 73%, 56%, 100%, and 56% of the age-related variance in SRT, CRT, MIVS, and MIVC, respectively.

Discussion

The present study aimed to describe age differences in speed of response and intraindividual variability in three population-based cohorts of adults aged 20–24, 40–44, and 60–64 years. It also evaluated predictors of speed and intraindividual variability, and age differences in the associations among the RT parameters and cognitive test performance. The approach taken here allowed for the evaluation of a range of potential correlates of RT performance that have previously been linked to age differences or age changes in cognitive performance.

The general findings of the study illustrate age differences in response times whereby older adults are slower than younger adults. Older adults were also less consistent in their responding than were younger adults on the CRT task, consistent with previous reports (Christensen, Griffiths, Mackinnon, & Jolcomb, 1997; Hultsch et al., 2002). There was no difference in consistency on the SRT task between the 40–44-year-olds and the 20–24-year-olds. We found

TABLE 4
Comparison of biomarkers and age on reaction time
parameters using hierarchical multiple regression

Model		R^2			
		SRT	CRT	MIVS	MIVC
1	1. Gender, height	.022	.014	.005	.003
	2. Age	.104	.210	.006	.030
	3. Biomarkers	.146	.232	.013	.034
2	1. Gender, height	.022	.014	.005	.003
	2. Biomarkers	.124	.145	.012	.022
	3. Age	.146	.232	.012	.034

Note: Incremental R^2 was significant at $p < .01$ for all steps in Models 1 and 2. Results did not differ according to whether age group was coded as a dummy variable or as a continuous variable (ages 20–24 = 1; ages 40–44 = 2, ages 60–64 = 3). Biomarkers included measures of vision, forced expiratory volume at one second, grip strength, and systolic blood pressure.

relatively small effect sizes for differences between age groups; however, our "old" sample was younger than samples used in other recent studies (e.g., Hultsch et al., 2002; Rabbitt et al., 2001). Therefore, the estimates of age differences are likely to be less reliable than those obtained in a laboratory situation over thousands of trials. Moreover, the present study yielded relatively gross measures of RT performance compared with those derived from experimental studies, precluding the evaluation of any sophisticated model of underlying processes.

We investigated a large number of predictors of reaction time and intraindividual variability from different domains. Theories by Hultsch et al. (2002) and Li and Lindenberger (1999) would predict that markers of neurological integrity would be most strongly associated with RT measures, and variables unrelated to neurological integrity would not be associated with response time and consistency. Our study included a measure of grip strength, which is known to reduce after neurological insult (Haaland, Temkin, Randahl, & Dikmen, 1994) and has been associated with biological ageing (Anstey & Smith, 1999). Visual function in ageing has been viewed by some authors as an indicator of brain ageing (Lindenberger & Baltes, 1994). Our study also included data on specific conditions previously associated with impaired or reduced neurocognitive function including diabetes, stroke, head injury, and hypertension. In our analyses, we found virtually no associations between medical conditions and RT performance. This may have been due to the relative health and youth of the samples compared with clinical and ageing studies that have found these conditions to be associated with cognitive performance. We did, however, find that our biomarkers explained a moderate proportion of variance in SRT and CRT and a small proportion of variance in MIVS and MIVC.

Of our biological markers, grip strength was associated with RT but not with intraindividual variability, suggesting that individuals with weaker grip are slower but no less consistent than their stronger peers. Likewise, vision was associated with slower performance but not with consistency of performance. It is possible that poorer vision and grip strength affect movement time and not decision time but the present study did not distinguish between these two components of the RT task. It would be valuable to follow up this finding in laboratory studies to determine whether specific biomarkers are more strongly associated with slowing versus intraindividual variability. FEV_1 was the only variable to be associated with all four RT measures. Although several studies have now shown that FEV_1 is correlated with RT and other measures of cognitive test performance, the reason for this is still not known (e.g., Anstey, 1999; Anstey, Windsor, Jorm, Christensen, & Rodgers, 2004; Christensen et al., 2001; van Boxtel et al., 1997). Some authors have suggested that FEV_1 is a marker of general biological age (Anstey et al., 1996; Anstey & Smith, 1999), or that it is related to cardiovascular fitness and lifestyle factors such as exercise and smoking (Emery, Pedersen, Svartengren, & McClearn, 1998). As a group, the biological markers were the most important set of predictors of SRT performance.

Lifestyle factors showed negligible associations with RT measures but depression was associated with CRT. This latter finding is consistent with previous research showing that depression is associated with cognitive slowing and poorer neuropsychological test performance (Austin et al., 1992; Christensen et al., 1997).

Results from the present study also show that biomarkers explain a large proportion of age-related variance in RT measures, although the proportion of variance explained was smaller than that found in a previous study that studied RT in relation to biomarkers conducted on a much older sample (e.g., Anstey, 1999). This difference is probably due to the inclusion of younger age cohorts in the present study. We expect that individual differences in rates of biological ageing will increase during the planned follow-up of the PATH Through Life Study and that greater age differences will be observed in future waves.

In comparison to laboratory studies (e.g., Rabbitt & Banerji, 1989) the present study is limited by the low number of reaction time trials which did not allow for the isolation of practice effects. Tests were not conducted in a laboratory setting, and the medical data were self-reported. However, the study has strengths in its large sample size and the use of measures of intraindividual variability that were independent of mean RT performance. We also note that a larger proportion of variance was not explained by the covariates examined. This probably reflects the fact that individual differences in RT performance occur in the normal healthy population and are due to general intellectual function rather than to health factors. However, the fact that associations were detected among some of the health and lifestyle variables and the biomarkers shows that these factors may affect brain function. The sizes of the associations among the health and biological variables and our RT measures were small and were detected due to our large sample size. Nevertheless, they are consistent with other reports in the literature and with earlier suggestions by Houx, Vreeling, and Jolles (1991) that suboptimal health and neurological risk factors affect cognitive development from young adulthood. From the point of view of cognitive ageing, it is important to identify even small effects if they are occurring in young adulthood as we still do not know when risk factors become important for determining cognitive decline. Research on older cohorts suggests that the factors identified in this study will become more important in age groups 65 and older (e.g., Anstey & Christensen, 2000). Population-based studies such as the one reported here reveal the importance of considering cognitive performance in the context of biological and health changes that occur in ageing. The results of this study also suggest that investigation of the association of specific biomarkers and RT performance may be a fruitful avenue for cognitive ageing researchers to pursue in the laboratory.

REFERENCES

Anstey, K. J. (1999). Sensorimotor and forced expiratory volume as correlates of speed, accuracy, and variability in reaction time performance in late adulthood. *Aging, Neuropsychology and Cognition, 6,* 84–95.

Anstey, K. J., & Christensen, H. (2000). Education, activity, health, blood pressure and apolipoprotein E as predictors of cognitive change in old age: A review. *Gerontology, 46,* 163–177.

Anstey, K. J., Lord, S. R., & Smith, G. A. (1996). Human functional age measurement: A review of empirical findings. *Experimental Aging Research, 22,* 245–266.

Anstey, K. J., Lord, S. R., & Williams, P. (1997). Strength in the lower limbs, visual contrast sensitivity and simple reaction time predict cognition in older women. *Psychology and Aging, 12,* 137–144.

Anstey, K. J., & Smith, G. A. (1999). Interrelationships among biological markers of aging, health, activity, acculturation and cognitive performance in older adults. *Psychology and Aging, 14,* 615–618.

Anstey, K. J., Windsor, T., Jorm, A. F., Christensen, H., & Rodgers, B. (2004). The association of pulmonary function with cognitive performance in early, middle and late adulthood. *Gerontology, 50,* 237–241.

Austin, M.-P., Ross, M., Murray, C., O'Carroll, R. E., Ebmeier, K. P., & Goodwin, G. M. (1992). Cognitive function in major depression. *Journal of Affective Disorders 25,* 21–30.

Birren, J. E. (1965). Age changes in speed of behavior: Its central nature and physiological correlates. In A. T. Welford & J. E. Birren (Eds.), *Behaviour, aging and the nervous system* (pp. 191–216). Springfield, IL: Thomas.

Bryan, J., & Luszcz, M. A. (2000). Measures of fluency as predictors of incidental memory among older adults. *Psychology and Aging, 15,* 483–489.

Caldwell, T. M., Rodgers, B., Jorm, A. F., Christensen, H., Jacomb, P. A., Korten, A. E., & Lynskey, M. T. (2002). Patterns of association between alcohol consumption and symptoms of depression and anxiety in young adults. *Addiction, 97,* 583–594.

Christensen, H., Dear, K., Anstey, K. J., Parslow, R., & Jorm, A. F. (in press). Within occasion intra-individual variability and pre-clinical diagnostic status: Is intraindividual variability an indicator of mild cognitive impairment? *Neuropsychology.*

Christensen, H., Griffiths, K., Mackinnon, A., & Jacomb, P. A. (1997). A quantitative review of cognitive deficits in depression and Alzheimer-type dementia. *Journal of the International Neuropsychological Society, 3,* 631–651.

Christensen, H., Korten, A. E., Mackinnon, A. J., Jorm, A. F., Henderson, A. S., & Rodgers, B. (2000). Are changes in sensory disability, reaction time, and grip strength associated with changes in memory and crystallized intelligence? A longitudinal analysis in an elderly community sample. *Gerontology, 46,* 276–292.

Christensen, H., Mackinnon, A., Jorm, A. F., Henderson, A. S., Scott, L. R., & Korten, A. E. (1994). Age differences in interindividual variation in cognition in community-dwelling elderly. *Psychology and Aging, 9,* 381–390.

Christensen, H., Mackinnon, A. J., Korten, A., & Jorm, A. F. (2001). The "common cause hypothesis" of cognitive aging: Evidence for not only a common factor but also specific associations of age with vision and grip strength in a cross-sectional analysis. *Psychology and Aging, 16,* 588–599.

Christensen, H., Mackinnon, A. J., Korten, A. E., Jorm, A. F., Henderson, A. S., & Jacomb, P. (1999). Dispersion in cognitive ability as a function of age: A longitudinal study of an elderly community sample. *Aging, Neuropsychology and Cognition, 6,* 214–228.

Deary, I. J., Der, G., & Ford, G. (2001). Reaction times and intelligences differences: A population-based cohort study. *Intelligence, 29,* 389–399.

Deary, I. J., Leaper, S. A, Murray, A. D., Staff, R. T., & Whalley, L. J. (2003). Cerebral white matter abnormalities and lifetime cognitive change: A 67-year follow-up of the Scottish Mental Survey of 1932. *Psychology and Aging, 18,* 140–148.

Dustman, R. E., Emmerson, R., & Shearer, D. (1994). Physical activity, age, and cognitive-neuropsychological function. *Journal of Aging and Physical Activity, 2,* 143–181.

Emery, C. F., Pedersen, N. L., Svartengren, M., & McClearn, G. E. (1998). Longitudinal and genetic effects in the relationship between pulmonary function and cognitive performance. *Journals of Gerontology: Series B, Psychological Sciences & Social Sciences, 53B,* 311.

Goldberg, D., Bridges, K., Duncan-Jones, P., & Grayson, D. (1988). Detecting anxiety and depression in general medical settings. *British Medical Journal, 297,* 897–899.

Haaland, K. Y., Temkin, N., Randahl., G., & Dikmen, S. (1994). Recovery of simple motor skills after head injury. *Journal of Clinical & Experimental Neuropsychology, 16,* 448–456.

Hill, R. D. (1989). Residual effects of cigarette smoking on cognitive performance in normal aging. *Psychology and Aging, 4*, 251–254.

Houx, P. J., Vreeling, F. W., & Jolles, J. (1991). Rigorous health screening reduces age effect on memory scanning task. *Brain and Cognition, 15*, 246–260.

Hultsch, D. F., & MacDonald, S. W. S. (2004). Intraindividual variability in performance as a theoretical window into cognitive aging. In R. A. Dixon, L. Bäckman, & L.-G. Nilsson (Eds.), *New frontiers in cognitive aging* (pp. 65–88). Oxford, UK: Oxford University Press.

Hultsch, D. F., MacDonald, S. W. S., & Dixon, R. A. (2002). Variability in reaction time performance of younger and older adults. *Journals of Gerontology: Psychological Sciences, 57B*, P101–P115.

Hultsch, D. F., MacDonald, S. W., Hunter, M. A., Levy-Bencheton, J., & Strauss, E. (2000). Intraindividual variability in cognitive performance in older adults: Comparison of healthy adults with mild dementia, adults with arthritis, and healthy adults. *Neuropsychology, 14*, 588–598.

Jorm, A. F., Anstey, K. J., Christensen, H., & Rodgers, B. (2004). Gender differences in cognitive abilities: The mediating role of health state and health habits. *Intelligence, 32*, 7–23.

Li, S.-C., Aggen, S. H., Nesselroade, J., & Baltes, P. (2001). Short-term fluctuations in elderly people's sensori-motor functioning predict text and spatial memory performance: The MacArthur Successful Aging Studies. *Gerontology, 47*, 100–116.

Li, S.-C., & Lindenberger, U. (1999). Cross-level unification: A computational exploration of the link between deterioration of neurotransmitter systems and dedifferentiation of cognitive abilities in old age. In L.-G. Nilsson & H. Markowitsch (Eds.), *Cognitive neuroscience and memory* (pp. 103–146). Toronto, Canada: Hogrefe & Huber.

Lindenberger, U., & Baltes, P. (1994). Sensory functioning and intelligence in old age: A strong connection. *Psychology and Aging, 9*, 339–355.

Lindenberger, U., Sherer, H., & Baltes, P. B. (2001). The strong connection between sensory and cognitive performance in old age: Not due to sensory acuity reductions operating during cognitive assessment. *Psychology and Aging, 16*, 196–205.

Luszcz, M. A., Bryan, J., & Kent, P. (1997). Predicting episodic memory performance of very old men and women: Contribution from age, depression, activity, cognitive ability and speed. *Psychology and Aging, 12*, 340–351.

Marmot, M. G., Davey Smith, G., Stansfeld, S., Patel, C., North, F., Head, J., et al. (1991). Health inequalities among British civil servants: the Whitehall II study. *Lancet, 337*, 1387–1393.

Martin, M., & Hofer, S. M. (2004). Intraindividual variability, change, and aging: Conceptual and analytical issues. *Gerontology, 50*, 7–11.

Morse, C. K. (1993). Does variability increase with age? An archival study of cognitive measures. *Psychology and Aging, 8*, 156–164.

Mueller, T., Benz, S., & Boernke, C. (2001). Delay of simple reaction time after levodopa intake. *Clinical Neurophysiology, 112*, 2133–2137.

National Health and Medical Research Council. (2001). *Australian alcohol guidelines: Health risks and benefits.* Canberra: NHMRC.

Nesselroade, J. R. (2004). Intraindividual variability and short-term change. Commentary. *Gerontology, 50*, 44–47.

Parsons, O. A., & Nixon, S. J. (1998). Cognitive functioning in sober social drinkers: A review of the research since 1986. *Journal of Studies on Alcohol, 59*, 180–190.

Rabbitt, P. M. A., & Banerji, N. (1989). How does very prolonged practice improve decision speed? *Journal of Experimental Psychology: General, 118*, 338–345.

Rabbitt, P. M. A., Donlan, C., Watson, P., McInnes, L., & Bent, N. (1995). Unique and interactive effects of depression, age, socioeconomic advantage, and gender on cognitive performance of normal healthy older people. *Psychology and Aging, 10*, 307–313.

Rabbitt, P., Osman, P., Moore, B., & Stollery, B. (2001). There are stable individual differences in performance variability, both from moment to moment and from day to day. *Quarterly Journal of Experimental Psychology, 54A*, 981–1003.

Salthouse, T. A. (1994). Aging associations: Influence of speed on adult age differences in associative learning. *Journal of Experimental Psychology: Learning, Memory, and Cognition, 20*, 1486–1503.

Salthouse, T. A. (1996). The processing speed theory of adult age differences in cognition. *Psychological Review, 3*, 403–428.

Saunders, J. B., Aasland, O. G., Babor, T. F., De La Fuente, J. R., & Grant, M. (1993). Development of the alcohol use disorders identification test (AUDIT): WHO collaborative project on early detection of persons with harmful alcohol consumption: II. *Addiction, 88*, 791–804.

Shafer, J. L., & Graham, J. W. (2002). Missing data: Our view of the state of the art. *Psychological Methods, 7*, 147–177.

Theodore, Z., & Mirsky, A. F. (1999). Reaction time indicators of attentional deficits in closed head injury. *Journal of Clinical and Experimental Psychology, 21*, 352–367.

van Boxtel, M. P., Paas, F. G., Houx, P. J., Adam, J. J, Teeken, J. C., & Jolles, J. (1997). Aerobic capacity and cognitive performance in a cross-sectional aging study. *Medicine and Science in Sports and Exercise, 29*, 1357–1365.

Ware, J. E., Kosinski, M., & Kellar, S. D. (1996). A 12-item Short-Form health survey: Construction of scales and preliminary tests of reliability and validity. *Medical Care, 34*, 220–233.

PrEview proof published online 6 August 2004

THE QUARTERLY JOURNAL OF EXPERIMENTAL PSYCHOLOGY
2005, 58A (1), 22–33

Ψ Psychology Press
Taylor & Francis Group

Hearing loss and perceptual effort: Downstream effects on older adults' memory for speech

Sandra L. McCoy and Patricia A. Tun

Brandeis University, Waltham, MA, USA

L. Clarke Cox

Boston University, Boston, MA, USA

Marianne Colangelo, Raj A. Stewart, and Arthur Wingfield

Brandeis University, Waltham, MA, USA

A group of older adults with good hearing and a group with mild-to-moderate hearing loss were tested for recall of the final three words heard in a running memory task. Near perfect recall of the final words of the three-word sets by both good- and poor-hearing participants allowed the inference that all three words had been correctly identified. Nevertheless, the poor-hearing group recalled significantly fewer of the nonfinal words than did the better hearing group. This was true even though both groups were matched for age, education, and verbal ability. Results were taken as support for an *effortfulness hypothesis*: the notion that the extra effort that a hearing-impaired listener must expend to achieve perceptual success comes at the cost of processing resources that might otherwise be available for encoding the speech content in memory.

The cognitive declines associated with normal ageing are well known and well described in the cognitive literature. These declines include reductions in the capacity of working memory (Salthouse, 1991; Wingfield, Stine, Lahar, & Aberdeen, 1988), attentional difficulties in inhibiting irrelevant stimuli (Barr & Giambra, 1990; Hasher & Zacks, 1988; Stoltzfus, Hasher, & Zacks, 1996), and slowing in many perceptual and cognitive operations (Cerella, 1994; Fisher & Glaser, 1996; Salthouse, 1996) All of these factors may contribute to the common complaint among older adults of increasing difficulty with memory for recently experienced events (Kausler, 1994).

Correspondence should be addressed to Arthur Wingfield, Volen National Center for Complex Systems (MS 013), Brandeis University, Waltham, MA 02454-9110, USA. Email: wingfield@brandeis.edu

This research was supported by NIH Grant AG19714 from the National Institute on Aging. We also gratefully acknowledge support from the W.M. Keck Foundation. The authors would like to thank Patrick Rabbitt, John Towse, and two anonymous reviewers for their helpful comments.

                    DOI:10.1080/02724980443000151

Although there is wide individual variability, the biological changes that accompany the ageing process also include an increased incidence of hearing loss, especially in the higher frequency ranges that are important for the accurate perception of speech (Morrell, Gordon-Salant, Pearson, Brant, & Fozard, 1996). It is clearly the case that the older adult's ability to recall what has been heard, whether from a spoken conversation with family or friends, or medication instructions from a health care provider, will depend significantly on the individual's ability to hear the full message. Speech in everyday environments is also often heard in noisy backgrounds, a factor known to further challenge the older auditory and cognitive systems (Gordon-Salant, 1987; Tun, 1998; Tun, O'Kane, & Wingfield, 2002; Tun & Wingfield, 1999; Working Group on Speech Understanding and Aging, 1988).

There is an additional concern, however, that arises even when the loudness and clarity of the speaker allow the listener with a mild-to-moderate hearing loss to correctly identify the speech being heard. This relates to what one may call an *effortfulness hypothesis*: the notion that the extra effort that a hearing-impaired listener must expend to achieve this perceptual success may come at the cost of processing resources that might otherwise be available for encoding the speech content in memory.[1]

The potential negative consequence of effortfulness in perceptual processing on subsequent memory performance was demonstrated in a classic set of experiments by Rabbitt (1968). Rabbitt (Exp. 1) showed poorer recall for strings of spoken digits by normal-hearing adults when the digits were noise masked, even when the level of masking still allowed accurate recognition of the to-be-recalled digits. As a further illustration, Rabbitt gave listeners 8-digit lists, temporally grouped into two 4-digit lists by a 2-s pause after the first 4 digits. He found that the first half of the list, whether presented in quiet or masked by noise, was less well recalled when the second half had been heard in noise than when it had been heard in quiet (Rabbitt, 1968, Exp. 2). As Rabbitt later summarized the implication of these findings, "the increased effort necessary to discriminate speech correctly through low levels of random noise may draw on information processing capacity which subjects can otherwise employ to rehearse the words they have to remember" (Rabbitt, 1991, p. 169).

Rabbitt (1991) expanded this principle by showing an analogous effect for older adults with mild hearing loss. In this case he showed that word lists were better recalled by individuals with good hearing than by those with mild hearing loss, even when both groups showed the ability to correctly repeat words presented at the same intensity level. As in the case of the noise-masking studies with normally hearing adults, Rabbitt argued that persons with impaired hearing may have to invest more processing resources to identify spoken words than do individuals with better hearing. This would have the effect of reducing available processing resources that might otherwise be deployed for maintenance or elaborative rehearsal to encode the words in memory for later recall. This general principle was reinforced by Murphy, Craik,

---

[1]We use the terms "resources" and "resource capacity" in Kahneman's (1973) original sense, to refer to a limited pool of attentional resources that must be allocated among tasks. In Kahneman's formulation, processing resources for a particular task will be diminished if access to the same resources is required for performance of multiple tasks that must be performed concurrently or in close sequence: in this case, perceptual processing of the spoken words and their encoding in memory. The more difficult or resource demanding a particular task, the fewer resources will be available for use elsewhere in the system. As such, Kahneman's notion of resource capacity is used in the same sense as Baddeley's (1996, 1998) notion of a limited-capacity central executive in working memory.

Li, and Schneider (2000) who used noise masking to simulate a hearing loss in young and older adults with good hearing. (See also discussions by Pichora-Fuller, Schneider, & Daneman, 1995; and Tun & Wingfield, 1999.)

However compelling this argument, there is a simpler account of why older adults with some degree of hearing loss might display poorer recall for spoken material than do older adults with good hearing. One might refer to this as a sensory account: the proposition that recall deficits of poor-hearing older adults are a direct consequence of an auditory system in which sensory registration is so degraded as to prevent the identification of lexical items necessary for encoding in memory and effective rehearsal. This strong version of a sensory account of recall deficits, however, must be modified in view of the substantial body of research that has demonstrated that linguistic context can moderate the effects of hearing loss. For example, when final words of spoken sentences are masked with noise, hearing loss produces smaller effects on word recognition in highly predictable sentence contexts than in low predictability contexts (Dubno, Ahlstrom, & Horwitz, 2000; Gordon-Salant & Fitzgibbons, 1997; see also Pichora-Fuller et al., 1995). Therefore, a purely sensory account must be modified to include not simply overall differences between good-hearing and poor-hearing listeners, but also larger recall differences for low-predictability material.

Although one should not underestimate how failures in initial perception can impact recall, in this experiment we ask whether not merely the degradation of sensory input but also the extra effort required for successful perception by older adults with hearing loss might even affect immediate recall of short, subspan messages. We chose for this study older adults with mild-to-moderate hearing loss because of the prevalence of this level of impairment and the fact that this group typically does not use hearing aids on a regular basis (National Academy on an Aging Society, 1999).

The test paradigm we chose was a running memory span, in which the participant was asked to listen carefully to a list of recorded words that would be stopped at any moment. When the list was stopped the task was to recall only the last three words heard. We chose a set size of three words because this is generally within the immediate memory span of healthy older adults in both simple (Kausler, 1994; Wingfield, Stine, Lahar, & Aberdeen, 1988) and running memory (Wingfield, Lahar, & Stine, 1989) span tests for spoken words.

Our first step in this test was to demonstrate that participants could recall the final word of the three-word set in order to ensure that both participants with hearing loss and participants with good hearing could correctly identify the words. For this purpose we relied on the well-known finding that word-list recall reflects a recency effect, in which the last items of a list, and especially the final item, show a very high level of recall. This is true for both short and long lists (Murdock, 1962), and it holds for older adults as well as for young adults (Kahana, Howard, Zaromb, & Wingfield, 2002; Kausler, 1994).

Our logic was as follows: If the final word in a set can be reported correctly by a listener, we can assume that he or she was just as likely to have correctly identified all three words in the set, which were all spoken by the same speaker at the same intensity level. That is, the ability to correctly report the final word would allow the inference that the listener had successfully identified, or achieved lexical access, for all three words. Thus, poorer recall of the first two words by a group with hearing loss, relative to a better hearing group, would be due not simply to an inability to correctly identify the words, as predicted by a purely sensory account. Instead, we suggest that such a differential failure of recall of the earlier words in the set would be due to the increased burden on processing resources experienced by the hearing loss group, who must expend greater effort to achieve perceptual success, or red-integration of a stimulus word from a weak trace (Neath, 2000; Newbigging, 1961). This drain on resources could deprive the participant of the necessary resources for adequate encoding of the materials in memory and thus result in poorer downstream recall. This is the essence of the effortfulness hypothesis.

To complete the full picture of everyday memory, albeit in microcosm, we wished also to examine recall performance when the to-be-recalled words were supported by contextual constraints. One would expect to see such facilitation, as it is well known that older adults, like young adults, benefit from linguistic context in the recognition of words heard under poor listening conditions. Indeed, it is a general principle of perception that the higher the probability of a stimulus, as determined, for example, by contextual constraints, the less sensory information is required for correct recognition (Morton, 1969). This includes listeners with good hearing recognizing words from just their acoustic onsets (Perry & Wingfield, 1994; Wingfield, Aberdeen, & Stine, 1991), listeners with good hearing recognizing words heard in background noise (Pichora-Fuller et al., 1995), and young and older adults with a mild-to-moderate hearing loss (Gordon-Salant & Fitzgibbons, 1997).

All of the studies cited above presented target words in the context of a grammatically coherent sentence. In such cases there are several sources of contextual constraint, including constraints on grammatical form class (the word "a" signals that the next word will be a count noun or an adjective) and semantic meaning (the sentence context "the train pulled into the" increases the likelihood of particular words such as "station," "tunnel," "siding," or "village").

In the interests of testing the generality of context effects as a balance against hearing loss in word recognition, we wished to determine whether one could facilitate recognition using linguistic constraints lacking ordinary syntactic and semantic structure. To this end we chose as stimuli so-called *statistical approximations* to English as a means of capturing the predictive quality of language based just on short-range associations (Miller & Selfridge, 1950; Moray & Taylor, 1960). Miller and Selfridge originally constructed these approximations by giving a participant several words of a sentence and asking him or her to guess what the next word might be. This sequence was then shown to another person who was asked to guess the next word, and so on, until a text of a desired length had been developed. The degree of contextual constraint is defined by the order of approximation: 1st order is text in which each word choice is based on one word of context ("realizing most so the together home and for were wanted"), 2nd order is text in which each word is based on two words of prior context ("sun was nice dormitory is I like chocolate cake"), 3rd order is text in which each word is based on three words of prior context ("family was large dark animal came roaring down the middle of my friends love books"), and so forth. These examples, taken from Miller and Selfridge (1950), show that as the orders of approximation are increased the resultant word sequences increase their resemblance to meaningful English, but only in regard to their short-range associations.

Based on prior studies (e.g., Murphy et al., 2000; Rabbitt, 1968, 1991) we had two predictions. The first was that older adults with age-related hearing loss would show poorer recall for the first two words of three-word recall sets than would age-matched older adults with good hearing, even when accurate recall of the final word of the three-word set implies that words not recalled had been correctly identified, albeit with greater effort on the part of the group with poorer hearing.

Our second prediction, based also on an effortfulness notion, was that the effect of hearing loss on recall would be reduced or eliminated with higher order approximations to English that increase the transitional probabilities of the stimulus words in the to-be-recalled word sets. This prediction is based on the assumption that this contextual support would facilitate perception (e.g., Morton, 1979), thus leaving more resources available for encoding the words in memory. By contrast, one would expect to see stronger effects of hearing loss on recall for word sets that do not provide contextual support. Of special note, we wished to determine whether one could demonstrate these effects not with relatively demanding memory tasks, or comprehension of complex discourse, but with simple recall of just three spoken words.

Method

Participants

The participants were 24 healthy, community-dwelling volunteers, 16 women and 8 men, ranging in age from 66 to 81 years ($M = 72.9$ years, $SD = 4.1$). All were native English speakers with good levels of education and verbal ability. All reported themselves to be in good health, with no history of stroke, Parkinson's disease, or other neuropathology that would compromise their ability to perform the research task.

Participants were tested audiometrically (air and bone conduction) to ensure that hearing loss was sensorineural in nature. Individuals with conductive or eighth nerve (retrocochlear) disorders were not used. Following otoscopic examination by an audiologist trained in otoscopy, tympanometry was conducted on all participants to document middle ear integrity and to help rule out conductive hearing loss. Distortion product otoacoustic emissions (DPOAEs) were obtained to help confirm cochlear hearing loss and to reject participants with possible auditory neuropathy (Starr, Picton, Sininger, Hood, & Berlin, 1996). Word recognition scores were also obtained, and subjects with results poorer than expected for their sensorineural hearing loss were excluded.

The participants were divided into two groups of 12 based on their puretone averages (PTAs) averaged across 1,000, 2,000, and 4,000 Hz, a frequency range known to be a good predictor of perceptual performance for speech (Humes, 1996). One group of 12 participants, referred to as the *better hearing* group, had PTAs of less than or equal to 25 dB in the better ear, which was the right ear for 7 of the participants. The PTAs of this group ranged in the better ear from 8.3 dB to 25.0 dB ($M = 21.4$ dB). The remaining 12 participants, referred to as the *hearing loss* group, had PTAs greater than 25 dB in the better ear, which was the right ear for 6 of the participants. Their PTAs ranged from 28.3 dB to 51.7 dB ($M = 35.7$ dB). Table 1 shows mean pure tone thresholds and standard deviations in the better (test) ear for the two participant groups across the range from 250 to 6000 Hz.

Although the two groups differed in hearing acuity they were equivalent in age [better hearing, $M = 72.5$ years, $SD = 4.7$; hearing loss, $M = 73.4$, $SD = 3.7$; $t(22) = 0.53$, *ns*], education [better hearing, $M = 16.5$ years, $SD = 1.8$; hearing loss, $M = 16.6$ years, $SD = 1.8$; $t(22) = 0.91$, *ns*], and verbal ability as assessed by the Shipley Vocabulary Test [Zachary, 1986; better hearing, $M = 16.5$, $SD = 2.2$; hearing loss, $M = 16.8$, $SD = 2.4$; $t(22) = 0.71$, *ns*].

Stimulus materials

The stimuli consisted of 16 strings, each 15 words in length, taken from Miller and Selfridge (1950). These represented four general degrees of contextual constraint, each comprising four lists. In decreasing order of contextual constraint these were (a) two lists each of 7th and 9th order of approximation to English, (b) two lists each of 4th and 5th order of approximation to English, (c) two lists each of 2nd

TABLE 1
Mean thresholds (in dB HL) and standard deviations
for the better hearing and hearing loss participants

Frequency (Hz)	Group			
	Better hearing		Hearing loss	
	M	SD	M	SD
250	15.8	4.7	20.0	8.0
500	16.3	3.8	24.6	6.6
1,000	13.8	4.3	22.9	7.5
2,000	18.8	7.1	34.2	8.2
3,000	24.6	8.9	46.7	11.3
4,000	31.7	11.3	50.0	13.7
6,000	45.8	12.9	56.3	11.1

Note: Data shown for better ear.

and 3rd order of approximation to English, and (d) two lists each of 0 and 1st order of approximation to English. For the 1st-order approximations each word was based on one word of prior context. The zero-order stimuli were random sequences of words that approximated the number of syllables in the other orders (e.g., "better write catch native evening bit position wish small proper grass").

In our analysis it is our intent to contrast higher order approximations with the 0- and 1st-order approximations. This is so because these two lowest level approximations were either not constrained by previous text (0 order) or constrained by only one word of previous text (1st order). For all of the orders of approximation from 2nd order and higher, each of the words to be recalled was constrained by at least two prior words. That is, even the first word in a three-word memory set had a minimum of two prior words of constraining context, as did the second and third words to be remembered. Thus, it is only 0- and 1st-order approximations that are not constrained to this degree.

All of the stimulus sequences were recorded by a female speaker of American English at a rate of one word per second to create a series of sound files using SoundEdit software (Macromedia, Inc., San Francisco, CA) for the Macintosh computer (Apple, Cupertino, CA). The lists were equated for sound intensity using a Larson-Davis 800B sound level meter (Larson Davis, Inc., Provo, UT).

Procedure

Each participant heard all 16 word-lists with order of presentation of word lists randomized between participants. Instructions were to listen carefully to each word list as it was presented. As soon as the list was finished, participants were prompted to recall the last three words by the appearance of three large asterisks on a computer screen directly in front of them. Participants were told to be ready for recall at any moment as the lists might be stopped at any time. To maintain this level of attention, the lists heard by each participant were randomly stopped for recall after 5, 7, 8, 10, 12, 13, 14, or 15 words. Regardless of list length, however, instructions were to recall just the last three words heard.

All testing was conducted in a sound-attenuated testing room, with the lists presented monaurally to the participant's better ear using Eartone 3A (E-A-R Auditory Systems, Aero Company, Indianapolis, IN) insert earphones. Stimuli were presented at a level of 75 dB HL to the better ear via a Maico MA 42 audiometer (Maico Diagnostics, Eden Prairie, MN) using Psyscope presentation software (Cohen, MacWhinney, Flatt, & Provost, 1993). Prior to the main experiment, participants completed a brief practice session in which they heard four word-lists of varying lengths and contextual constraint to familiarize them with the experimental instructions and report procedures. None of these practice lists was used in the main experiment.

Results

The recall test performance is summarized in Figure 1 for the better hearing (left panel) and hearing loss (right panel) groups. The vertical bars in each panel show the average percentage of correct recall for the first two words of the three-word sets for the various orders of approximation. For ease of presentation we have clustered the higher constraint approximations into three groups (from left to right: combined 7th and 9th order, combined 4th and 5th order, combined 2nd and 3rd order). The single vertical bars on the right in each panel show the mean percentage of correct recall for the first two words of the low contextual constraint group (combined 0 and 1st order).

As indicated previously, an important check for the analysis of word recall was to ensure that the last word of each of the three-word sets was recalled correctly. This high level of accuracy would allow the presumption that the first two words of the set had also been heard. This criterion was amply met: Across all approximation levels, the mean accuracy in reporting the final words of the three-word recall sets was 99.5% correct for the better hearing group and 98.2% for the hearing loss group. As a very conservative check on presumed perceptual registration of these to-be-remembered words, we show in Figure 1 accuracy scores only for those cases where the final words of the three-word sets were reported correctly. All analyses to be described below were also conducted on just these cases.

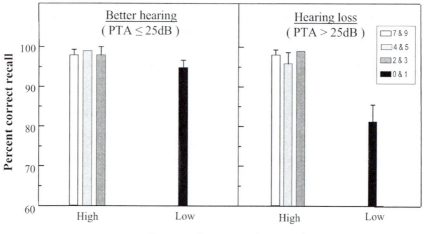

Figure 1.   Percentage of correct recall for the first two words of three-word recall sets for word sequences with high contextual constraints (2nd-through 9th-order approximations to English) and low contextual constraints (0- and 1st-order approximations). Data are shown for better hearing participants (pure tone average, PTA, less than or equal to 25 dB HL; left panel) and for participants with hearing loss (PTA greater than 25 dB HL; right panel). Error bars represent one standard error. Error bars are absent where they were too small to plot.

Inspection of Figure 1 shows that, for both groups, recall levels for the first two words of each three-word recall set are at ceiling or near ceiling for the three high contextual constraint groups (2nd through 9th orders of approximation), but that the recall level is lower when the level of constraint is low (0 and 1st orders of approximations). Importantly, this latter effect is differentially greater for the hearing loss group than for the better hearing group. These trends were confirmed by a series of analyses of variance (ANOVAs) conducted on these data.

We first conducted a 4 (approximation level: 7th & 9th, 4th & 5th, 2nd & 3rd, 0 & 1st) × 2 (hearing: better hearing, hearing loss) mixed design omnibus ANOVA, with approximation level as a within-participants factor and hearing group as a between-participants factor. The appearance in Figure 1 that order of approximation had a significant effect on recall was confirmed by a significant main effect of approximation level, $F(3, 66) = 9.34$, $MSE = 0.063$, $p < .001$. There was also a significant main effect of hearing group, $F(1, 22) = 7.76$, $MSE = 0.005$, $p < .025$. The observation that the effect of hearing loss depended on the order of approximation of the stimulus set was confirmed by a significant Hearing Group × Approximation Level interaction, $F(3, 66) = 4.20$, $MSE = 0.063$, $p < .01$.

To verify the impression in Figure 1 that the source of this interaction was in the effect of hearing on the low constraint sets (0 and 1st order) we first conducted a subsidiary two-way ANOVA on just the higher order approximation stimuli (the three approximation groups ranging from 2nd through 9th order), excluding the combined 0- and 1st-order data. As we can see, with this small recall ensemble, presented with these degrees of contextual constraint, performance was virtually at ceiling. As would thus be expected, this analysis failed to show significant main effects of either approximation level, $F(2, 44) < 1$, $MSE = 0.004$, or hearing group, $F(1, 22) < 1$, $MSE = 0.003$, nor was there a significant Approximation Level × Hearing Group interaction, $F(2, 44) < 1$, $MSE = 0.004$. By contrast, when we conducted a one-way ANOVA comparing the two hearing groups on just the low constraint sets (0 and 1st order) there was a significant difference between the hearing groups, $F(1, 22) = 8.65$, $MSE = 0.001$, $p < .01$.

As part of this analysis, however, we required a further test of our assumption that the greater number of errors made by the poor hearing group in the low context conditions was due not to a failure of perceptual identification of the words, but to a detrimental effect on memory encoding resulting from increased effort in perceptual processing of the stimulus words. To the extent that this is correct, one would expect to see no effect of participants' hearing acuity on recall of the final word of a three-word set, but one would expect to see a significant difference between the two hearing groups on the prior two words.

Planned-comparison testing conducted on the three serial positions of the recall sets confirmed this expectation: There was no significant difference between the good and poor hearing groups on recall accuracy for the final word of the three-word sets (good hearing, $M = 100\%$ correct; poor hearing, $M = 97.9\%$; $SD = 0.07$), on either a two- or a one-tailed significance test, $t(11) = 1.00$, ns. In contrast, hearing acuity had a significant effect on recall of the second-to-last word of the three-word set (good hearing, $M = 100\%$; poor hearing, $M = 87.5\%$; $SD = 0.17$), $t(11) = 2.57$, $p < .05$, and on recall of the first word of the three-word set (good hearing, $M = 89.6\%$; $SD = 0.13$; poor hearing, $M = 72.9\%$; $SD = 0.25$), $t(11) = 2.06$, $p < .05$. (Inspection of these accuracy rates offers a suggestion of a graded effect of hearing acuity, with the difference between the good and poor hearing groups increasing as one proceeds backward in serial position. An ANOVA conducted on these data, however, failed to show a significant Hearing Group × Serial Position effect due, most probably, to the generally high levels of recall for both groups.)

Discussion

As Rabbitt (1968) originally noted, we are often forced to listen to speech over a poor telephone line (or today over cell phones with a weak signal) or speech partially masked by environmental noise. In the case of many older adults, these environmental contributors to less-than-clear speech are further compounded by a hearing loss, especially in the higher frequency ranges that affect consonant recognition (Morrell et al., 1996).

Such losses in signal clarity, whether a consequence of ambient noise, hearing loss, or both, need not necessarily be sufficient to produce errors in recognition. The question we raise, however, is whether the perceptual and inferential efforts required for the successful recognition of a degraded signal may take a toll on processing resources that might otherwise be used for downstream operations. Such potentially vulnerable downstream operations would include the ability to encode the materials in memory through rehearsal or to comprehend text meaning at a propositional level, often in the face of rapid speech with complex syntax. Such effects could lead not only to the reduced memory performance seen here but also, potentially, to the perhaps erroneous impression of reduced cognitive function in the listener. Indeed, one could entertain an analogous concern in the case of vision, where even modest sensory impairment might have significant secondary effects on downstream processes such as memory (Dickinson & Rabbitt, 1991).

The present results have shown that the added perceptual effort required for successful recognition by participants with a mild-to-moderate hearing loss was sufficient to affect memory performance when recall of just three words was required. This illustrates that the perceptual effort required to successfully identify words may affect recall in a situation far less demanding than the memory tasks used in the prior studies of participants with hearing loss (Rabbitt, 1991) or the effects of noise on recall by participants with good hearing (Murphy et al., 2000; Rabbitt, 1968).

To isolate the source of this effect it was necessary that we showed that the recall failures for the low-constraint words by the hearing loss group were not due to a failure to identify the words, albeit with some effort. Because both groups correctly reported the final words of the three-word sets, we can infer that they also identified the prefinal words, which were recorded by the same speaker and at the same intensity. We thus conclude that the larger number of recall failures for the prefinal words by the hearing loss group was not due to a failure of recognition, but to the necessary allocation of greater processing resources to achieve this successful identification. This point was emphasized in our analysis, which used only those cases where the final word was reported correctly.

These data go beyond prior studies that have used meaningful sentences to supply contextual support for word recognition for degraded words (e.g., Perry & Wingfield, 1994; Pichora-Fuller et al., 1995; Wingfield et al., 1991) or with young and older adults with hearing loss (Gordon-Salant & Fitzgibbons, 1997). The current work shows that such constraints operate even with statistical approximations to English that mimic the predictive quality of natural language but without conveying semantic coherence (Miller & Selfridge, 1950; Moray & Taylor, 1960). Indeed, so long as each of the words to be recalled was constrained by at least two prior words (i.e., 2nd-order approximations and higher) hearing acuity had no effect on recall. As indicated earlier, the reason this is so lies in the nature of statistical approximations to English and our use of three-word memory sets. That is, with 2nd-order approximations every word in the three-word memory set is always constrained by at least two previous words. Thus, it is only 0- and 1st-order approximations that are not constrained to this degree.

The constraints offered by the higher orders of approximation may have operated to facilitate the recognition of the target words either by increasing their likelihood (Morton, 1969, 1979) or by decreasing the number of potential lexical possibilities (Marslen-Wilson, 1990) as the words were being heard. They may also have aided in retrospective recognition of words whose identity had originally been unclear (Grosjean, 1985; Wingfield, Alexander, & Cavigelli, 1994). Our presumption is that any or all of these effects might reduce the perceptual burden on the listener's processing resources. This would, in turn, leave more resources available for encoding the words in memory, resulting in more successful recall.

It should be recognized that the higher order approximations may have also affected performance by listeners using the transitional probabilities between the words to aid in reconstructive operations during the act of recall itself (Potter & Lombardi, 1990). None of these influences, however, would operate for the lower order approximations, and it was here that hearing acuity showed its effect. For older adults with hearing loss, the extra effort necessary to successfully recognize the words had a significant effect on memory for what had been heard.

In the case of everyday speech comprehension, and memory for what has been heard, the task takes on far more complexity than the simple recall task used here. Successful comprehension of everyday discourse must rely not only on lexical identification of the individual words, but also on the determination of the syntactic relations among the words and the development of a full coherence structure for what has been heard (e.g., Kintsch, 1988). In this more challenging world of comprehension and recall of rapid and sometimes complex speech, our results, and that of others (Murphy et al., 2000; Pichora-Fuller et al., 1995; Rabbitt, 1968, 1991), suggest a need on the part of the professional community to be sensitive to the possibility raised here: that the extra perceptual effort expended on the initial stages of speech recognition by listeners with even mild hearing loss may cause measurable failures in the downstream operations of comprehension and memory for what has been heard.

In this latter regard it should be noted that in this study we examined only people with hearing loss less than 50 dB. The nature of these data would lead us to presume that individuals with hearing loss greater than 50 dB would need to expend an even greater degree of perceptual effort to effect successful comprehension. It is the case that many older adults, as well as the general public, can be highly sensitive to even the smallest sign of cognitive decline (Erber, Prager, Williams, & Caiola, 1996). The present data support the argument that downstream effects of perceptual effort due to hearing loss might lead one to overestimate the degree of cognitive decline in an older listener. Alternatively, when cognitive decline is present, a performance decline might be further exacerbated by the combination of hearing loss and the burden on resources necessary to achieve perceptual success.

REFERENCES

Baddeley, A. D. (1996). The concept of working memory. In S. Gathercole (Ed.), *Models of short-term memory* (pp. 1–28). Hove, UK: Psychology Press.

Baddeley, A. D. (1998). The central executive: A concept and some misconceptions. *Journal of the International Neuropsychological Society, 4*, 523–526.

Barr, R. A., & Giambra, L. M. (1990). Age-related decrement in auditory selective attention. *Psychology and Aging, 3*, 597–599.

Cerella, J. (1994). Generalized slowing and Brinley plots. *Journal of Gerontology: Psychological Sciences, 49*, 65–71.

Cohen, J. D., MacWhinney, B., Flatt, M., & Provost, J. (1993). Psyscope: An interactive system for designing and controlling experiments in the psychology laboratory using Macintosh computers. *Behavior Research Methods, Instruments, and Computers, 25*, 257–271.

Dickinson, C. M., & Rabbitt, P. M. A. (1991). Simulated visual impairment: Effects on text comprehension and reading speed. *Clinical Vision Sciences, 6*, 301–308.

Dubno, J. R., Ahlstrom, J. B., & Horwitz, A. R. (2000). Use of context by young and aged adults with normal hearing. *Journal of the Acoustical Society of America, 107*(1), 538–546.

Erber, J. T., Prager, I. G., Williams, M., & Caiola, M. A. (1996). Age and forgetfulness: Confidence in ability and attributions for memory failures. *Psychology and Aging, 11*, 310–315.

Fisher, D. L., & Glaser, R. A. (1996). Molar and latent models of cognitive slowing: Implications for aging, dementia, depression, development, and intelligence. *Psychonomic Bulletin and Review, 3*, 458–480.

Gordon-Salant, S. (1987). Age-related differences in speech recognition performance as a function of test format and paradigm. *Ear and Hearing, 8*, 270–276.

Gordon-Salant, S., & Fitzgibbons, P. J. (1997). Selected cognitive factors and speech recognition performance among young and elderly listeners. *Journal of Speech, Language, and Hearing Research, 40*, 423–431.

Grosjean, F. (1985). The recognition of words after their acoustic offset: Evidence and implications. *Perception and Psychophysics, 38*, 299–310.

Hasher, L., & Zacks, R. T. (1988). Working memory, comprehension, and aging: A review and a new view. In G. H. Bower (Ed.), *The psychology of learning and motivation: Advances in research and theory* (Vol. 22). San Diego: Academic Press.

Humes, L. E. (1996). Speech understanding in the elderly. *Journal of the American Academy of Audiology, 7*, 161–167.

Kahana, M. J., Howard, M., Zaromb, F., & Wingfield, A. (2002). Age dissociates recency and lag recency effects in free recall. *Journal of Experimental Psychology: Learning, Memory, and Cognition, 28*, 530–540.

Kahneman, D. (1973). *Attention and effort.* Englewood Cliffs, NJ: Prentice-Hall.

Kausler, D. M. (1994). *Learning and memory in normal aging.* San Diego, CA: Academic Press.

Kintsch, W. (1988). The role of knowledge in discourse comprehension: A construction-integration model. *Psychological Review, 95*, 163–182.

Marslen-Wilson, W. D. (1990). Activation, competition, and frequency in lexical access. In G. T. M. Altmann (Ed.), *Cognitive models of speech processing* (pp. 148–172). Cambridge, MA: MIT Press.

Miller, G. A., & Selfridge, J. A. (1950). Verbal context and the recall of meaningful material. *American Journal of Psychology, 63*, 176–185.

Moray, N., & Taylor, A. (1960). Statistical approximations to English. *Language and Speech, 3*, 7–10.

Morrell, C. H., Gordon-Salant, S., Pearson, J. D., Brant, L. J., & Fozard, J. L. (1996). Age- and gender-specific reference ranges for hearing level and longitudinal changes in hearing level. *Journal of the Acoustical Society of America, 100*, 1949–1967.

Morton, J. (1969). Interaction of information in word recognition. *Psychological Review, 76*, 165–178.

Morton, J. (1979). Facilitation in word recognition: Experiments causing change in the logogen model. In P. A. Kolers, M. E. Wrolstad, & H. Bouma (Eds.), *Processing visual language.* New York: Plenum Press.

Murdock, B. B. (1962). The serial position effect in free recall. *Journal of Experimental Psychology, 64*, 482–488.

Murphy, D. R., Craik, F. I. M., Li, K. Z. H., & Schneider, B. A. (2000). Comparing the effects of aging and background noise on short-term memory performance. *Psychology and Aging, 15*, 323–334.

National Academy on an Aging Society. (1999, December). Hearing loss: A growing problem that affects quality of life. *National Academy on an Aging Society, Number 2.*

Neath, I. (2000). Modeling the effects of irrelevant speech on memory. *Psychonomic Bulletin and Review, 7*, 403–423.

Newbigging, P. L. (1961). The perceptual redintegration of frequent and infrequent words. *Canadian Journal of Psychology*, *15*, 123–131.

Perry, A. R., & Wingfield, A. (1994). Contextual encoding by young and elderly adults as revealed by cued and free recall. *Aging and Cognition*, *1*, 120–139.

Pichora-Fuller, M. K., Schneider, B. A., & Daneman, M. (1995). How young and old adults listen to and remember speech in noise. *Journal of the Acoustical Society of America*, *97*, 593–607.

Potter, M. C., & Lombardi, L. (1990). Regeneration in the short-term recall of sentences. *Journal of Memory and Language*, *29*, 633–654.

Rabbitt, P. M. A. (1968). Channel capacity, intelligibility and immediate memory. *Quarterly Journal of Experimental Psychology*, *20*, 241–248.

Rabbitt, P. M. A. (1991). Mild hearing loss can cause apparent memory failures which increase with age and reduce with IQ. *Acta Otolaryngolica, Supplementum 476*, 167–176.

Salthouse, T. A. (1991). *Theoretical perspectives on cognitive aging*. Hillsdale, NJ: Lawrence Erlbaum Associates, Inc.

Salthouse, T. A. (1996). The processing-speed theory of adult age differences in cognition. *Psychological Review*, *103*, 403–428.

Starr, A., Picton, T., Sininger, Y., Hood, L., & Berlin, C. (1996). Auditory neuropathy. *Brain*, *199*, 741–753.

Stoltzfus, E. R., Hasher, L., & Zacks, R. T. (1996). Working memory and aging: Current status of the inhibitory view. In J. R. Richardson (Ed.), *Working memory and cognition* (pp. 66–88). New York: Oxford University Press.

Tun, P. A. (1998). Fast noisy speech: Age differences in processing rapid speech with background noise. *Psychology and Aging*, *13*, 424–434.

Tun, P. A., O'Kane, G. O., & Wingfield, A. (2002). Distraction by competing speech in young and older adult listeners. *Psychology and Aging*, *17*, 453–467.

Tun, P. A., & Wingfield, A. (1999). One voice too many: Adult age differences in language processing with different types of distracting sounds. *Journal of Gerontology: Psychological Sciences*, *54B*, P317–P327.

Wingfield, A., Aberdeen, J. S., & Stine, E. A. L. (1991). Word onset gating and linguistic context in spoken word recognition by young and elderly adults. *Journal of Gerontology: Psychological Sciences*, *46*, P127–P129.

Wingfield, A., Alexander, A. H., & Cavigelli, S. (1994). Does memory constrain utilization of top-down information in spoken word recognition? Evidence from normal aging. *Language and Speech*, *37*, 221–235.

Wingfield, A., Lahar, C. J., & Stine, E. A. L. (1989). Age and decision strategies in running memory for speech: Effects of prosody and linguistic structure. *Journal of Gerontology: Psychological Sciences*, *44*, P106–P113.

Wingfield, A., Stine, E. A. L., Lahar, C. J., & Aberdeen, J. S. (1988). Does the capacity of working memory change with age? *Experimental Aging Research*, *14*, 103–107.

Working Group on Speech Understanding and Aging. (1988). Speech understanding in aging. *Journal of the Acoustical Society of America*, *83*, 859–895.

Zachary, R. (1986). *Shipley Institute of Living Scale, Revised manual*. Los Angeles: Western Psychological Services.

PrEview proof published online 7 July 2004

THE QUARTERLY JOURNAL OF EXPERIMENTAL PSYCHOLOGY
2005, 58A (1), 34–53

Ψ Psychology Press
Taylor & Francis Group

Age-related declines in context maintenance and semantic short-term memory

Henk J. Haarmann

University of Maryland, College Park, USA

Gemma E. Ashling

Goldsmiths College, University of London, UK

Eddy J. Davelaar and Marius Usher

Birkbeck College, University of London, UK

This study reports age-related declines in context maintenance (Braver et al., 2001) and semantic short-term memory (STM) and evidence for a relation between the two. A group of younger and older adults completed a context maintenance task (AX-CPT), a semantically oriented STM task (conceptual span), a phonologically oriented STM task (digit span), and a meaning integration task (semantic anomaly judgement). In the AX-CPT task, a target response is required to the probe letter "X" but only when it is preceded by the letter "A" (the context). Either three (short interference) or six distractor letters (long interference) were presented between the cue and the probe. Results indicated an age-related deficit in context maintenance. Age-related declines were also observed for conceptual span and semantic anomaly judgement but not for digit span. Context maintenance was correlated with conceptual span and semantic anomaly judgement but not with digit span. These correlations were largely mediated by age differences, which also explained variance that was unique to (and not shared among) context maintenance, conceptual span, and semantic anomaly judgement.

It is well known that healthy ageing reduces information processing speed (Cerella, 1985; Myerson, Hale, Wagstaff, Poon, & Smith, 1990; Salthouse, 1996) and results in performance declines in various cognitive functions, including working memory (Morris, Craik, & Gick, 1990; Verhaeghen & Salthouse, 1997), inhibition (Hasher, Stoltzfus, Zacks, & Rypma, 1991; Hasher & Zachs, 1988; West & Alain, 2000; Zacks & Hasher, 1997), attention (Anderer, Pascual-Marqui, Semlitsch, & Saletu, 1998), and episodic memory (Craik, 1977; Moscovitch & Winocur, 1992). Furthermore, older adults show patterns of task performance that suggest

Correspondence should be addressed to Henk Haarmann at the Center for the Advanced Study of Language, University of Maryland, College Park, MD 20742, USA. Email: hhaarmann@comcast.net

EJD was supported by the Economic and Social Research Council (T0262701312).

http://www.tandf.co.uk/journals/pp/02724987.html   DOI:10.1080/02724980443000214

age-related declines in various forms of attention, including selective attention (Brink & McDowd, 1999; Panek, Rush, & Slade, 1984; Spieler, Balota, & Faust, 1996; West & Baylis, 1998; West & Bell, 1997), divided and/or alternating attention (Brouwer, Waterink, Van Wolffelaar, & Rothengatter, 1991; Jensen & Goldstein, 1991; Korteling, 1993), and sustained attention (Filley & Cullum, 1994; Parasuraman & Nestor, 1991). Older adults take longer to respond on many tasks from very simple perceptual tasks to more complex cognitive tasks (Cerella, 1985; Myerson et al., 1990). Ageing also affects executive function, as indicated, for example, by age-related declines on neuropsychological tests for assessing prefrontal dysexecutive syndrome, such as the Wisconsin Card Sorting Test (Daigneault, Braun, & Whitaker, 1992), the fluency test (Keys & White, 2000), and the trail making test (Keys & White, 2000), even when speed of processing is controlled for. Finally, within the domain of episodic memory, age-related declines are especially apparent on tasks that involve free recall (Craik & Jennings, 1992), temporal order memory (Parkin, Walter, & Hunkin, 1995), source memory (Spencer & Raz, 1994), and release from proactive inhibition (Dobbs, Aubrey, & Rule, 1989).

One of the major challenges for a theory of cognitive ageing is to provide a unifying account for the age-related declines that are observed in the various cognitive domains, in a manner that is consistent with what is known about the neurobiological effects of ageing (Braver et al., 2001; Moscovitch & Winocur, 1992). Theories of ageing have tried to explain age-related performance declines across a variety of tasks in terms of a deficit in a single underlying cognitive function or a small set of cognitive functions, including processing speed (Myerson et al., 1990; Salthouse, 1996), working memory capacity (Craik, Morris, & Gick, 1990; Light & Anderson, 1985; Salthouse, 1992), inhibition (Hasher & Zacks, 1988; Zacks & Hasher, 1997), and attention (West & Bell, 1997). Recently, Braver, Barch, Cohen, and their colleagues have proposed a theory of cognitive ageing that has the potential to unify various previous theories (Braver et al., 2001; Braver & Barch, 2002). Their proposal is that cognitive ageing involves a working memory deficit in the ability to represent, maintain, and update information about task context. As a result, information about task context is used less effectively in governing the use of task-relevant information, explaining age-related problems on a variety of tasks in terms of a common mechanism. For example, in the Stroop task, the task instructions ("name ink colour") must be actively represented and maintained in working memory to bias attention allocation and response selection toward the ink colour dimension of a visually presented word. In the Stroop task, an age-related deficit in context representation and/or maintenance may appear as a problem in selective attention and/or a problem in inhibiting processing of the irrelevant task dimension (i.e., word reading; Braver et al., 2001). In dual-task paradigms, there are frequent shifts between tasks, requiring a continuous updating of task context. Thus, an age-related deficit in the representation, maintenance, and/or updating of task context may appear as a problem in dividing attention between two tasks. The same age-related deficit may interfere with performance on working memory tasks, which, due to their simultaneous storage and processing demands, involve a dual-task component and a need to frequently update the task context (Braver et al., 2001). Finally, age-related declines in episodic memory, such as, free recall, recall of temporal order, and source memory, may also be due to a problem in the representation, maintenance, and/or updating of context (Braver et al., 2001), since such tasks require integration of outputs from long-term memory with relevant contextual information or strategic cues (Moscovitch & Winocur, 1992;

Perfect, 2003). The theory that ageing impairs the processing of context in working memory is consistent with neurobiological theories of ageing according to which age-related cognitive declines are due to deficits in the executive function of the prefrontal cortex (PFC), resembling the deficits of neuropsychological patients with PFC damage (Moscovitch & Winocur, 1992; Perfect, 2003). Such deficits may be the expression of an underlying deficit in the processing of task context in a specific region within the PFC, the dorso-lateral PFC (DL-PFC; Braver & Barch, 2002; Braver et al., 2001; MacPherson, Phillips, & Della Sala, 2002). Indeed, neuroimaging data indicate that the DL-PFC supports the processing of task context in working memory and is activated differently during the maintenance of task context in old adults from the way it is in young adults (i.e., showing a decline instead of increase of activation across time; Barch, Braver, Racine, & Satpute, 2001).

One of the most direct pieces of evidence for an age-related deficit in the processing of context in working memory has been obtained with a modified version of the AX-CPT test (Braver et al., 2001). The AX-CPT test is an adaptation of the classic continuous performance test (CPT; Rosvold, Mirsky, Sarason, Bransome, & Beck, 1956), which has been especially designed to place a demand on the processing of task-relevant contextual information in working memory (Cohen, Barch, Carter, & Servan-Schreiber, 1999; Servan-Schreiber, Cohen, & Steingard, 1996). Participants are presented with a series of letters and have to give a target response to each occurrence of the letter "X" (i.e., the target) but only when it is preceded by the letter "A" (valid cue), which serves as the context. The experimental condition in which this happens is known as AX. In all other conditions, including BX (invalid cue followed by a target), AY (valid cue followed by a nontarget), and BY (invalid cue followed by nontarget), a nontarget response is required. The letter "B" is used to indicate any letter other than the cue "A", whereas the letter "Y" is used to indicate any letter other than the target "X". In the ageing study by Braver et al. (2001), AX trials occurred much more frequently than each of the other three trial types (e.g., 70% versus 10% each), creating a strong bias to respond incorrectly with a target response in the BX and AY condition and, therefore, increasing the demands on the use of context information (i.e., valid vs. invalid cue; Cohen et al., 1999). Poor context representation and/or maintenance should *increase* errors in the BX condition, since the noncue (B) is less likely to be in working memory when the target (X) is presented and since the target response is a prepotent response due to high proportion of AX trials. By contrast, poor context representation and/or maintenance should *decrease* errors in the AY condition, since the cue (A) is less likely to be in working memory and create a bias towards a target response when a nontarget (Y) is presented. These context maintenance problems should be exacerbated when the delay between the context (a cue or noncue) and the probe (a target or nontarget) is made longer and/or filled with intervening distractor letters (Braver & Barch, 2002; Braver et al., 2001). To test this latter prediction, Braver et al.'s (2001) study manipulated the properties of the cue–probe interval (4.9 s). In a baseline condition it was unfilled, whereas in an interference condition three distractor letters (requiring a nontarget response) were presented during the interval. A degraded condition, identical to the baseline condition except for visual degradation of the cue and probe letter, was included to control for task difficulty.

The results of the Braver et al. (2001) study provided evidence for a context maintenance deficit in older adults (Barch et al., 2001). In the baseline condition, compared to young adults, older adults showed a trend towards more BX errors, fewer AY errors, reduced context sensitivity (as indicated by a d' measure using BX errors for false alarms), and slower responses on AX and BX (but not AY) trials. This pattern was significant and amplified in the interference condition, which placed a greater demand on context maintenance, strongly suggesting an age-related impairment in context maintenance. Both the interference and the degraded condition showed an increase in target errors relative to the baseline condition. However, unlike interference, perceptual degrading did not affect nontarget errors, suggesting that the interference effects on BX and AY errors were not caused by an increase in the general level of task difficulty (Braver et al., 2001) but by an impairment in context maintenance. This interpretation was confirmed by the simulation results of a neurocomputational model, which assumed that ageing impairs context maintenance and updating in the DL-PFC (Braver et al., 2001), consistent with neuroimaging results (Barch et al., 2001). When such a deficit was simulated, the model showed that increasing the cue–probe interval decreases performance on BX trials and increases performance on AY trials. The intact model, by contrast, showed no change in performance on BX trials and even a slight increase in AY errors with increased delay.

The proposal that ageing affects a working memory component that processes context information raises the issue of whether this component is related to short-term memory (STM) for information about the identity of previous lexical/semantic stimuli. This issue arises especially since STM may be viewed as the storage component of working memory (Cowan, 1999; Engle, Tuholski, Laughlin, & Conway, 1999; Haarmann, Davelaar, & Usher, 2003). One possibility is that there is no relation between working memory for context and short-term memory for identity information. As Braver et al. (2001) pointed out, this might explain why ageing is associated with declines in performance on complex working memory tasks, but with no or much smaller declines in standard STM tasks, such as digit span (Fisk & Warr, 1996; Humes, Nelson, Pisoni, & Lively, 1993). Whereas complex working memory tasks, such as reading span (Daneman & Carpenter, 1980) and operation span (Turner & Engle, 1989), place large demands on the representation, active maintenance, and updating of context, standard STM tasks, such as digit span, may incur those demands to a much lesser extent. For example, operation span requires solving a sequence of arithmetic problems, while maintaining digits (or words) presented in between problems for subsequent recall. Thus, operation (but not digit) span requires a continuous updating of the internal representation of the task instructions from a focus on arithmetic to one on digit recall. Nevertheless, another possibility is that there is a relation between working memory for context and STM for identity information. This is suggested by the need for context maintenance to allow semantic disambiguation in language processing. For example, in order to select the contextually appropriate meaning of an ambiguous word at the end of a sentence (e.g., whether the word *bank* refers to the edge of a river or a financial institution) one must be able to maintain the specific meanings of one or more prior words as part of its semantic context (e.g., *"Because the river was so beautiful, they decided to go for a walk along the bank"*; Swinney, 1979). There is evidence that schizophrenia patients with positive thought disorder have difficulties maintaining context information in both a semantic disambiguation task (Bazin, Perruchet, Hardy-Bayle, & Feline, 2000; Cohen & Servan-Schreiber, 1992) and an AX-CPT task (Braver & Barch, 2002; Braver et al., 2001), suggesting that the mechanisms supporting STM for (semantic) identity information and context maintenance could be related.

If indeed such a relation exists, then the question arises of how to explain the finding of more severe age-related deficits on working memory tasks (e.g., reading span, operation span) than on standard span tasks, such as digit span (Fisk & Warr, 1996; Humes et al., 1993). The latter type of task may rely primarily on the classic phonological STM (Baddeley, 1986, 1992; Burgess & Hitch, 1999; Warrington & Shallice, 1969), which may not place a large demand on context maintenance, especially since it uses a specialized mechanism for retaining phonological codes (i.e., articulatory rehearsal of phonologically decaying codes). Recent neuropsychological findings by Martin and colleagues (Freedman & Martin, 2001; Martin & Romani, 1994; Martin, Shelton, & Yaffee, 1994; Romani & Martin, 1999) suggest that verbal STM consists not only of a phonological STM but also of a semantic STM, which maintains information about the identity of a small set of word meanings. They reported a double dissociation between two types of STM deficit. One patient, E.A, had a greater phonological than semantic STM impairment, and three patients, A.B., M.L., and G.R., had a greater semantic than phonological STM impairment (Freedman & Martin, 2001; Martin & Romani, 1994; Martin et al., 1994; Romani & Martin, 1999). Patient E.A. but not A.B. showed the patterns of effect typically associated with a phonological STM deficit including (a) impaired rhyme probe recognition, (b) a reversed modality effect (i.e., better performance in the visual than auditory modality), (c) lack of a phonological similarity effect in the visual modality, and (d) lack of a word length effect in both modalities. By contrast, patient A.B. but not E.A. showed a pattern of effects that indicated a deficit in semantic STM, including (a) severely impaired category probe recognition, (b) absence of a lexicality effect (i.e., words were not better recalled than nonwords), (c) problems with semantic attribute judgements (e.g., "Which is softer, cotton or sandpaper?"), and (d) problems with on-line semantic anomaly judgement, especially when the memory load is high (e.g., "*Jeeps*, men, and women were *walking* the streets"; Martin & Romani, 1994). Additional evidence for a semantic STM also comes from a recent cognitive study showing that lexical semantic effects are observed at recency in immediate free recall, even after contributions from long-term memory are factored out and also after contributions from phonological STM are minimized through articulatory suppression (Haarmann & Usher, 2001). This is also consistent with findings indicating the existence of semantic strategies that can eliminate word length and similarity effects in word span tasks even for subjects whose span is in the normal range (Logie, Della Sala, Laiacona, Chalmers, & Wynn, 1996).

Given such dissociable systems within verbal STM, it seems possible that the part of working memory that maintains information about task context is related to semantic but not phonological STM. This idea is consistent with the results of a recent correlation study with healthy young adults (Haarmann et al., 2003), showing that semantic but not phonological STM correlates well with performance on more complex cognitive tasks, including semantic anomaly judgement, text comprehension, and verbal problem solving. While phonological STM was assessed with a nonword span test requiring serial recall, semantic STM was assessed by means of the conceptual span test (Haarmann et al., 2003), which had been designed to maximize the contribution of semantic STM. In the *conceptual span* task, participants are presented with a memory list of nine randomly ordered words, consisting of three words in each of the three semantic categories. The memory list is followed by the name of one of the categories, and participants try to recall the words in the memory list belonging to that category. Since conceptual span uses a semantic cued recall procedure and does not require serial recall of the three words within a category, it is likely to primarily engage semantic STM and to involve only a minimal contribution of phonological STM.[1] Moreover, this span measure does not require alternation between memory encoding and production, as more complex span measures do. Nevertheless, the conceptual span test outperformed a complex span measure, the reading span (Daneman & Carpenter, 1980), in predicting semantic anomaly judgement and verbal problem solving (Haarmann et al., 2003), suggesting an important role for semantic STM in complex cognitive tasks.

Overview of the current study

The present study had three major aims, namely (a) to replicate and extend the finding of an age-related context maintenance deficit in the AX-CPT task, (b) to examine whether there is an age-related deficit in semantic (but not phonological STM), and (c) to test the hypothesis that there is a relation between the systems for context maintenance and semantic (but not phonological) STM. The semantic and the phonological STM abilities are tested with the conceptual span (described above) and the digit span, respectively. The digit span was used as it is one of the most standard tests (included in the Wechsler IQ test; test–retest reliability of .83; Wechsler, 1981) and is traditionally related to the phonological loop.

In discussing their results, Braver et al. (2001) pointed out that "a strong claim of our theory is that inhibitory deficits in healthy older adults will be greatest under task conditions in which successful inhibition is dependent upon actively maintaining context information over a delay period. This claim remains to be tested" (p. 20). Although in Braver et al., the age effect on AY errors in the interference condition was as predicted, the effect of interference on the AY errors in the older group did not show the predicted improvement (relative to baseline). It is possible, however, that the comparison between the interference and the baseline conditions involves processes additional to context maintenance. Therefore, in the present study, we manipulated the difficulty of maintaining context information in the AX-CPT task, by contrasting a short and long interference condition during which three and six distractor letters were presented, respectively. To ensure encoding of these distractor letters and to prevent rehearsal of the cue, participants read the cue and distractor letters out loud. In addition, we intermixed trials belonging to the long and short conditions, rather than presenting them in separate blocks (as in Braver et al., 2001), to ensure that differences are not due to strategy variations between the two conditions (e.g., different encoding of context cue or increased attention) but can be attributed to the amount of time over which the context is maintained and exposed to interference. Finally, in order to obtain a more sensitive measure of performance, we used a speeded performance measure by imposing a 1-s response deadline. Notice that although older people are known to be sensitive in particular to time pressure, our main interest focuses on the predicted within-group effect of interference interval on performance. Accordingly, maintenance of the cue is more difficult in the long than in the short interference condition. The added maintenance difficulty reduces the ability of an invalid cue to inhibit a target response on BX trials. It furthermore reduces the ability of a valid cue to create a bias towards a target response on AX and AY trials. Hence, if older

---

[1]This is suggested by the absence of word length effects in semantic category cued recall (Haarmann et al., 2003).

adults have a deficit in maintaining context information (i.e., valid vs. invalid cue) in working memory, then they should produce more AX and BX errors but fewer AY errors in the long than in the short interference condition.

Using this rationale, we defined an index of context maintenance, based on the equation (AX short − AX long) + (BX short − BX long) + (AY long − AY short), where AX, BX, and AY refer to the error percentages on the corresponding trial types and short and long to the short and long interference condition. Semantic STM was assessed with the conceptual span test, while phonological STM was assessed with a digit span test. If the systems for context maintenance and semantic (but not phonological) STM are related, then there should be an age-related decline not only in context maintenance in the AX-CPT task but also in conceptual (but not digit) span. In addition, the index of context maintenance should correlate positively with conceptual span, whereas it should not correlate with digit span. We expected the correlation to be mediated largely by age-related effects, because ageing may affect overlapping or adjacent systems (in the prefrontal cortex) that support context maintenance and semantic STM. To assess the role of such a system for performance on a complex cognitive task that involves the on-line storage and integration of word meanings, a speeded anomaly judgement task requiring detection of semantic errors among the words in a sentence was included as well.

Method

Participants

Participants in the study were 43 young adults (age range 21–37 years) and 36 older adults (age range 66–85 years). The young adult group included 29 females and 14 males, while the older adult group included 23 females and 13 males. Young participants were recruited from Birkbeck College and from University College London, while older participants were recruited from a geriatric day centre (Edith Cavell House of Peterborough Hospital), from a residential home for the Elderly (Tanglewood), and from Birkbeck College in London. Informed consent was obtained in accordance with the institutional review board, and a small cash payment was given in return for participation. Inclusion criteria for all participants included (a) normal or corrected normal (20/30) vision and (b) at least 5 years of formal education. In addition, participants were excluded for (a) non-English native language, (b) lifetime history of psychiatric disorders or substance dependence, on the basis of *Diagnostic and Statistical Manual of Mental Disorders* (4th ed.; American Psychiatric Association, 1994) criteria, (c) evidence of dementia (on the basis of using *DSM-IV* criteria), or (d) history or evidence of any cognitive and/or neurological disorder or head trauma or other sensory, motor, or medical problems that could affect cognition or performance. There were no known differences between the older adults recruited from the three different sites in terms of cognitive or physical background, other than that the older adults at the day centre and residential home (but not at Birkbeck College) were provided with meals and recreational activities in a protective setting. All participants were ambulatory, except for two older adults at the residential home who used walking aids. Focused contrasts indicated that the young and older adults did not differ on educational level. The demographic characteristics of both participant groups are shown in Table 1.

Tests

Each participant was tested individually and performed four tests, given in the same order—namely, digit span, conceptual span (Haarmann et al., 2003), AX-CPT, and anomaly judgement. A test

TABLE 1
Demographic characteristics

Characteristic	Young adults			Older adults		
	M	SD	%	M	SD	%
Age[a]	26.8	3.9		74.8	5.7	
Education[a]	14.84	1.6		14.36	2.0	
% female			67			64
% right-handed			91			88

[a]In years.

session lasted about 40 minutes. Presentation of all tests was visual and controlled by a laptop computer. In the digit and conceptual span tests, the experimenter recorded participants' spoken responses manually using a score sheet. In the AX–CPT and anomaly judgement tasks, the computer recorded both response choice and response time with 1-ms accuracy, using a button box with designated yes and no buttons.

Digit span.   On each trial, participants silently read a random sequence of digits (1 to 9), presented at a computer-controlled rate of one digit/s. Immediately after the offset of the last digit, a question mark appeared, and participants attempted to recall aloud all digits in the set in their order of presentation. Testing started at a set size of two digits. There were two trials per set size. The set size was increased with one digit if there was at least one correct response (i.e., all words recalled in correct order). A participant's digit span was defined as the largest set size at which a correct response was obtained.

Conceptual span.   On each trial, participants silently read a sequence of nine nouns (in small letters) followed by a category name (in capital letters), presented at a computer-controlled rate of 1 word/s. The nine words consisted of three groups of three nouns, with each group belonging to a different semantic category, and were presented in a random order. Participants were instructed to try to recall aloud the three nouns in the named category in any order (e.g., *lamp, pear, tiger, apple, grape, elephant, horse, fax, phone, FRUIT?* Answer: *pear grape apple*). Categories and words were sampled at random from six semantic categories with eight nouns each. There were 2 practice trials and 10 test trials. A participant's conceptual span was defined as the number of words recalled across the 10 test trials (the maximum possible score was 30).

AX–CPT.   The letter sequences used for the AX–CPT task comprised a three-by-two design, crossing the factors trial type (AX, BX, or AY) and delay (short or long). Each letter sequence consisted of a cue letter (the context), several distractor letters, and a probe letter. The cue A and probe X refer to the actual letters A and X, while the cue B and probe Y refer to any other randomly selected letter in the alphabet (except "K", since it is visually similar to X and Y). In the short and long delay condition, three and six randomly selected distractor letters (different from the cue and the probe) intervened between the cue and probe letter, respectively. AX, BX, and AY sequences occurred with 70, 15, and 15%, respectively, half of them occurring in the short delay condition and the other half in the long delay condition. A total of 120 letter sequences (trials) were presented in random order across two blocks with a brief break in between. There were six practice trials. On each trial, a fixation cross appeared for 1,000 ms, followed by the presentation of the cue, the distractors, and the probe, one at a time at 550 ms per letter. All stimuli were shown centrally on a white background in 65-point uppercase Lucida font.

The cue letter and the distractor letters were shown in red, whereas the probe letter was shown in black. Participants were instructed to say out loud the cue letter and the distractor letters as they saw each of them, to ensure encoding and prevent rehearsal of the cue. They were instructed to otherwise ignore the distractor letters when monitoring for targets. Participants were further instructed to respond to the probe letter by pressing a yes button on AX trials and a no button otherwise, as quickly and accurately as possible. The assignment of buttons (left vs. right button) to answers ("yes" versus "no" answer) was counterbalanced across the participants in each age group. To prevent ceiling level performance, participants had to respond within 1,000 ms from the onset of the probe letter. Responses that were slower than this limit were recorded as incorrect. The computer recorded both response choice and response time with 1-ms accuracy. The response initiated the next trial.

Anomaly judgement. This test came from a previous study (see Haarmann et al., 2003, Exp. 2, for details). This test consisted of 68 sentences. They were presented in a random order, one word at a time at a base rate of 450 ms (plus 30 ms for every additional letter in a word). Half of the sentences were semantically sensible, and half were semantically anomalous, including either an absurd (i.e., semantically anomalous) adjective–noun combination or an absurd noun–verb combination, but not both (e.g., "*The boys admired the* **curly**, *new* **car** *of the secretary in the office*", "*He* **lifted** *the bright* **sun** *outside the factory*", bold type shown for illustrative purposes only). Participants silently read each sentence word by word and had to press a no button as soon as the sentence stopped making sense and to press a yes button if at the end of the sentence it turned out the sentence was sensible. There was a 1.5-s response deadline to prevent ceiling level performance. Participants received feedback to indicate whether or not their response was correct and whether or not it occurred within the deadline. The computer recorded both response choice and response time with 1-ms accuracy.

Data analysis

Average error rates (misses plus false alarms) and RTs (for correct trials only) were calculated per subject per condition in the AX-CPT task. They were then entered as data points into mixed-factor analyses of variance (ANOVA) with age (young or old) as a between-subjects factor and delay (short or long) as a within-subjects factor. Error type (BX or AY) was an additional within-subjects factor in the ANOVAs of nontarget trials (Braver et al., 2001). Separate ANOVAs were carried out for target (i.e., AX) and nontarget trials (i.e., BX and AY trials), because of their different response requirements (target button vs. nontarget button press) and their different frequencies of occurrence (i.e., 70% for AX trials, 15% for each of the nontarget trials) (Braver et al., 2001; Servan-Schreiber et al., 1996). Significant interactions were broken down into lower order interactions and/or simple main effects with further ANOVAs. ANOVAs were also calculated for each of the other measures (i.e., conceptual span, digit span, and anomaly judgement accuracy) separately, with age (young or old) as a between-subjects factor. For purposes of correlation and regression analyses, a single variable, "context maintenance", was calculated as an aggregate measure of the delay effect on the error rate across the three trial types, as follows: (AX short − AX long) + (BX short − BX long) + (AY long − AY short), where AX, BX, and AY denote error percentages on the corresponding trial types, and short and long refer to the short and long delay condition. A lower score on this variable indicates greater problems with context maintenance, since such problems are expected to increase AX and/or BX errors and to decrease AY errors in the long condition relative to the short condition (Braver et al., 2001). First-order and partial product moment correlations were calculated among age, context maintenance, conceptual span, digit span, and anomaly judgement. The partial correlation analyses were augmented with several stepwise hierarchical regressions. In anomaly judgement, older adults showed a much higher percentage of trials on which the 1,500-ms response deadline was surpassed than did young adults ($M = 59\%$ old adults vs. $M = 16\%$ young adults). We therefore calculated two measures of anomaly judgement—Anomaly Judgement 1 and Anomaly Judgement 2—which did and did not, respectively, take the deadline into account, in order to assess its effect on the results. Anomaly Judgement 1 took the deadline into account by scoring only responses prior to the deadline as correct (1) or incorrect (0), while scoring correct and incorrect responses past the deadline as if they were "don't know" responses (.5). Several participants showed a tendency to be over-rejecting in the anomaly judgement task. To correct for response bias, A' was used as an accuracy measure in this task. A' provides an unbiased estimate of the proportion correct in a two-alternative forced-choice procedure (Pollack & Norman, 1964) and was calculated as $A' = 0.5 + (y - x)(1 + y - x)/4y(1 - x)$, where x = false alarm rate, and y = hit rate (Grier, 1971; Linebarger, Schwartz, & Saffran, 1983).

Results

AX-CPT accuracy

Figure 1 shows the average performance accuracy in the AX-CPT task as a function of age, delay, and error type. The analysis of error rates on target trials (AX) revealed main effects of age, $F(1, 77) = 138.42$, $p < .001$, and delay, $F(1, 77) = 69.36$, $p < .001$, and an interaction of age and delay, $F(1, 77) = 25.72$, $p < .001$, due to an increase in AX errors with increased age and delay and due to a larger delay effect for older adults, $F(1, 35) = 70.21$, $p < .001$, than for young adults, $F(1, 42) = 6.91$, $p < .05$. However, when expressed in relative rather than absolute terms, young and older adults showed almost equal delay effects (50% and 45% more AX

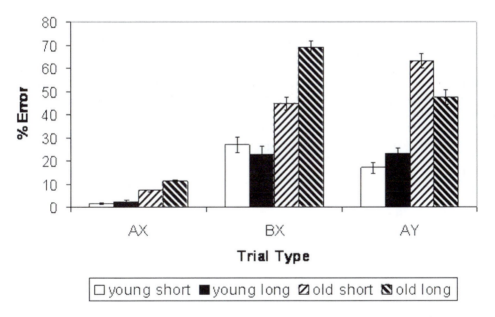

Figure 1. Percentage of error in the AX-CPT task as a function of trial type, age, and delay. Error bars depict standard errors of the means. Old adults made more AX, BX, and AY errors than did young adults. Old adults made more AX and BX errors but fewer AY errors in the long than in the short delay condition, suggesting a problem with context maintenance.

errors, respectively[2]). The analysis of error rates on nontarget trials (BX and AY) strongly suggested the presence of a context maintenance deficit in old but not young adults. There was an
interaction of delay and error type, $F(1, 77) = 22.43$, $p < .001$, and an interaction of age, delay,
and error type, $F(1, 77) = 64.37$, $p < .001$, due to different effects of age and delay on the BX
versus AY errors. For BX errors, there were main effects of age, $F(1, 77) = 50.82$, $p < .001$, and
delay, $F(1, 77) = 28.20$, $p < .001$, and an interaction of age and delay, $F(1, 77) = 55.93$,
$p < .001$, due to the fact that older adults produced more BX errors than did young adults and
due to the fact that older adults produced more BX errors in the long than in the short delay
condition, $F(1, 35) = 76.18$, $p < .001$, whereas young adults did not. Young adults showed
more BX errors in the short than in the long delay condition, but this effect fell short of
significance, $F(1, 42) = 2.55$, $p < .12$. For AY errors, there were main effects of age,
$F(1, 77) = 149.94$, $p < .001$, and delay, $F(1, 77) = 5.02$, $p < .05$, and an interaction of age and
delay, $F(1, 77) = 26.58$, $p < .001$, due to the fact that older adults produced more AY errors
than did young adults and due to opposite effects of delay in young versus older adults.
Whereas AY errors increased with delay in young adults, $F(1, 42) = 4.90$, $p < .05$, they
decreased with delay in old adults, $F(1, 35) = 23.68$, $p < .001$. The pattern of more BX errors
and fewer AY errors in the long than in the short condition obtained for older adults suggests
that they have a deficit in context maintenance. Such a deficit was also indicated by an age
effect on d' context,[3] $F(1, 77) = 73.54$, $p < .001$, which was larger in the long than in the short
delay condition, $F(1, 77) = 42.52$, $p < .001$, replicating Braver et al. (2001).

AX-CPT response times

Table 2 lists the average RTs and standard errors in the AX-CPT task as a function of age,
delay, and error type. The analysis of RTs on target trials (AX) revealed a main effect of age,
$F(1, 77) = 274$, $p < .001$, due to an age-related slowing in response times. The analysis of RTs
on nontarget trials (BX and AY) revealed a main effect of age, $F(1, 77) = 275$, $p < .001$, an
interaction between error type and age, $F(1, 77) = 5.25$, $p < .05$, and an interaction among
error type, age, and delay, $F(1, 77) = 5.58$, $p < .05$, reflecting the following pattern of results.
For RTs on AY trials, there was a main effect of age, $F(1, 77) = 265$, $p < .001$, due to slower
responses for the older group. For RTs on BX trials, there was not only a main effect of age,
$F(1, 77) = 238$, $p < .001$, but also an interaction of age and delay, $F(1, 77) = 4.60$, $p < .01$, due
to a delay effect in older, $F(1, 35) = 6.33$, $p < .05$, but not young adults, $F < 1$. Older adults
responded more slowly on BX trials in the long than in the short delay condition.

Age effects on other tasks

Table 3 shows descriptive statistics for context maintenance in the AX-CPT task, conceptual
span, digit span, and anomaly judgement accuracy for young and old adults. Ageing effects were
found for all task measures except digit span. Compared to young adults, older adults showed

---

[2]The relative percentage change in error rate was calculated as (long − short)/((long + short)/2), where short
and long designate error rates in the short and long delay conditions, respectively.

[3]The d' context provides a focused and unbiased measure of context sensitivity, which is based on AX hits and BX
false alarms and corrects for perfect hit rates (1.0) and false alarms (0.0) with a correction factor (i.e., hits $= 2^{-(1/N)}$ and
false alarms $= 1 - 2^{-(1/N)}$, where N equals the number of target and nontarget trials, respectively; Braver et al., 2001).

TABLE 2
AX-CPT response times[a]

Trial type	Delay	Young		Old	
		M	SE	M	SE
AX	Short	277	17	609	17
	Long	277	12	623	16
BX	Short	295	15	611	16
	Long	282	15	636	19
AY	Short	309	14	629	18
	Long	312	14	605	14

[a]In ms.

TABLE 3
Descriptive statistics of all task measures

Measure	Age group					
	Young[a]			Old[b]		
	M	SD	Range	M	SD	Range
Context maintenance[c]	9.3	25.8	−46.8–55.6	−44.2	30.3	−93.7–26.2
Conceptual span	20.02	2.99	14–25	11.22	2.19	7–17
Digit span	4.4	1.29	2–7	4.14	1.15	2–6
Anomaly Judgement 1[d]	0.91	0.09	0.62–1	0.69	0.16	0.38–0.96
Anomaly Judgement 2[e]	0.95	0.06	0.71–1	0.81	0.13	0.45–0.98

[a]$N = 43$. [b]$N = 36$. [c]Context maintenance = (AX short − AX long) + (BX short − BX long) + (AY long − AY short), where AX, BX, and AY denote the error percentages in the corresponding trial types, and short and long refer to the length of the delay in the AX-CPT task. [d]A prime measure, which scored only responses within the deadline as correct (0) or incorrect (1) and treated responses beyond it as "don't know" answers (.5). [e]A prime measure, which ignored whether or not the responses were made within the deadline.

poorer context maintenance, $F(1, 77) = 71.99$, $p < .001$, conceptual span, $F(1, 77) = 214.36$, $p < .001$, and anomaly judgement, $F(1, 77) = 65.34$, $p < .001$ (Anomaly Judgement 1), $F(1, 77) = 39.81$, $p < .001$ (Anomaly Judgement 2). However, older adults did not differ from young adults on digit span, $F < 1$. In anomaly judgement, ageing had a larger negative impact when the response deadline was imposed on scoring (see Table 3), and ageing had a negative impact not only on performance accuracy, but also on RT (for correct trials only), $F(1, 77) = 55.02$, $p < .001$, excluding a speed–accuracy trade-off explanation of the effect.

Correlation and regression analyses

Table 4 lists the size and p values of the product moment correlations among context maintenance, conceptual span, digit span, anomaly judgement, and years of age. Significant correlations of a moderate to large size were found among context maintenance, conceptual

TABLE 4
Correlations among task measures and age

Measure	Conceptual span	Digit span	Anomaly Judgement[b] 1	Anomaly Judgement[b] 2	Age
Context maintenance	.60**	.07	.42**	.39**	−.67**
Partial corr.[a]	.03, age				−.38**, conceptual span
Conceptual span	–	−.06	.61**	.58**	−.87**
Partial corr.[a]					−.79**, context maintenance
Digit span	–	–	.03	−.02	−.08
Anomaly Judgement 1	–	–	–	.86**	−.67**
Anomaly Judgement 2	–	–	–	–	−.59**

[a]Partial correlations among context maintenance, conceptual span, and age, and the variable that is controlled for.
[b]See the data analysis section or Table 3 for an explanation of the difference between Anomaly Judgements 1 and 2.
*$p < .05$; **$p < .01$.

span, anomaly judgement, and years of age, whereas digit span did not correlate with any of these three measures. The correlation between conceptual span and anomaly judgement ($r = .58$) was of similar magnitude ($z = .58$, $p = .56$, $N_1 = 79$, $N_2 = 64$, two-tailed)[4] as the one obtained in a previous study with young adults ($r = .51$; Haarmann et al., 2003). The correlations involving the Anomaly Judgements 1 and 2 measures were of similar magnitude, with one exception. Age correlated better, $t(76) = 1.77$, $p = .04$, one-tailed, with Anomaly Judgement 1 than with Anomaly Judgement 2. This difference in the size of the correlation with age was to be expected given that older adults had greater difficulty in responding within the deadline (41% of all trials) than young adults (84% of all trials) due to their age-related slowing and given that the Anomaly Judgement 1 but not Anomaly Judgement 2 measure took the deadline into account.

Table 4 also lists the partial correlations (a) between context maintenance and conceptual span, controlling for age, (b) between age and context maintenance, controlling for conceptual span, and (c) between age and conceptual span, controlling for context maintenance. The correlation between context maintenance and conceptual span was abolished when age was controlled for, consistent with the notion of age-related effects upon a system that supports common aspects of context maintenance and semantic STM. However, there appeared to be additional age-related effects upon context maintenance above and beyond those shared with semantic STM, suggested by the finding that the correlation between age and

_____

[4]The test for the significance of the difference between independent correlations (i.e., comparing correlations obtained from two samples) was computed with the indepcor.exe program, accompanying an article by Crawford, Mychalkiw, Johnson, and Moore (1996). This program implements Howell's (1997) procedures for such a test, following which both correlations are first converted to Fisher's z', and the difference between them is divided by the standard error of the difference to yield a normal curve deviate (z).

context maintenance was reduced but not abolished when conceptual span was controlled for. To further test this, context maintenance was regressed onto conceptual span (entered first) and age (entered second). Conceptual span accounted for 27% of the variance in context maintenance, $R^2 = 27$, $F(1, 77) = 28.52$, $p < .001$, which was entirely shared with age. Age added another 21.5% of unique variance, R^2 change $= 21.5$, $F(1, 76) = 26.99$, $p < .001$. Together, conceptual span and age accounted for 48.5% of the variance in context maintenance, $R^2 = 48.5$, $F(2, 76) = 35.85$, $p < .001$. The correlation between age and conceptual span was somewhat reduced but remained highly significant, and age still explained 62% of the variance on conceptual span when context maintenance was controlled for, consistent with the existence of age-related effects that are unique to semantic STM.

Age-related effects upon anomaly judgement may be associated with common effects on semantic STM and context maintenance, with additional unique effects of context maintenance, and with still further unique effects of age. To test this, anomaly judgement (Anomaly Judgement 2) was regressed onto conceptual span (entered first), context maintenance (entered second), and age (entered third). Conceptual span accounted for 17% of the variance in anomaly judgement, $R^2 = 17$, $F(1, 77) = 17.09$, $p < .001$, which was entirely shared with both context maintenance and age. While context maintenance did not add any further significant variance over and beyond conceptual span, R^2 change $= 0.02$, $F(1, 76) = 2.09$, $p = .15$, age added another 17% of variance, R^2 change $= 17$, $F(1, 75) = 20.26$, $p < .001$. Together, conceptual span, context maintenance, and age accounted for 34% of the variance in anomaly judgement, $R^2 = 34$, $F(3, 75) = 14.87$, $p < .001$. An identical regression analysis that used the Anomaly Judgement 1 instead of Anomaly Judgement 2 measure yielded analogous results, supporting the same conclusions. These results are consistent with the notion that anomaly judgement is affected by a factor that accounts for shared variance among ageing, semantic STM, and context maintenance and by one or more additional age-related factors.

Discussion

The main focus of the AX-CPT analysis is the error rates, which already include a temporal deadline (the response-time analysis mirrors the error rates, despite the response deadline that may diminish the range of the effects). The different error patterns of young and older adults on the AX-CPT task provide further support for the proposal of an age-related deficit in the maintenance of context information in working memory (Braver et al., 2001). On nontarget trials, young adults produced an equal amount of BX errors in the short and long interference condition and more AY errors in the long than in the short interference condition. This error pattern indicates that the added delay and interference in the long interference condition did not affect the ability of young adults to maintain the context letter (i.e., the cue). Moreover, the longer maintenance of the cue may have increased the a priori bias towards a target response on AY trials, explaining why AY errors increased with delay in young adults. By contrast, older adults produced more BX errors and fewer AY errors in the long than in the short interference condition. This error pattern indicates that the added delay and/or interference had a negative effect on the ability of older adults to maintain the context letter in working memory. On BX trials, a loss of context information across the delay makes it more difficult to use the invalid cue to inhibit the prepotent target response, explaining the increase in BX errors with delay. On AY trials, a loss of context information across the delay reduces the ability of the valid cue to create an inadvertent bias towards the prepotent target response, explaining the decrease in AY errors with delay.

These error patterns are consistent with the theory of Braver et al. (2001) for an age-related context maintenance deficit. As expected (since responses were scored under a deadline), older people made more errors than did the younger ones in all conditions. As predicted, however, the increase in interference led to an increase in AY errors rate for the young subjects but to a decrease for the older ones. This data pattern was not obtained in Braver et al., which focused on between-group effects. A number of procedural differences can explain the subtle variation in the results. First, while in the Braver et al. study, the difficulty in context maintenance was manipulated by adding interference within an unfilled cue–probe delay interval, in our study we lengthened the duration of the filled cue–probe delay interval. Second, while in Braver et al.'s study, the trials in the easy and difficult context maintenance condition were presented in separate blocks, we intermixed the trials, reducing the likelihood that effects of task condition reflect strategy variations (e.g., difference in the encoding of the context cue or increased attention). Third, we used a shorter response deadline, and we did not provide response feedback. This is likely to explain why older adults in our study had a larger overall error rate. Despite these subtle differences, we believe that our results provide complementary data supporting the context theory of ageing, by demonstrating within-group effects of interference predicted by this theory.

A prominent theory of cognitive ageing is that it involves a global decline in processing speed (Myerson et al., 1990; Salthouse, 1996). While this theory explains an important aspect of the reaction time data in the AX–CPT task (i.e., the overall slower response times in older adults), it is insufficient to explain all age effects on reaction time in the AX–CPT task, in particular on AY trials (Braver et al., 2001). The processing speed theory of ageing predicts that the slowest condition in young adults will show the largest age effect on reaction time (Brinley, 1965; Cerella, 1985; Myerson et al., 1990) and that reaction times in all conditions correlate positively with age. However, Braver et al. (2001) found that AY trials, while being the slowest condition in young adults, did not show the largest age effect on reaction time, and that AY reaction times correlated negatively with age, after factoring out a global decline in processing speed. Furthermore, the processing speed theory of ageing predicts that factors affecting processing difficulty, such as interference, should have effects that are in the same direction in young and older adults. However, this was not the case for AY trials, where young adults had more difficulty in the long than in the short interference condition, whereas the reverse was true for older adults.

In addition to the evidence for an age-related decline in context maintenance, the span and anomaly judgement data suggest that there may be an age-related decline in semantic STM. The results for the two span tasks revealed negative effects of ageing on conceptual span but not on digit span. Conceptual span relies to a large extent on the contribution of semantic STM (Haarmann et al., 2003). In contrast, digit span may primarily rely on phonological STM, due to the relatively shallow meaning of digits and due to the fact that serial recall of digits relies on their sequential rehearsal in the phonological loop (Baddeley, 1986). This is consistent with neuropsychological data showing that patients with phonological STM deficits are impaired in this test (e.g., patient E.A. above or K.F. reported by Warrington & Shallice, 1969). Moreover, the digit span is less likely to be contaminated by semantic/visual strategies, which affect word span tests (Logie et al., 1996).[5] Despite the procedural differences (cued vs. serial recall), the span results may therefore suggest that there is an age-related deficit in semantic STM but not in phonological STM. Such a selective deficit is consistent with the semantic anomaly judgement findings. Semantic anomaly judgement is dependent on semantic STM for the active maintenance of word meanings in order to support their on-line integration and to allow detection of semantic errors (Haarmann et al., 2003; Hanten & Martin, 2000; Martin & Romani, 1994). In line with this task analysis, we found a positive correlation between anomaly judgement and conceptual (but not digit) span and age-related performance declines on both tasks.

Our claim that the age-related decline in conceptual span reflects a semantic STM impairment can only be accepted tentatively at the present time. The present study used a nonclustered version of conceptual span, where words from different semantic categories are randomly mixed in a memory list and thus need to be clustered into their respective category to support category-cued recall. As a result, the nonclustered version of the conceptual span may measure not only semantic STM, but also clustering ability, which may engage cognitive functions other than semantic STM. It would, therefore, be of much relevance to determine whether there is an age-related effect on a clustered version of conceptual span, where words are grouped by their category, and clustering ability is less required. We predict this to be the case, however, on the basis of a correlational study where we find that both the clustered and the nonclustered versions of the conceptual span show high correlations with reading comprehension and problem solving in young adults (Haarmann et al., 2003). Finally, it is possible that (although constructed as a storage-only test) the conceptual span may still capture individual differences in the ability to control attention (Kane, Bleckley, Conway, & Engle, 2001; Kane & Engle, 2000). It is currently an open question as to what extent the construct of semantic STM and the ability to control attention rely on a common underlying cognitive mechanism.

In addition to investigating whether there is evidence for age-related deficits in context maintenance and semantic STM, this study sought to investigate whether there is a relation between these two cognitive functions. Consistent with the existence of such a relation, there was a positive correlation of context maintenance with conceptual span and with anomaly judgement, while neither of these measures correlated with digit span. From a theoretical perspective, two hypotheses regarding the relation between cognitive decline in context maintenance and in semantic STM can be contrasted. First, it is possible that in contextual tasks such as the AX-CPT, task-relevant representations (e.g., A preceding an X) are created on-line (and from scratch) for the task and are utilized to bias information processing. The brain system involved in this function is, according to this hypothesis, distinct from the system involved in active maintenance of semantic information. The two systems may, however, be located within adjacent areas of the frontal cortex (Braver & Bongiolatti, 2002) and may both therefore to some degree be affected by ageing, explaining the source of the age-mediated correlation between context maintenance (in AX-CPT) and semantic STM (in conceptual span). The second hypothesis is that context representations are not built for each task from scratch but are rather piggybacking on top of system engaged in the maintenance of lexical-semantic information (Gabrieli, Poldrack, & Desmond, 1998). Further (behavioural,

---

[5]Most of the subjects reported using a covert rehearsal strategy in the digit span test and only a very small minority of subjects (< 5%) reported using a visual strategy.

neuropsychological, and imaging) studies, which explicitly contrast delayed semantic judgements and contextual word meaning disambiguation, are necessary to determine whether and how semantic STM and context maintenance are related.

While ageing may affect overlapping or separate mechanisms for context maintenance and semantic STM, our data suggest that ageing has additional effects as well. The partial correlations and regression analyses indicated that ageing accounts for variance in context maintenance, conceptual span, and anomaly judgement beyond the age-related variance that is shared by those measures. This may indicate that ageing affects not only a common mechanism that contributes to all three measures but also additional, task-specific mechanisms. Based on the present data, we can only speculate as to what those additional ageing effects may be. A deficit in the ability to update context information in working memory may interfere more with its activation in the long than in the short condition (due to the presence of more distractor letters in the long condition) and thus account for additional ageing effects on the context maintenance measure. A deficit in the ability to cluster word meanings belonging to a cued category may account for additional ageing effects on conceptual span, while a deficit in the ability to integrate word meanings into a sentence representation may account for additional ageing effects on anomaly judgement.

The present findings suggest several theoretically motivated directions for future research. To obtain further evidence for a relation between context maintenance and semantic STM, one could use a semantic disambiguation task and vary the interference (i.e., number of intervening words) between the context word (e.g., river) and the ambiguous target word (e.g., bank). A similar interference manipulation may be also applied in a delayed semantic judgement task. The hypothesis that there is overlap in the mechanisms for context maintenance and semantic STM predicts a strong association between the effect of interference in these tasks. Further research should also contrast indices of semantic and phonological STM that are more similar in (number of) items and response requirements. This could be done, for example, by contrasting cued recall with a semantic category versus a rhyme cue.

In conclusion, the results of this study suggest that the age-related deficit in the processing of information about task context (Braver et al., 2001) is in part due to a problem in the maintenance of that information in working memory and that there is an age-related decline in semantic but not phonological STM. The results of this study further suggest that there might be a relation between context maintenance and semantic STM, such that context maintenance depends on semantic STM. Additional studies are needed to further evaluate this possibility and differentiate it more conclusively from a model in which context maintenance and semantic STM are supported by separate cognitive mechanisms. These studies should utilize behavioural experiments, complex correlational analysis, and functional neuroimaging, as well as comparison of young and older adults. Such a use of convergent methodology will help characterize the interplay between context maintenance and semantic STM in controlling cognition and action in young and older adults.

REFERENCES

American Psychiatric Association. (1994). *Diagnostic and statistical manual of mental disorders* (4th ed.). Washington, DC: American Psychiatric Association.

Anderer, P., Pascual-Marqui, R. D., Semlitsch, H. V., & Saletu, B. (1998). Differential effects of normal aging on sources of standard N1, target N1 and target P300 auditory event-related brain potentials revealed by low resolution electromagnetic tomography (LORETA). *Electroencephalography and Clinical Neurophysiology, 108*, 160–174.

Baddeley, A. D. (1986). *Working memory* (Oxford Psychology series No. 11). Oxford, UK: Clarendon Press.

Baddeley, A. D. (1992). Is working memory working? The fifteenth Bartlett lecture. *Quarterly Journal of Experimental Psychology, 44A*, 1–31.

Barch, D. M., Braver, T. S., Racine, C. A., & Satpute, A. B. (2001). Cognitive control deficits in healthy aging: Neuroimaging investigations. *Neuroimage, 13*, S1025.

Bazin, N., Perruchet, P., Hardy-Bayle, M. C., & Feline, A. (2000). Context-dependent information processing in patients with schizophrenia. *Schizophrenia Research, 45*, 93–101.

Braver, T. S., & Barch, D. M. (2002). A theory of cognitive control, aging cognition, and neuromodulation. *Neuroscience and Biobehavioral Reviews, 26*(7), 809–817.

Braver, T. S., Barch, D. M., Keys, B. A., Carter, C. S., Cohen, J. D., Kaye, J. A., et al. (2001). Context processing in older adults: Evidence for a theory relating cognitive control to neurobiology in healthy aging. *Journal of Experimental Psychology: General, 130*, 746–763.

Braver, T. S., & Bongiolatti, S. R. (2002). The role of frontopolar cortex in subgoal processing during working memory. *Neuroimage, 15*, 523–536.

Brink, J. M., & McDowd, J. M. (1999). Aging and selective attention: An issue of complexity or multiple mechanisms. *Journal of Gerontology: Psychological Sciences, 54*, 30–33.

Brinley, J. F. (1965). Cognitive sets, speed and accuracy of performance in the elderly. In A. T. Welford & J. E. Birrent (Eds.), *Behavior, aging, and the nervous system* (pp. 114–149). Springfield, IL: Charles C. Thomas.

Brouwer, H., Waterink, W., Van Wolffelaar, P. C., & Rothengatter, T. (1991). Divided attention in experienced young and older drivers: Lane tracking and visual analysis in a dynamic driving simulator. *Human Factors, 33*, 573–582.

Burgess, N., & Hitch, G. J. (1999). Memory for serial order: A network model of the phonological loop and its timing. *Psychological Review, 106*, 551–581.

Cerella, J. (1985). Information processing rates in the elderly. *Psychological Bulletin, 98*, 67–83.

Cohen, J. D., Barch, D. M., Carter, C., & Servan-Schreiber, D. (1999). Context-processing deficits in schizophrenia: Converging evidence from three theoretically motivated cognitive tasks. *Journal of Abnormal Psychology, 108*, 120–133.

Cohen, J. D., & Servan-Schreiber, D. (1992). Context, cortex, and dopamine: A connectionist approach to behavior and biology in schizophrenia. *Psychological Review, 99*, 45–77.

Cowan, N. (1999). An Embedded-Processes Model of working memory. In A. Miyake & P. Shah (Eds.), *Models of working memory: Mechanisms of active maintenance and executive control* (pp. 62–101). Cambridge, UK: Cambridge University Press.

Craik, F. I. M. (1977). Age differences in human memory. In J. E. Birren & K. W. Schaie (Eds.), *Handbook of the psychology of aging* (pp. 384–420). New York: Van Nostrand Reinhold.

Craik, F. I. M., & Jennings, J. M. (1992). Human memory. In F. I. M. Craik & T. A. Salthouse (Eds.), *The handbook of aging and cognition* (pp. 51–110). Hillsdale, NJ: Lawrence Erlbaum Associates, Inc.

Craik, F. I. M., Morris, R. G., & Gick, M. (1990). Adult age differences in working memory. In G. Vallar & T. Shallice (Eds.), *Neuropsychological impairments of short-term memory* (pp. 247–267). Cambridge, UK: Cambridge University Press.

Crawford, J. R., Mychalkiw, B., Johnson, D. A., & Moore, J. W. (1996). WAIS-R short-forms: Criterion validity in healthy and clinical samples. *British Journal of Clinical Psychology, 35*, 638–640.

Daigneault, S., Braun, C. M. J., & Whitaker, H. A. (1992). Early effects of normal aging on perseverative and non-perseverative prefrontal measures. *Developmental Neuropsychology, 8*, 99–114.

Daneman, M., & Carpenter, P. A. (1980). Individual differences in working memory and reading. *Journal of Verbal Learning and Verbal Behavior, 19*, 450–466.

Dobbs, A. R., Aubrey, J. B., & Rule, B. G. (1989). Age-associated release from proactive inhibition: A review. *Canadian Psychologist, 30*, 331–344.

Engle, R. W., Tuholski, S. W., Laughlin, J. E., & Conway, A. R. A. (1999). Working memory, short-term memory and general fluid intelligence: A latent variable approach. *Journal of Experimental Psychology: General, 128,* 309–331.

Filley, C. M., & Cullum, C. M. (1994). Attention and vigilance functions in normal aging. *Applied Neuropsychology, 1,* 29–32.

Fisk, J. E., & Warr, P. (1996). Age and working memory: The role of perceptual speed, the central executive, and the phonological loop. *Psychology and Aging, 11,* 316–323.

Freedman, M. L., & Martin, R. C. (2001). Dissociable components of short-term memory and their relation to long-term learning. *Cognitive Neuropsychology, 18,* 193–226.

Gabrieli, J. D. E., Poldrack, R. A., & Desmond, J. E. (1998). The role of left prefrontal cortex in language and memory. *Proceedings of the National Academy of Sciences, 95,* 906–913.

Grier, J. B. (1971). Nonparametric indexes for sensitivity and bias: Computing formulas. *Psychological Bulletin, 75,* 424–429.

Haarmann, H. J., Davelaar, E. J., & Usher, M. (2003). Individual differences in semantic short-term memory capacity and reading comprehension. *Journal of Memory and Language, 48,* 320–345.

Haarmann, H. J., & Usher, M. (2001). Maintenance of semantic information in capacity-limited item short-term memory. *Psychonomic Bulletin & Review, 8(3),* 568–578.

Hanten, G., & Martin, R. C. (2000). Contributions of phonological and semantic short-term memory to sentence processing: Evidence from two cases of closed head injury in children. *Journal of Memory and Language, 43,* 335–361.

Hasher, L., Stoltzfus, E. R., Zacks, R. T., & Rypma, B. (1991). Age and inhibition. *Journal of Experimental Psychology: Learning, Memory, and Cognition, 17,* 163–169.

Hasher, L., & Zachs, R. T. (1988). Working memory, comprehension and aging: A review and a new view. In G. H. Bower (Ed.), *The psychology of learning and motivation XXII* (pp. 193–225). New York: Academic Press.

Howell, D. C. (1997). *Statistical methods for psychology* (4th ed.). Belmont, CA: Duxbury Press.

Humes, L. E., Nelson, K. J., Pisoni, D. B., & Lively, S. E. (1993). Effects of age on serial recall of natural and synthetic speech. *Journal of Speech and Hearing Research, 36,* 634–639.

Jensen, G. D., & Goldstein, L. (1991). A microcomputerized task assessment of cognitive change in normal elderly and young adults. *Experimental Aging Research, 17,* 119–121.

Kane, M. J., Bleckley, M. K., Conway, A. R. A., & Engle, R. W. (2001). A controlled-attention view of working-memory capacity. *Journal of Experimental Psychology: General, 130,* 169–183.

Kane, M. J., & Engle, R. W. (2000). Working-memory capacity, proactive interference, and divided attention: Limits on long-term memory retrieval. *Journal of Experimental Psychology: Learning, Memory, and Cognition, 26,* 336–358.

Keys, B. A., & White, D. A. (2000). Exploring the relationship between age, executive abilities, and psychomotor speed. *Journal of the International Neuropsychological Society, 6,* 76–82.

Korteling, J. E. (1993). Effects of age and task similarity on dual-task performance. *Human Factors, 35,* 99–113.

Light, L. L., & Anderson, P. A. (1985). Working-memory capacity, age, and memory for discourse. *Journals of Gerontology, 40,* 737–747.

Linebarger, M. C., Schwartz, M., & Saffran, E. M. (1983). Sensitivity to grammatical structure in so-called agrammatic aphasics. *Cognition, 13,* 361–392.

Logie, R. H., Della Sala, S., Laiacona, M., Chalmers, P., & Wynn, V. (1996). Group aggregates and individual reliability: The case of verbal short-term memory. *Memory and Cognition, 24,* 305–321.

MacPherson, S. E., Phillips, L. H., & Della Sala, S. (2002). Age, executive function, and social decision making: A dorsolateral pre-frontal theory of cognitive aging. *Psychology and Aging, 17,* 598–609.

Martin, R. C., & Romani, C. (1994). Verbal working memory and sentence comprehension: A multiple-components view. *Neuropsychology, 9(4),* 506–523.

Martin, R. C., Shelton, J. R., & Yaffee, L. S. (1994). Language processing and working memory: Neuropsychological evidence for separate phonological and semantic capacities. *Journal of Memory and Language, 33,* 83–111.

Morris, R. G., Craik, F. I. M., & Gick, M. L. (1990). Age differences in working memory tasks: The role of secondary memory and the central executive system. *Quarterly Journal of Experimental Psychology, 42A,* 67–86.

Moscovitch, M., & Winocur, G. (1992). The neuropsychology of memory and aging. In F. I. M. Craik & T. A. Salthouse (Eds.), *Handbook of aging: Cognition* (pp. 315–372). Hillsdale, NJ: Lawrence Erlbaum Associates, Inc.

Myerson, J., Hale, S., Wagstaff, D., Poon, L. W., & Smith, G. A. (1990). The information-loss model: A mathematical theory of age-related cognitive slowing. *Psychological Review*, *97*, 475–487.

Panek, P. E., Rush, M. C., & Slade, L. A. (1984). Locus of the age–Stroop interference relationship. *Journal of Genetic Psychology*, *145*, 209–216.

Parasuraman, R., & Nestor, P. G. (1991). Attention and driving skills in aging and Alzheimer's disease. *Human Factors*, *33*, 539–557.

Parkin, A. J., Walter, B. M., & Hunkin, N. M. (1995). Relationships between normal aging, frontal lobe function, and memory for temporal and spatial information. *Neuropsychology*, *9*, 304–312.

Perfect, T. (2003). Memory aging as frontal lobe dysfunction. In M. A. Conway (Ed.), *Cognitive models of memory* (pp. 315–339). Cambridge, MA: MIT Press.

Pollack, L., & Norman, D. A. (1964). A non-parametric analysis of recognition experiments. *Psychonomical Science*, *1*, 125–126.

Romani, C., & Martin, R. (1999). A deficit in the short-term retention of lexical-semantic information: Forgetting words but remembering a story. *Journal of Experimental Psychology: General*, *128*, 56–77.

Rosvold, H. E., Mirsky, A. F., Sarason, I., Bransome, E. D., & Beck, L. H. (1956). A continuous performance test of brain damage. *Journal of Consulting Psychology*, *20*, 343–350.

Salthouse, T. A. (1992). Working-memory mediation of adult age differences in integrative reasoning. *Memory and Cognition*, *20*, 413–423.

Salthouse, T. A. (1996). The processing-speed theory of adult age differences in cognition. *Psychological Review*, *103*, 403–428.

Servan-Schreiber, D., Cohen, J. D., & Steingard, S. (1996). Schizophrenic deficits in the processing of context. A test of a theoretical model. *Archives of General Psychiatry*, *53*, 1105–1112.

Spencer, W. D., & Raz, N. (1994). Remembering facts, source, and context: Can frontal dysfunction explain adult age differences? *Psychology and Aging*, *9*, 149–159.

Spieler, D. H., Balota, D. A., & Faust, M. E. (1996). Stroop performance in healthy younger and older adults and in individuals with dementia of the Alzheimer's type. *Journal of Experimental Psychology: Human Perception and Performance*, *22*, 461–479.

Swinney, D. A. (1979). Lexical access during sentence comprehension: (Re)consideration of context effects. *Journal of Verbal Leaning and Verbal Behavior*, *18*, 645–659.

Turner, M. L., & Engle, R. W. (1989). Is working memory capacity task dependent? *Journal of Memory and Language*, *28*, 127–154.

Verhaeghen, P., & Salthouse, T. A. (1997). Meta-analyses of age-cognition relations in adulthood: Estimates of linear and nonlinear age effects and structural models. *Psychological Bulletin*, *122*, 231–249.

Warrington, E. K., & Shallice, T. (1969). The selective impairment of auditory verbal short-term memory. *Brain*, *4*, 885–896.

Wechsler, D. (1981). *Wechsler Adult Intelligence Scale–Revised*. New York: Psychological Corporation.

West, R., & Alain, C. (2000). Age-related decline in inhibitory control contributes to the increased Stroop effect observed in older adults. *Psychophysiology*, *37*, 179–189.

West, R., & Baylis, G. C. (1998). Effects of increased response dominance and contextual disintegration on the Stroop interference effect in older adults. *Psychology and Aging*, *13*, 206–217.

West, R., & Bell, M. A. (1997). Stroop color–word interference and electroencephalogram activation: Evidence for age-related decline in the anterior attentional system. *Neuropsychology*, *11*, 421–427.

Zacks, R., & Hasher, L. (1997). Cognitive gerontology and attentional inhibition: A reply to Burke and McDowd. *Journals of Gerontology: Series B. Psychological Sciences and Social Sciences*, *52*, 274–283.

PrEview proof published online 6 August 2004

THE QUARTERLY JOURNAL OF EXPERIMENTAL PSYCHOLOGY
2005, 58A (1), 54–71

Ψ Psychology Press
Taylor & Francis Group

Memory for proper names in old age: A disproportionate impairment?

Peter G. Rendell

Australian Catholic University, Fitzroy, Victoria, Australia

Alan D. Castel

University of Toronto, Toronto, Canada

Fergus I. M. Craik

Rotman Research Institute, Toronto, Canada

A common complaint of older adults is that they have trouble remembering names, even the names of people they know well. Two experiments examining this problem are reported in the present article. Experiment 1 tested episodic memory for surnames and occupations; older adults and younger adults under divided attention performed less well than did full attention younger adults, but showed no disproportionate loss of name information. Experiment 2 examined the ability to name photographs of public figures and of uncommon objects; this experiment therefore tested retrieval from semantic memory. In this case adults in their 70s did show an impairment in recall of names of known people, but not of known objects. Further analyses revealed systematic relations between naming, recognition, and rated familiarity of the categories used. Familiarity largely determined the proportions of recognizable items that were named in a prior phase. Overall, little evidence was found for a disproportionate age-related impairment in naming in either episodic or semantic memory.

Correspondence should be addressed to Fergus Craik, Rotman Research Institute, Baycrest Centre, 3560 Bathurst St., Toronto, Canada, M6A 2E1. Email: craik@psych.utoronto.ca

This research was supported by a grant from the Natural Sciences and Engineering Research Council of Canada (NSERC) to Fergus Craik, a NSERC postgraduate scholarship and support from Soroptomists International and the Scottish Rite Foundation to Alan Castel, and an Australian Catholic University Large Grant to Peter Rendell. Peter Rendell was on research leave at the University of Toronto during this project, and has now returned to the Australian Catholic University. We are grateful to Patrick Rabbitt and two anonymous reviewers for very helpful comments on previous versions of the manuscript. We would like to thank Sharyn Kreuger for help with the experiments and analysis and Jennie Sawula for help with the preparation of the manuscript. We would also like to thank Sandra Priselac, Amy Siegenthaler, and Thomas Graham for providing access to images of famous people and Robyn Westmacott for information that helped with selecting appropriate famous people.

http://www.tandf.co.uk/journals/pp/02724987.html   DOI:10.1080/0272498044300188

One of the commonest complaints by older adults is an increased difficulty in remembering proper names. This difficulty often occurs at social gatherings when the older person forgets the names of people he or she has just been introduced to; but it also occurs as a failure to recollect well-known names—personal friends as well as names of celebrities and public figures. The first example may simply reflect the well-established inefficiency of new learning associated with ageing, but the second example appears to be a clear case of an age-related problem of retrieval. The present article reports two studies of ageing and name retrieval, the first involving new learning, and the second involving retrieval of previously established information. The general question motivating both experiments was whether there is a special difficulty associated with name recall in older adults; that is, do older adults show a disproportionate impairment in name recall relative to the retrieval of other types of information? Previous research has shown that proper names are the linguistic category most likely to cause retrieval difficulties in normal adults (Maylor & Valentine, 1992) and that proper name recall is the only linguistic problem for some brain-injured patients (see Valentine, Brennan, & Brédart, 1996, for a review). This issue is important both at the behavioural and at the neuropsychological level, as a disproportionate impairment might suggest that brain regions and networks involved in proper name encoding and retrieval are particularly affected by the ageing process, resulting in the behavioural consequences of specific memory failures. Alternatively, it may simply reflect the fact that naming people is a particularly difficult task.

The existing evidence regarding this issue is mixed. First, questionnaire studies in which people rate their own cognitive abilities strongly confirm that older adults perceive themselves to have problems with name retrieval. In fact, forgetting names was by far the largest age-related problem reported in one study (Maylor, 1997). A second source of evidence is diary studies in which adults of different ages record their memory failures over several days or weeks. In one such study, Cohen and Faulkner (1986) found that a group of older adults (mean age 71 years) reported more memory blocks for names than did either a young or a middle-aged group (mean ages 31 and 47 years, respectively). The majority of name blocks occurred for the names of friends or relatives whose names were rated as well known and usually easy to retrieve, suggesting that retrieval failure results from some fluctuation in the efficiency of the retrieval process. In a similar study, Burke, MacKay, Worthley, and Wade (1991) also found that older adults reported a greater incidence of tip-of-the-tongue (TOT) states than did their younger counterparts, and that the age difference was greatest for proper names. Further analysis of the proper names showed that age differences were greater for names of acquaintances than for names of famous people. One plausible reason for this difference is that "place names and famous names may take on a sort of borrowed semanticity (and perhaps associated imagery as well), which links them into the semantic network. Proper names of ordinary people lack semantic associations, and it is this semantic isolation that causes retrieval problems" (Cohen & Faulkner, 1986, p.195).

In the category of laboratory studies, Burke et al. (1991) found that older adults experienced more TOT states for the names of famous people than did younger participants, although Maylor (1997) points out that when TOTs were expressed as a proportion of unsuccessful retrievals, the age differences were similar for nouns, adjectives, verbs, and names. In a more recent study, Evrard (2002) presented photographs of everyday objects and famous people (the task was to name the object or person as rapidly as possible) and found significantly greater percentages of TOT responses for proper names, a greater incidence of TOTs for the group of older adults, and a significant age by word type interaction, suggesting a disproportionate age-related problem in lexical access to proper names. In line with this result, Maylor and Valentine (1992) presented evidence for a disproportionate slowing of naming on the part of older adults. Finally, in a thoughtful article, Maylor (1997) showed that whereas older adults were less able to retrieve proper names than were their younger counterparts, this age-related difficulty was no more severe for the final stage of recalling the name than it was for such prior stages as face recognition and retrieval of relevant semantic information (Bruce & Young, 1986). That is, according to Maylor there is no compelling evidence to suggest a *disproportionate* age-related impairment in the recall of names. One further point that is unclear is whether any age-related difficulty with name retrieval is purely a semantic memory phenomenon, or whether it is also found in episodic memory. That is, are proper names (or perhaps just names of people) inherently difficult to acquire and remember, possibly reflecting their specificity of reference (Craik, 2002)?

The present experiments were carried out in an attempt to cast further light on these important issues; the first experiment examined episodic memory for newly learned names, and the second investigated semantic memory—the ability to name pictures of public figures and uncommon objects. In Experiment 1, we capitalized on the ingenious study by McWeeny, Young, Hay, and Ellis (1987) in which the investigators tested younger adults and contrasted memory for unambiguous surnames (e.g., Hyde, Rothwell) and occupations (e.g., architect, grocer) with that for surnames that are also names of occupations (e.g., Baker, Cook). McWeeny and her colleagues found that ambiguous labels were better recalled when they were presented as occupations than as names. That is, it is harder to recall that a person's name is Baker than to recall that his occupation is a baker. We argued that if older adults do have a specific difficulty in learning and recalling names of people, then they should show a greater drop than do their younger counterparts in the ability to recall ambiguous labels when they are surnames than when they are occupations. Furthermore, it may be the case that situations of reduced attentional resources (e.g., divided attention) in younger adults might lead to comparable impairments to that of older adults in terms of name and occupation recall. In Experiment 2 we presented photographs of famous people and uncommon objects for participants to name. The same photographs were then presented in two further phases; in the first of these, participants were given a multiple-choice identification test to check whether they could select the correct name, and in the final phase they rated how well they knew the photographed person or object. This procedure allowed us to examine age differences in failures to recall the names of people and objects that participants knew well. Again, if older adults have a disproportionate problem with proper name recall then, relative to young adults, they should fail to recall a larger proportion of names of people or objects that they do in fact know; further, this age-related difference should be greater for the names of people than for the names of objects.

EXPERIMENT 1

Three groups of participants studied photographs of unfamiliar male faces, each of which was labelled with a name and an occupation (e.g., "Mr. Stevens is a lawyer") and later attempted to recall these labels when shown the series of faces. The three groups were one group of older adults, one group of younger adults who studied the faces and labels under full attention, and one group of younger adults who studied the faces and labels under conditions of divided attention (DA). The reason for running the third group was to explore the possibility that division of attention might produce a pattern of results similar to that produced by the effects of ageing. Previous research has shown such similarities (Castel & Craik, 2003; Craik, 1982; Troyer & Craik, 2000), and it was hoped that inclusion of the young divided attention group might help to elucidate the factors relevant to remembering names.

Method

Participants

A total of 24 older adults (14 women, 10 men, mean age = 70.2 years, mean number of years of education = 14.2) participated in the study and were offered $10 to cover their expenses for participation. A total of 24 undergraduate students from the University of Toronto (14 women and 10 men, mean age = 22.9 years, mean number of years of education = 15.8) comprised the young full attention group (young-FA); they had volunteered to participate and received course credit for participation. A second group of 24 undergraduates from the University of Toronto (18 women and 6 men, mean age = 19.1 years, mean number of years of education = 13.6) comprised the young divided attention group (young-DA); they were also volunteers who received course credit for participation. The young-FA group was drawn from second- and third-year university courses, whereas the young-DA group was drawn from first year courses; the groups therefore differed in their years of education, $t(43) = 7.27$, $p < .001$. The young-FA group had also received more education than had the older group, $t(46) = 3.10$, $p < .01$, as is often the case in cognitive ageing studies. However, the older adult group and the young-DA group did not differ in this respect, $t(46) = 1.32$, $p > .10$.

Materials and design

Photographs of 16 male faces were chosen from a pool of nonfamous middle-aged faces maintained by the Psychology Department at the University of Toronto. The selection of the faces was based on the criteria that none of the faces had facial hair or wore glasses, and the photos of the faces were cropped such that they were free of any background information. They were in black and white and were presented on a VGA computer screen. Eight "ambiguous" names (names that could also be an occupation, e.g., Mr. Baker) and eight "unambiguous" names (names that are not typically thought of as occupations, e.g., Mr. Stevens) were then chosen from the Toronto telephone book and were matched for frequency of occurrence (based on the procedure used by McWeeny et al., 1987). These 16 names were then randomly assigned to the faces and were paired with either an ambiguous occupation (e.g., barber) or an unambiguous occupation (e.g., lawyer). The occupations were normed and matched for frequency of occurrence. In total, there were four different "types" of name–occupation pairs, each with four exemplars: (a) unambiguous name–unambiguous occupation (e.g., Mr. Edwards is a lawyer), (b) unambiguous name–ambiguous occupation (e.g., Mr. Stevens is a cook), (c) ambiguous name–unambiguous occupation (e.g., Mr. Singer is a banker), (d) ambiguous name–ambiguous occupation (e.g., Mr. Baker is a barber). A complete list of the materials is presented in Appendix A. Two different versions of the face–name–occupation slides were constructed such that ambiguous names in one version served as ambiguous occupations in the other version, and vice versa. This counterbalancing technique was between subjects and allowed for a between-subject comparison of how well these words were remembered when they served as names and when they referred to occupations.

Procedure

Participants were tested singly and were told that they would be presented with faces, as well as the name and occupation of the person, on the computer screen. They were told that their task was to remember the person's name and occupation for a later memory test, in which they would be presented with the face, and that they would be asked to recall as much information as possible (name or occupation or both) associated with the face. The 16 slides were presented twice during the study phase (in the same order), and all of the information was presented visually. Thus, on each slide, below the photo of the face, the phrase "Mr X is a Y" was printed in 32-point Times New Roman font. Each slide was presented for 10 seconds, followed immediately by the next slide. In total, the study phase took just over 5 minutes to complete. Participants then began the recall phase, in which they were presented with the faces one at a time (for 10 seconds each) and attempted to recall the associated name and occupation; the order of presentation was different from that of the study phase.

In addition to studying the stimuli, participants in the DA condition also carried out a secondary task (digit monitoring) during the study phase of the experiment. The digit-monitoring task consisted of an auditory presentation of single digits ranging from zero to nine in a random order. Twelve hundred digits were spoken by a female voice and recorded on a tape recorder at a rate of one digit every 1.5 seconds, producing a 30-minute long recording. The participant's task was to monitor the series of digits for target sequences defined as "three successive odd digits" (e.g., 3,9,1, or 9,5,1) and to report the targets to the experimenter. The lags between target sequences ranged from 6 to 19 digits, with a mean lag of 12.5 digits. Each participant was exposed to 14 target sequences during the study phase of the experiment, and performance on this task was recorded by the experimenter. The retrieval phase of the experiment was performed under full attention conditions for all participants.

Results and discussion

The overall recall performance for the three groups is shown in Figure 1 with the means collapsed over both types of names and occupations (ambiguous and unambiguous). This overall pattern shows that occupations were better recalled than surnames, and that the advantage for occupations was similar for all three groups (i.e., there was no evidence for a disproportionate impairment for names for the older adults relative to the other two groups, although all three groups remembered fewer names than occupations). The figure also shows that the young-FA group performed at a higher level than did the old and young-DA groups; these

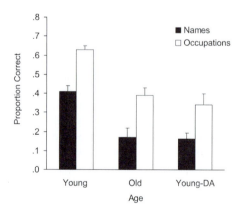

Figure 1. The mean overall proportions of correctly recalled names and occupations for younger adults, divided attention younger adults (young-DA), and older adults in Experiment 1. Error bars represent standard errors of the mean.

TABLE 1
The mean proportions of correctly recalled names (ambiguous and unambiguous) and
occupations (ambiguous and unambiguous) for each group in Experiment 1

| | Names | | | | Occupations | | | |
| | Ambiguous | | Unambiguous | | Ambiguous | | Unambiguous | |
	M	SD	M	SD	M	SD	M	SD
Young-FA	.43	.25	.40	.24	.62	.24	.64	.23
Old	.14	.11	.21	.17	.30	.16	.50	.19
Young-DA	.12	.15	.19	.18	.28	.19	.41	.15

last two groups performed comparably, with both showing a similar impairment for names relative to occupations. The young-DA group detected 81% of the target sequences in the digit-monitoring task, confirming that they had divided their attention between auditory monitoring and the study of the visual material. To provide greater detail, the data are also presented split down into ambiguous and unambiguous items in Table 1. The table confirms the superior recall of occupations over surnames, even when the words were identical (baker vs. Baker) in the ambiguous case, and it confirms the higher performance of the young-FA group. There is also some suggestion that unambiguous items are better recalled than ambiguous items in the old and young-DA groups, but not in the young-FA group. A three-way analysis of variance (ANOVA; Group × name/occupation × ambiguity) on these data revealed main effects of group, $F(2, 69) = 24.97$, $MSE = 0.09$, $p < .001$, of name/occupation, $F(1, 69) = 207.60$, $MSE = 0.02$, $p < .001$, and ambiguity, $F(1, 69) = 26.92$, $MSE = 0.06$, $p < .001$. The interaction between name/occupation and ambiguity was reliable, $F(1, 69) = 6.85$, $MSE = 0.03$, $p = .01$, showing that unambiguous labels had a greater recall advantage in the case of occupations than with surnames. The only other interaction to approach significance was that between ambiguity and group, $F(2, 69) = 2.90$, $MSE = 0.02$, $p = .06$, signaling a trend for the superior recall of unambiguous words to be confined to the old and young-DA groups. A further $2 \times 2 \times 2$ ANOVA comprising only the old and young-DA groups revealed no main effect of group and no interactions involving groups (all $Fs < 1$).

The results of Experiment 1 confirm the interesting finding of McWeeny and colleagues (1987) that the same words are better recalled when they are presented as occupations rather than as names, and that this holds true for both younger and older adults. We endorse the suggestions of previous researchers (e.g., Cohen & Burke, 1993; Cohen & Faulkner, 1986) that this superiority is probably due to the greater semantic richness of such occupational terms as baker, cook, and carpenter than that of their counterparts as surnames (Baker, Cook, and Carpenter), especially perhaps in situations like the present one in which these surname labels were associated episodically to previously unknown faces. The drop in recall performance from occupations to surnames was equivalent for all three groups, however, disconfirming the hypothesis that older adults would be disproportionately disadvantaged by the switch to proper names. This experiment thus provided no support for the notion that name recall is especially penalized by the ageing process.

Other results of interest include the superior recall of unambiguous words (e.g., Jones, architect) and that this finding was confined to the old and young-DA groups (for young-FA, unambiguous mean = .52, ambiguous mean = .53; Table 1). Speculatively, the reduced efficiency of encoding processes in the young-DA, and presumably also in the old, group had a greater deleterious effect on ambiguous words, leading perhaps to confusion at retrieval as to whether the word had been a name or an occupation. It should be noted that errors (e.g., recalling an incorrect name or occupation for a given face) were similar for all three groups, with incorrect name recall occurring on 5–8% of all trials (5% for young-DA, 6% for older adults, and 8% for young-FA), and incorrect occupation recall occurring on 11–13% of all trials (11% for both young-DA and older adults, and 13% for young-FA). Finally, the experiment provides a further illustration of the similarity between the effects of divided attention and ageing on human memory (e.g., Castel & Craik, 2003; Craik, 1982; Troyer & Craik, 2000). The similarity goes beyond the simple demonstration of poorer performance in the old and young-DA groups; it is also seen in the comparable reduction in recall of name and occupation words, and in the comparable asymmetry in the reduction of ambiguous and unambiguous words relative to the young-FA group.

In summary, Experiment 1 showed that older adults recalled fewer newly learned names than did younger adults, but that this age-related loss was proportional to the age-related loss in memory for names of occupations. Apparently older adults have no special difficulty with people's names in episodic memory. Experiment 2 examined possible age differences in the ability to name photographs of public figures and relatively uncommon objects. It thus dealt with the recall of names from semantic memory.

EXPERIMENT 2

In overview, younger and older adults were shown two separate series of 36 photographs; one series was of public figures, and the other was of uncommon objects. The participant's task was to name the person or object. If they were unable to provide a name, participants rated how well they thought they knew the name on a 4-point scale. If they did produce a name, participants rated their confidence in their answer on a 4-point scale. After viewing all 36 photographs in this first phase, participants were shown the complete set again in a second phase. The purpose of the second phase was to see whether the participant could recognize the correct name. To this end, we provided a list of the 36 correct names plus 36 similar distractors, mixed together in alphabetic order. The participant selected a name that matched the current photograph and again indicated his or her confidence in the choice on a 4-point rating scale. The series of 36 photographs was then shown for a third time; in this phase each photograph was named by the experimenter, and the participants' task was to rate how familiar the person or object (plus its name) was to them. The entire procedure was then repeated for the second series of 36 photographs.

This three-phase design enabled us to determine which names of faces or objects each participant knew—as indicated by correct identification in Phase 2 plus high rated familiarity in Phase 3. The person's ability to name the photograph in Phase 1 was then expressed as the number of people and objects named as a proportion of people and objects they actually knew. Naming latencies were also recorded. The main points of interest were to check whether older adults were less able to name photographs of items they knew, whether there were any differences between the ability to name people as opposed to objects, and whether the ability to name was affected by the familiarity of the category from which stimuli were drawn. Preliminary evidence suggested that adults older than 70 years might be particularly vulnerable to naming problems, so three groups of participants were tested: young adults, young-old adults (mean age = 67 years), and older old adults (mean age = 73 years).

Method

Participants

A total of 60 adults participated in the experiment: 20 young (mean age = 21.3 years), 20 young-old (mean age = 66.9 years), and 20 old-old (mean age = 73.4 years). Table 2 summarizes the characteristics of the three age groups. The groups did not differ significantly on their health self-ratings or on their number of years of education ($F < 1$ in both cases). The young adults were undergraduates from the University of Toronto; they volunteered to participate and received course credit for participating. The older adults were community dwelling participants who were offered $10 to cover their expenses. Given that the study involved familiarity with the names of famous people and of objects connected with North American culture, it was important to ascertain that our groups were reasonably homogeneous in this respect. Table 2 demonstrates that all participants had lived in Canada or the US for a large part of their lives, and that nearly all had spoken English all their life.

Materials

There were two sets of items: pictures of 36 famous faces and pictures of 36 somewhat uncommon objects. Each set comprised six categories, with six items in each category. The "famous faces" stimuli were photographs of public figures, mostly in colour, taken against a plain background and without such context cues as sports clothes or professional equipment. For each person depicted we selected the name

TABLE 2
The characteristics of participants in Experiment 2

		Young adult[a]		Young-old[a]		Old-old[a]	
		M	SD	M	SD	M	SD
Age[b]		21.25	3.02	66.85	1.35	73.40	2.76
Sex	Number of men	7		4		5	
	Number of women	13		16		15	
Health self ratings[c]		2.05	0.89	2.00	0.92	1.95	0.94
Education: years completed		15.90	1.62	16.27	2.52	16.10	3.16
Years living in Canada/US		18.50	5.12	56.80	16.20	66.40	13.08
Years speaking English		18.95	5.06	66.65	1.46	72.90	3.23

[a]$n = 20$. [b]In years.
[c]Participants rated their own health on scale of 1 (excellent) to 5 (poor).

of a similar distractor person to be used in the recognition test in the second phase of the study. Half of the famous faces depicted women, and half depicted men. The six categories plus their paired distractors are shown in Appendix B. The final set of 36 photographs was chosen after conducting pilot tests with 5 older and 4 younger adults; the personalities were selected so that all participants would find the set reasonably challenging and so that floor and ceiling effects would be avoided. Pictures of objects were also selected so that participants of all ages would find them challenging but possible; the final selection was again made after considering pilot results from 5 older and 4 young adults. Half of the 36 objects were living things, and half were manmade objects, again organized into six categories of six items each (Appendix B). The object images were obtained from the Hemera Photo-Objects 50,000 Volumes 1 and 2. Photo-objects are photographic images of objects without the surrounding background. They were in colour and were presented on a VGA computer screen.

In the second phase of the experiment, participants were presented with a typed sheet of 72 names after each block of items (famous faces or objects). In the case of famous faces, the task sheet had two separate alphabetic lists of men and women. The sheet for objects had two separate alphabetic lists of living and nonliving objects. The sheets were organized in this way to facilitate participants' ability to check the list rapidly (although this phase was untimed). In each recognition set the target names and distractors were mixed and presented on one sheet in a large font that could be easily read.

Half of the participants in each group were given the famous faces first, and half were given the objects first. Additionally, there were two different random orders of the items within each set; half of the participants in each age group were given one order, and the remainder were given the other order. The items were shown in the same order in each phase.

Procedure

Phase 1: Naming task.   Participants were tested singly. After filling in a brief questionnaire giving basic biographical information (Table 2), participants were told that we were interested in people's ability to recollect names of famous people and of objects. They were also told that after pro-viding a name they had to rate each item as to how certain they were that the name was correct: 1 = very uncertain; 2 = fairly uncertain; 3 = fairly certain; and 4 = very certain. Each face or object to be named was exposed for 10 seconds; if participants could not remember the name in that time, they were asked whether they had any idea of the name. Again a 4-point rating scale was used in which 1 = no idea, 2 = some idea, 3 = fairly sure, and 4 = certainly know name, but just cannot recall it. Participants were then given a practice trial in which the use of the rating scales was rehearsed, and the importance of first giving the full name of the person or object as quickly as possible was stressed.

In the main part of the experiment each picture was shown for a maximum of 10 seconds, followed by a blank screen. As soon as the participant said the name of the item, the experimenter pressed a key that brought up the blank screen. This key press also recorded the response latency. If no response was given by the participant, the blank screen appeared after 10 seconds. While the screen was blank, par-ticipants rated the certainty of knowing the item name (whether of not they had recalled the name) and then the experimenter pressed a key that displayed the image of the next item.

Phase 2: Recognition task.   This phase immediately followed Phase 1. Participants were given the appropriate recognition task sheet and were told that they would be shown the same series of pic-tures again but this time they had to select the name of the person or object from the sheet. For the famous faces, participants were informed that the recognition sheet of 72 names was organized alpha-betically and that men and women were listed separately. For the objects, they were informed that the list of names was organized alphabetically and as separate lists of living and nonliving objects. After selecting a name from the list (in their own time), participants were required to give a 4-point certainty rating where 1 = complete guess, 2 = possibly correct, 3 = fairly sure, and 4 = complete certainty. As in Phase 1, the experimenter recorded the responses said aloud by the participant. The experimenter exposed the next slide as soon as participants made their selection and had given their rating.

Phase 3: Familiarity ratings. This phase followed immediately after Phase 2. Participants were informed that they would see the same pictures for a third time, but that this time the experimenter would say aloud the name of the famous person or object as it was presented. They were then told that their task was to rate how familiar the combination of name and person (or object) was, using a 4-point rating scale (1 = never encountered, 2 = some slight experience, 3 = fairly well known, and 4 = extremely familiar). It was emphasized that they were required to rate the familiarity of the object/person as pictured in combination with the name. The pictures were shown in the same order as in the first two phases. Participants responded by saying the rating aloud, and the experimenter recorded their responses. After participants had given their response, the experimenter initiated the presentation of the next item.

Results and discussion

The principal results are shown in Table 3 and Figure 2. The main measure of interest is the proportion of known items named (see Figure 2), for the two types of item and three age groups, but other measures are also provided to give a fuller picture. The first line in Table 3 shows the number of public figures ("faces") and objects named out of the 36 presented. This number declined with age for faces, but increased somewhat with age for objects. A 3 × 2 ANOVA (Age Group × Type of Item) revealed that age was not a significant main effect, $F(2, 57) = 2.92$, $MSE = 32.09$, $p = .062$, but that the Age × Item interaction was significant, $F(2, 57) = 7.09$, $MSE = 29.96$, $p = .002$. The main effect of item was also significant, $F(1, 57) = 34.27$, $MSE = 29.96$, $p < .001$. That is, objects were more easily named than famous faces, and this was particularly true for the older participants. Within each type of item, age was a significant simple main effect for naming faces, $F(2, 57) = 4.69$, $p = .013$, and for naming objects, $F(2, 57) = 5.28$, $p = .008$. The age-related trend was different in the two cases, however, with the old-old group being poor at naming public figures, but the young adults being worst at

TABLE 3
The overall results from Experiment 2

| | Faces | | | | | | Objects | | | | | |
| | Young adult | | Young-old | | Old-old | | Young adult | | Young-old | | Old-old | |
	M	SD	M	SD	M	SD	M	SD	M	SD	M	SD
Number named[a]	14.9	5.5	14.3	7.3	9.6	5.1	15.9	5.9	20.8	4.3	19.7	4.8
Number recognized[a]	24.2	4.9	24.9	8.1	21.5	7.1	25.1	4.9	30.8	3.7	31.0	3.5
Proportion known[b]	.64	.14	.64	.24	.56	.19	.65	.14	.81	.11	.78	.15
Proportion of known items named	.64	.16	.57	.17	.46	.13	.65	.17	.71	.12	.68	.11
Reaction time[c]	3.15	0.47	4.13	0.74	4.31	0.79	3.28	0.63	3.55	0.60	3.72	0.68

Note: See text for a more detailed description of the measures.
[a]Out of all 36 faces and 36 objects.
[b]*Known* was defined as items recognized and also given familiarity rating 3 or 4.
[c]Reaction time in seconds for correctly named items, regardless of familiarity rating.

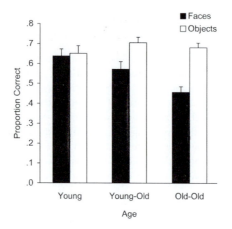

Figure 2.   The mean proportions of items correctly named as a proportion of those recognized for items rated 3 and 4 for familiarity in Experiment 2. Error bars represent standard errors of the mean.

naming uncommon objects. Clearly this pattern of results may well reflect the specific public figures and objects chosen, but it is interesting to note that whereas the old–old and young–old groups do not differ in their ability to name objects, the old–old group is significantly poorer than the young–old group at naming faces (Tukey post hoc test, $p = .042$).

The number of items recognized in Phase 2 shows a similar pattern. Overall, the main effect of age was only marginally significant, $F(2, 57) = 3.12$, $MSE = 32.78$, $p = .052$, and the Age × Item interaction was significant, $F(2, 57) = 6.18$, $MSE = 30.50$, $p = .004$. Table 3 shows that for faces, young and young–old groups recognized the same number of public figures, but the old–old group recognized somewhat fewer; tests of simple effects showed that age was not a significant effect, however, $F(2, 57) = 1.38$, $p = .260$. For objects, in contrast, age was a significant simple main effect, $F(2, 57) = 13.73$, $p = .001$, and Tukey post hoc tests revealed that the two older groups recognized the same number ($p = .979$), but the young group recognized significantly fewer than did both older age groups ($p < .001$). The same pattern occurs in the proportions of items that were known to participants—where "known" is defined as an item that was selected correctly in the recognition phase and was also given a familiarity rating of 3 or 4 in the third phase. Age approached significance as a main effect ($p = .064$), and the age by item interaction was significant, $F(2, 57) = 4.10$, $MSE = 0.03$, $p = .022$. Age was not significant for the proportion of known public figures ($p = .348$) but age was a significant simple main effect for the proportion of known objects $F(2, 57) = 8.71$, $p = .001$. Post hoc tests revealed that the two older groups knew the same proportion of objects ($p = .668$), but the young group knew significantly fewer objects than did both older age groups ($p < .001$).

For each participant we calculated the number of items "known" as those recognized in Phase 2 that were also given a familiarity rating of 3 or 4 in Phase 3. We then calculated the proportion of these known items correctly named in Phase 1. The results are shown in Figure 2. An overall ANOVA on these data revealed that age was not a reliable main effect, $F(2, 57) = 2.89$, $MSE = 0.02$, $p = .064$, but that the age by item interaction was highly reliable, $F(2, 57) = 6.68$, $MSE = 0.02$, $p = .002$. The interaction reflects the finding that naming of known objects did not change with age ($F < 1$), but age was a significant simple main effect for the naming of known public figures, $F(2, 57) = 7.25$, $p = .002$. Tukey post hoc tests revealed that the old-old named a significantly lower proportion of known public figures than did the young ($p < .001$) and the young-old ($p = .05$), but the young and young-old groups named the same proportion ($p = .370$). Additionally, known objects were named more often than faces by the young-old, $F(1, 57) = 10.53$, $p = .002$, and by the old-old, $F(1, 57) = 30.17$, $p < .001$, but not by the young group, $F < 1$ (as shown in Figure 2).

Since we considered this analysis the most revealing, we checked the validity of the results by re-analysing the data taking items as the random factor. That is, we calculated the proportion of participants who named each item given that it was known to them, as defined above. Items were blocked into categories (e.g., musicians, politicians, games, fruit) and separate 3 (age groups) × 6 (categories) ANOVAs were run for the faces and objects. For faces, the ANOVA revealed a main effect of age $F(2, 60) = 8.43$, $MSE = 0.02$, $p < .001$, showing that the old-old named fewer people that they knew. The effect of category was also significant, $F(5, 60) = 4.04$, $MSE = 0.09$, $p < .01$, as was the interaction between age and category, $F(10, 60) = 7.76$, $MSE = 0.02$, $p < .001$. Thus some categories gave participants more difficulty than others (e.g., Canadian politicians = .33; popular musicians = .67), and there were marked age difference in this respect (e.g., classic actors were named often by the old-old group, .71, but infrequently by the young group, .38, whereas contemporary actors showed the opposite trend, old-old = .37, young = .78). Bear in mind, however, that all of the naming proportions are of the items that were well known to the participants. A similar ANOVA was run on an item analysis of the object data. This analysis showed a main effect of age, $F(2, 60) = 3.16$, $MSE = 0.02$, $p = .049$, and no effect of category ($F < 1$) but a significant age by category interaction, $F(10, 60) = 4.02$, $MSE = 0.02$, $p < .001$. The proportions of known items named by each group and category are shown in Appendix C. The finding that the proportion of well-known items named varied substantially from category to category was unexpected and is considered in a following section. It should be emphasized that the item analysis yielded essentially the same result as the analysis by participants—there was no effect of ageing on object naming (means were .60, .68, and .67 for young, young-old, and old-old, respectively) but there was a significant effect of ageing on the naming of people (means were .52, .57, and .43 for the young, young-old, and old-old, respectively).

Finally, the bottom line in Table 3 shows mean naming latencies for the different groups and item types. An ANOVA on these data yielded significant main effects of age, $F(2, 57) = 14.24$, $MSE = 0.50$, $p < .001$, and of item type, $F(1, 57) = 9.79$, $MSE = 0.38$, $p < .01$, as well as a significant interaction between age and item type, $F(2, 57) = 4.45$, $MSE = 0.38$, $p < .05$. Table 3 shows that reaction time increased systematically with age as expected; it also shows that naming persons took longer than naming objects—but only for the two older groups; the young adults showed a nonsignificant trend in the opposite direction.

Familiarity: In order to be "fair" to the various age groups, the categories of objects and names included in the experiment were chosen such that some would be more familiar to young adults and some more familiar to older adults. The item analysis showed that this happened, both at the level of categories and at the level of items (e.g., George Clooney was named by 20 out of 20 young adults, 7 out of 20 young-old, and 3 out of 20 old-old, whereas Judy Garland was named by 0, 11, and 16 young, young-old, and old-old adults, respectively). We expected these asymmetries, but argued that a valid estimate of age-related naming problems could be obtained by conditionalizing on those items that each participant knew—defined as items that were correctly recognized in Phase 2 and also rated "fairly well known" or "extremely familiar" in Phase 3. However (prompted by reviewers of a previous draft), it also seemed worthwhile to check whether the ability to name people or objects varied as a function of the item's familiarity, even if the item was correctly identified in Phase 2. Accordingly, for each category we calculated the ratio of items correctly named in Phase 1 over items correctly recognized in Phase 2, and we plotted this ratio against the average rated familiarity of each category. These calculations were performed separately for each age group and separately for objects and public figures.

If the ratio of items named to items recognized is independent of familiarity the scatterplot should be random, but Figures 3a and 3b show that the relation is highly lawful. For categories of high mean familiarity, the ratio of items named to items recognized was also high. For the faces data (Figure 3a) the correlation between familiarity and the name/recognized ratio was $r(16) = +.88$, and for the objects data (Figure 3b) the corresponding correlation was $r(16) = +.71$, both $p < .01$. It is also clear from Figure 3 that there were no systematic differences associated with age group; the ratio of items named to items recognized is strongly influenced by rated familiarity in all three age groups.

One possible reason for the strong relationship between the named/recognized ratio and familiarity is that prior success, or lack of success, at naming each item in Phase 1 influences the familiarity rating that it is given in Phase 3 (cf. Valentine, Hollis, & Moore, 1998). A stronger reason is provided by the scatterplots shown in Figure 4, however. These graphs plot the probability of naming and recognizing items as a function of familiarity. For both the faces data and the object data, recognition performance is higher than naming performance, and both recognition and naming functions are well fitted by linear functions. It is also clear from the figures that the ratio of named to recognized items will therefore decline

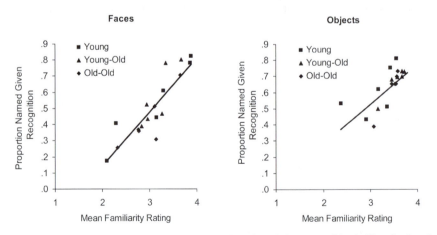

Figure 3. The mean proportions of items correctly named in Phase 1 given recognition in Phase 2, plotted as a function of mean rated familiarity of each category in Experiment 2. Data from faces stimuli are shown in the left panel (3a), and data from the object stimuli are shown in the right panel (3b). The regression lines represent the best-fit linear function for all data points (see text for details).

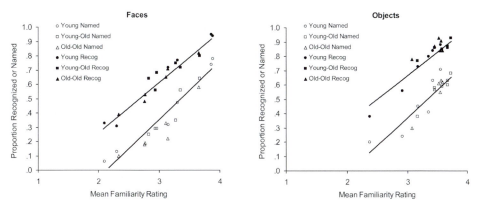

Figure 4. The mean proportions of items correctly named in Phase 1 (open symbols) and correctly recognized in Phase 2 (filled symbols) as a function of rated familiarity (Phase 3) for each category and age group in Experiment 2. Faces stimuli are shown in the left panel (4a), and object stimuli are shown in the right panel (4b). The regression lines represent the best-fit linear functions for correctly named and correctly recognized items for all age groups (see text for details).

systematically from highly familiar to less familiar categories. It is important to note that for both recognition and naming, younger and older adults appear to lie on the same function. Although in the faces data the old-old group has a lower mean familiarity rating (2.96) than either the young-old group (3.17) or the young adult group (3.10), these differences were not significant by a one-way ANOVA, $F(2, 57) = 1.26$, $MSE = 0.23$, $p > .05$. For the objects data, familiarity ratings rose with age (means were 3.13, 3.45, and 3.54 for young, young-old, and old-old groups, respectively), and in this case the differences were significant, $F(2, 57) = 10.22$, $MSE = 0.09$, $p < .001$.

Figures 3 and 4 make it clear that naming and the ratio of named to recognized items are strongly determined by familiarity. Does this mean that the age-related drop in ability to name known faces reported in the previous section simply reflects an age-related reduction in familiarity? We argue against this possibility on two grounds; first, there is no reliable age-related decrease in mean familiarity ratings, and, second, the previously reported ratio was the proportion of known items named, where "known" signified recognized items that were also given familiarity ratings of 3 or 4. The ratio thus controls for familiarity, or at least restricts consideration to well-known faces and objects. Finally, Figure 4a reveals that the naming data for faces in the old-old group tend to fall beneath the best-fit function for the whole group (five of the six categories fall below the function) whereas five of the six categories for the young group fall either on or above the line. Our conclusion is therefore that whereas familiarity is a strong predictor of naming ability, there is an additional negative effect of ageing on naming public figures that does not appear to apply to the naming of objects.

In summary, Experiment 2 showed that older adults, especially those over 70 years of age, were less able than their younger counterparts to name public figures that they demonstrably knew. This age-related trend was not found for the ability to name uncommon objects, however. Further analyses showed that the ratio of named to recognized stimuli declined systematically as a function of the mean familiarity of each category, calculated from the familiarity ratings given in Phase 3 (Figure 3), and that absolute probabilities of correct naming (Phase 1) and correct recognition (Phase 2) also declined systematically as rated familiarity declined (Figure 4). The strong relation between familiarity and the named/recognized ratio (Figure 3) is thus understandable in terms of the declining functions for naming and recognition shown in Figure 4. Given that both functions decline linearly with decreasing familiarity, it follows that the proportion of recognized items that were named also declines as familiarity declines. The old-old group's relative inability to name recognizable faces may thus be driven partly, but not wholly, by their lower rated familiarity for some of these categories.

GENERAL DISCUSSION

The principal objective of the study was to gather further evidence on the question of whether older adults suffer a disproportionate loss in memory for names, relative to memory for other types of information. The two experiments reported here appeared at first to yield contradictory answers to this question: Experiment 1 found equivalent age-related losses for surnames and occupations, whereas Experiment 2 showed that adults in their 70s were as good as young adults at recollecting the name of known objects, but were substantially poorer than young adults at recollecting the names of known public figures. One obvious difference between the experiments is that Experiment 1 involves new learning and the episodic pairing of labels (whether "surname" or "occupation") with previously unknown faces, whereas Experiment 2 involves the retrieval of well-learned information. In a previous study, Cohen and Faulkner (1986) also found equivalent age-related losses in proper names and other types of information (places, occupations, hobbies) when the material was previously unknown and presented in an episodic learning situation. As in the present Experiment 1, Cohen and Faulkner found that surnames were recalled less well than occupations (although in their experiment the exemplars were different words).

One further finding from Experiment 1 was the equivalent pattern of results shown by the older adults and the young-DA group, which is similar to other experiments involving comparisons between ageing and divided attention in terms of memory performance (e.g., Castel & Craik, 2003). Relative to the young adults working under full attention, both groups showed proportionate age-related decrements in recall of names and occupations. In the present Experiment 1, the young-DA group worked under divided attention conditions at encoding only—retrieval was performed under full attention conditions. A tentative conclusion is therefore that the parallel memory loss for names and occupations shown by the older adults is attributable to an encoding deficit. This conclusion further differentiates the two present experiments, with Experiment 1 illustrating an age-related encoding impairment and Experiment 2 illustrating an age-related problem of retrieval.

In order to equate the knowledge base for naming in Experiment 2, we conditionalized naming ability on items that were known to each participant, where "known" was defined as items that were recognized in Phase 2 and were also rated "fairly well known" or "extremely familiar" in Phase 3. On this basis, the data showed that naming ability declined with age for famous faces but not for uncommon objects. It should be noted, however, that this age-related decline is not necessarily a disproportionate impairment; it may very well be the case that other relevant cognitive operations show comparable losses in our older group (cf. Maylor, 1997). Nonetheless, compared with the ability to name known objects, the older groups showed some impairment. The young adults named the same proportion of known faces (.64) as known objects (.65), but for the young-old group the proportions were .57 and .71, respectively, and for the old-old group the proportions were .46 and .68, respectively.

These comparisons must be treated cautiously, however, in light of the analyses shown in Figures 3 and 4. The ratio of named to recognized items declined as a function of declining familiarity of categories used (Figure 3), and this relationship is understandable in terms of the relative decline of naming and recognition shown in Figure 4. Given that there are no obvious differences among the age groups in these functions, we concluded that the age-related impairment in naming faces is partly but not wholly attributable to a corresponding decline in rated familiarity for the categories used.

This conclusion immediately raises the question of what factors determine rated familiarity. Clearly the major determinant must be exposure to the name and face of the public figure, or the name and appearance of the object. The names of the Canadian politicians used in the study (see Appendix B) are probably not well known outside of Canada, for example. Recency of usage is a second likely factor, as are the variables of naming success and recognition success from Phases 1 and 2. The relative salience of these and other factors, and how they interact to give rise to the final experience of familiarity at different ages, are interesting questions for further research.

REFERENCES

Bruce, V., & Young, A. W. (1986). Understanding face recognition. *British Journal of Psychology, 77,* 305–327.

Burke, D. M., MacKay, D. G., Worthley, J. S., & Wade, E. (1991). On the tip of the tongue: What causes word finding failures in young and older adults? *Journal of Memory and Language, 30,* 542–579.

Castel, A. D., & Craik, F. I. M. (2003). The effects of aging and divided attention on memory for item and associative information. *Psychology and Aging, 18,* 873–885.

Cohen, G., & Burke, D. M. (1993). Memory for proper names: A review. *Memory, 1,* 249–263.

Cohen, G., & Faulkner, D. (1986). Memory for proper names: Age differences in retrieval. *British Journal of Developmental Psychology, 4,* 187–197.

Craik, F. I. M. (1982). Selective changes in encoding as a function of reduced processing capacity. In F. Klix, S. Hoffman, & E. Van der Meer (Eds.), *Cognitive research in psychology* (pp. 152–161). Berlin: DVW.

Craik, F. I. M. (2002). Human memory and aging. In L. Bäckman & C. von Hofsten (Eds.), *Psychology at the turn of the millennium* (pp. 261–280). Hove, UK: Psychology Press.

Evrard, M. (2002). Ageing and lexical access to common and proper names in picture naming. *Brain and Language, 81,* 174–179.

Maylor, E. A. (1997). Proper name retrieval in old age: Converging evidence against a disproportionate impairment. *Aging, Neuropsychology, and Cognition, 4,* 211–226.

Maylor, E. A., & Valentine, T. (1992). Linear and nonlinear effects of aging on categorizing and naming faces. *Psychology and Aging, 7,* 317–323.

McWeeny, K. H., Young, A. W., Hay, D. C., & Ellis, A. W. (1987). Putting names to faces. *British Journal of Psychology, 78,* 143–149.

Troyer, A. K., & Craik, F. I. M. (2000). The effects of divided attention on memory for items and their context. *Canadian Journal of Experimental Psychology, 54,* 161–171.

Valentine, T., Brennan, T., & Brédart, S. (1996). *The cognitive psychology of proper names.* London: Routledge.

Valentine, T., Hollis, J., & Moore, V. (1998). On the relationship between reading, listening, and speaking: It's different for people's names. *Memory & Cognition, 26,* 740–753.

PrEview proof published online 6 August 2004

APPENDIX A

Materials used in Experiment 1

Unambiguous names
Dixon, Flynn, Gilmour, Graham, Gordon, Harrison, Spencer, Waddell

Ambiguous names / occupations
Baker, Barber, Bishop, Butler, Carpenter, Cook, Farmer, Gardener, Mason, Mechanic, Merchant, Painter, Potter, Singer, Tailor, Usher

Unambiguous occupations
Actor, Banker, Butcher, Doctor, Engineer, Lawyer, Teacher, Politician

APPENDIX B

Experiment 2 stimulus items organized into the six categories for each set of items

	Faces			*Objects*	
Category	*Target name*	*Distractors*	*Category*	*Target name*	*Distractors*
Actor	Cary Grant	Jimmy Stewart	Games	Backgammon	Cribbage
(classic)	Rock Hudson	Gregory Peck		Bishop	
				(chess piece)	Rook
	Sydney Poitier	Harry Belafonte		Canteen	Knapsack
	Elizabeth Taylor	Vivienne Leigh		Croquet	Lawn bowls
	Judy Garland	Grace Kelly		Crossbow	Javelin
	Sophia Loren	Gina Lollabrigida		Shuttlecock	
				(or birdie)	Lawn dart
Actor	Bill Murray	Dan Aykroyd	Kitchen	Garlic press	Tea infuser
(contemporary)	George Clooney	Pierce Brosnan		Honey dipper	
				(or stick)	Meat tenderizer
	Kevin Costner	Martin Sheen		Ladle	Baster
	Jodie Foster	Helen Hunt		Mortar & pestle	Dough blender
	Julia Roberts	Michelle Pfeiffer		Tongs	Jar opener
	Sandra Bullock	Demi Moore		Whisk	Egg separator
Music	Elton John	Billy Joel	Tools	Allen keys	Wrench
(singers)	Mick Jagger	David Bowie		Chisel	Gouger
	Paul McCartney	George Harrison		Hacksaw	Coping saw
	Cher	Barbra Streisand		Sickle (or scythe)	Hedge clipper
	Geri Halliwell	Jennifer Lopez		Trowel	Trencher
	Shania Twain	Sheryl Crow		Wood planer	Sander
Politician	Arthur Eggleton	Paul Martin	Animals	Bobcat	Cougar
	Dalton McGuinty	Howard Hampton	(+ birds,	Doberman	Rottweiler
	John Manley	Brian Tobin	bugs &	Holstein	Jersey
	Alexa McDonough	Eleanor Caplan	insects)	Praying mantis	Longhorn beetle
	Anne McLellan	Ethel Blondin-			
		Andrew		Puffin	Toucan
	Madeleine Albright	Golda Meir		Salamander	Chameleon

APPENDIX B (Cont.)

	Faces			Objects	
Category	Target name	Distractors	Category	Target name	Distractors
Sport	Andre Agassi	Pat Rafter	Flowers	African violet	Agapanthus
	Mats Sundin	Chris Pronger		Arum lily	Orchid
	Mike Tyson	George Foreman		Crocus	Cyclamen
	Catriona Le				
	May Doan	Susan Auch		Hyacinth	Daffodil
	Jenny Capriati	Monica Seles		Iris	Tulip
	Michelle Kwan	Tara Lipenski		Poppies	Zinnia
Television	Andy Rooney	Walter Cronkite	Fruit	Artichoke	Broccoli
(celebrity)	Jay Leno	Mike Bullard	(+ vege-	Eggplant	Zucchini
	Peter Jennings	Ron McLean	tables &	Ginger	Garlic
	Anne Robinson	Sandy Rinaldo	nuts)	Leek	Onion
	Connie Chung	Katie Couric		Lychee	Paw paw
	Dianne Sawyer	Andrea Thomson		Pistachio nuts	Hazel nuts

APPENDIX C

For Experiment 2, the proportions of "known" items
named by each age group and category

	Young	Young-old	Old-old
Faces			
Classic actor	.38	.82	.71
Contemporary actor	.78	.53	.37
Musicians	.81	.74	.45
Politicians	.19	.46	.34
Sport	.57	.42	.31
TV celebrities	.40	.46	.38
Objects			
Games	.82	.69	.72
Kitchen utensils	.51	.67	.71
Tools	.47	.72	.68
Animals	.63	.52	.46
Flowers	.41	.74	.77
Fruit and vegetables	.78	.74	.67

THE QUARTERLY JOURNAL OF EXPERIMENTAL PSYCHOLOGY
2005, 58A (1), 72–97

Ψ Psychology Press
Taylor & Francis Group

Searching from the top down: Ageing and attentional guidance during singleton detection

Wythe L. Whiting and David J. Madden

Duke University Medical Center, Durham, NC, USA

Thomas W. Pierce

Radford University, Radford, VA, USA

Philip A. Allen

University of Akron, Akron, OH, USA

Previous investigations of adult age differences in visual search suggest that an age-related decline may exist in attentional processes dependent on the observer's knowledge of task-relevant features (top–down processing). The present experiments were conducted to examine age-related changes in top–down attentional guidance during a highly efficient form of search, singleton detection. In Experiment 1 reaction times to detect targets were lower when target features were constant (feature condition) than when target features were allowed to vary between trials (mixed condition), and this reaction time benefit was similar for younger and older adults. Experiments 2 and 3 investigated possible interactions between top–down and bottom–up (stimulus-driven) processes. Experiment 2 demonstrated that search times for both age groups could be improved when targets varied on an additional feature from distractors (double-feature condition) but only when top–down control was available (feature search). In Experiment 3, the availability of top–down guidance enabled both younger and older adults to override the distracting effects of a noninformative spatial location cue. These findings indicate that top–down attentional control mechanisms interact with bottom–up processes to guide search for targets, and that in the context of singleton detection these mechanisms of top–down control are preserved for older adults.

Correspondence should be addressed to Wythe L. Whiting, Department of Psychology, Washington & Lee University, Lexington, VA 24450, USA. Email: whitingw@wlu.edu

Wythe L. Whiting is now at the Department of Psychology, Washington and Lee University.

This research was supported by grants R37 AG02163 and T32 000029 from the National Institute on Aging. We are grateful to Susanne M. Harris, Sara Moore, Niko Harlan, and Leslie Crandell Dawes for technical assistance. Barbara Bucur and Julia Spaniol provided helpful comments on a draft of this article.

http://www.tandf.co.uk/journals/pp/02724987.html   DOI:10.1080/02724980443000205

A considerable debate has existed for some time as to how and when target features in a display are identified by the observer (Logan, 2004; Quinlan, 2003; Wolfe, 1998, 2003). Different configurations of target and nontarget (distractor) features lead to markedly different levels of performance. When the target is a singleton whose features are unique and separable from those of the distractors (e.g., a red target among green distractors), reaction time (RT) tends to be independent of the number of distractors (or to even decrease at larger display sizes), expressed as a zero or negative RT × Display Size slope. If, however, a target is a conjunction of distractor features (e.g., a red vertical target among red horizontal and green vertical distractors), RT tends to increase monotonically as a function of increasing display size, yielding a positive RT slope. These different patterns of the RT × Display Size function represent a continuum of search efficiency, anchored by the two extremes of a highly efficient search (zero or negative RT slope) and a more difficult search (positive RT slope). This continuum of search difficulty, in turn, depends on the degree of featural similarity among the display items, with higher levels of search efficiency resulting from low target–distractor similarity, high similarity among distractors, or both (Duncan & Humphreys, 1989).

A common component of current models of visual search is a central or master map of activation, which represents the summation of signals from the constellation of features in the display (Found & Müller, 1996; Müller, Heller, & Ziegler, 1995; Treisman, 1988; Wolfe, 1994). Observers base their target detection response on the relative saliency, in terms of the degree of activation, of the features in this map. Activation is enhanced not only by stimulus-driven or bottom–up processes, such as featural similarity, but also by top–down processes such as the observer's general knowledge of task goals and specific information about target probabilities (Yantis, 1998). To use an everyday example, in trying to find one's car in a parking lot, one could simply walk down every aisle of the lot until the particular combination of colour, size, and shape in a given car activated a correct identification, in a bottom–up manner. Alternatively, the search process is made considerably easier by top–down processes such as remembering that one's car was parked in the far northwest corner of the lot.

Top–down attentional guidance is of obvious importance in conjunction search tasks, in which knowledge of the set of features distinguishing the target from the distractors is a necessary component of target identification. Top–down guidance can also be valuable, however, in highly efficient search tasks involving the detection of a featural singleton. Bravo and Nakayama (1992) demonstrated this principle with a two-choice discrimination task (left/right orientation of a shape), in which the target shape was always a colour singleton. When the particular colour of the singleton was not predictable (i.e., either a red target among green distractors or vice versa), discrimination RT decreased with increasing display size, suggesting a bottom–up search process in which mutual suppression of similar target features (Duncan & Humphreys, 1989; Kastner & Ungerleider, 2000) occurred at the larger display sizes. When, in contrast, the singleton and distractor colours remained constant across trials, RT was lower and relatively constant across display size, suggesting a significant top–down contribution from the observer's knowledge of the target and distractor colours.

Wolfe, Butcher, Lee, and Hyle (2003) obtained similar results in a singleton detection paradigm (i.e., *yes/no* response regarding target presence), in which the singleton target features were either blocked (consistent across trials) or mixed (varied across trials). Wolfe et al. proposed that top–down attentional guidance sets weights in the activation map of display features, in a manner that optimizes the signal to noise ratio. Variation in the target and distractor features across trials decreases the signal to noise ratio, thus increasing RT, even though the search remains efficient in terms of a zero slope for the RT × Display Size function. In this model, the top–down weighting of specific features is implemented by both an explicit mechanism defined by the observer's intentions and an implicit mechanism based on the repetition priming of features across trials (Maljkovic & Nakayama, 1994). Müller and colleagues have developed a similar account, although they emphasize the weighting of target dimensions, rather than individual features, in the activation map (Found & Müller, 1996; Krummenacher, Müller, & Heller, 2001, 2002; Müller, Heller, & Ziegler, 1995).

Adult age differences in visual search and top–down control

Evidence from a large body of research has confirmed what is frequently observed outside the laboratory: In tasks that rely heavily on visual search and discrimination, older adults are typically slower and less accurate than younger adults (Madden & Whiting, 2004; McDowd & Shaw, 2000; Schneider & Pichora-Fuller, 2000). Whether these age differences represent attention specifically, rather than a decline in sensory processing and/or generalized slowing of information processing, is a matter of debate. There is, in addition, considerable evidence that older adults are comparable to younger adults in the ability to improve search performance when a stimulus dimension defines task-relevant information. This age constancy in attentional guidance has been most clearly evident when the task provides observers with advance information regarding the spatial location or other characteristics of the target (Madden & Plude, 1993).

Whether some bottom–up processes may be insulated from age-related decline, or whether there is any change associated specifically with top–down attentional guidance, is less clear. Manipulating target motion coherence of distractors in a visual search task, Folk and Lincourt (1996) found that older adults were less successful than younger adults at top–down inhibition of distractors, a finding later supported by Watson and Maylor (2002). Research using noninformative onset singletons as a means of capturing attention (or an eye movement) suggests that under some conditions older adults are more vulnerable than younger adults to attentional capture, perhaps as result of a decline in the ability to inhibit the irrelevant singleton (Colcombe et al., 2003; Kramer, Hahn, Irwin, & Theeuwes, 2000; Pratt & Bellomo, 1999). In some forms of conjunction search, however, top–down knowledge of either the proportion of features shared by targets and distractors (Humphrey & Kramer, 1997) or the homogeneity of distractors (Madden, Pierce, & Allen, 1996) leads to comparable levels of improvement in search for younger and older adults, implying some preservation of top–down control. In these latter studies, the specification of top–down processing is difficult because featural similarity (and thus bottom–up processing) varies across task conditions. However, a preservation of top–down attentional control during conjunction search has also been reported when the features of individual displays are equated across task conditions (Madden, Whiting, Cabeza, & Huettel, 2004).

The present experiments

Previous investigations of age differences in top–down attentional guidance have addressed this issue primarily in the context of difficult task conditions (e.g., moving distractors) or inefficient search performance as evidenced by positive display size slopes. The goal of the present experiments was to determine whether age differences in top–down attentional control would be evident in a very efficient form of search, singleton detection. Our general design was a singleton search task, similar to that of Wolfe et al. (2003), in which the target differed from a set of homogeneous distractors on at least one feature. As noted previously, younger adults' performance in this type of search task typically yields RT × Display Size slopes that are either zero or negative, implying a rapid detection process, and there is a further decline in mean RT with the addition of top–down control.

As in the Wolfe et al. (2003) research, participants in the present experiments responded regarding the presence or absence of a line bar that could differ in colour, size, or orientation from a set of homogeneous distractors. In each of three experiments, the amount of top–down information available during search was defined in terms of whether the target and distractor features either remained constant within trial blocks, thus encouraging top–down guidance (feature condition), or varied across trials within a block (mixed condition), thus allowing bottom–up processes to predominate.

Within this general framework, we explored age differences in relation to several issues: First, is top–down attentional guidance limited to the activation of target features? Wolfe et al. (2003) reported several findings suggesting that top–down guidance affects the activation of target features at a relatively early stage of perceptual identification. Wolfe et al., however, did not analyse RT for target-absent trials in detail. Because the activation of target features on these latter trials is minimal (limited to the activation of target-similar distractors), the presence of top–down effects on target-absent trials would indicate some influence of top–down control on the decision and response selection processes following target identification (Chun & Wolfe, 1996; Cohen & Magen, 1999). Second, how do bottom–up and top–down mechanisms interact in search performance? Featural similarity effects, for example, can be influenced by top–down control (Hodsoll & Humphreys, 2001; Krummenacher et al., 2001), and this interaction between top–down and bottom–up effects may vary in relation to age, even if top–down guidance in isolation is relatively preserved. Third, how do top–down and bottom–up mechanisms interact in preventing attentional capture? Previous research with younger adults suggests that top–down attentional guidance can reduce attentional capture by an irrelevant singleton (Peterson & Kramer, 2001). In exploring this latter issue we investigated whether older adults could successfully use top–down guidance to reduce an attentional capture effect (Colcombe et al., 2003; Kramer et al., 2000; Pratt & Bellomo, 1999).

EXPERIMENT 1

In this experiment we varied the amount of top–down control available during singleton detection. In each of three search conditions, the target differed from the distractors in a single feature (i.e., colour, size, or orientation). During the feature condition, the target's features remained constant across all trials within a block, and observers were explicitly instructed of target features (e.g., "target will always be a red line"). In the opposing search condition—mixed—targets could differ in colour, size, or orientation from distractors, thus minimizing the amount of top–down information available to guide search.[1] An intermediate condition was also included in which observers were told the dimension of the target (e.g., "target will always be a different colour"), though the specific feature value was allowed to vary between trials within a block, thus creating a degree of uncertainty about the target's specific feature value.

If older adults are as capable of benefiting from top–down guidance as are younger adults, as has been demonstrated for conjunction search (Humphrey & Kramer, 1997; Madden et al., 1996, 2004), then the decrease in search RT in the feature and dimension conditions, relative to the mixed condition, should be at least as great for older adults as for younger adults. An age-related decline in top–down guidance (Folk & Lincourt, 1996; Watson & Maylor, 2002), in contrast, would be evident as a less pronounced difference in RT across the search conditions. In this experiment we also examined the top–down effects on target-absent trials as well as on target-present trials, to assess potential top–down guidance beyond the level of target activation.

Method

Participants

A total of 24 younger adults between 18 and 28 years of age ($M = 21.5$ years) and 24 older adults between 60 and 81 years of age ($M = 66.8$ years) participated in Experiment 1. Testing was conducted at the Duke University Medical Center (Durham, NC), Radford University (Radford, VA), and the University of Akron (Akron, OH). The older participants were healthy, community-dwelling individuals who possessed at least a high-school education. The younger participants were university students and staff. Within each age group, 12 participants (6 women) were tested at Duke, and 6 participants (3 women) were tested at each of the Radford and Akron sites.

Participants completed a vocabulary measure (Salthouse, 1993) and a computer administered digit-symbol substitution test (Salthouse, 1992). Corrected visual acuity was at least 20/40 for each participant, and all participants were screened for normal colour vision using Dvorine or Ishihara colour plates. Participant characteristics (e.g., education, acuity, and psychometric performance) are presented in Table 1. Analyses of these data indicated that there were no Age Group × Testing Site interactions in the psychometric data, and thus the data were averaged across the three testing sites.

Apparatus and stimuli

The experimental task was created and run using E-Prime© software. At each testing site, stimuli were presented using either a Pentium II or Pentium III processor microcomputer and CRT monitor (either 17- or 20-in.). On each trial, participants viewed a display of 4, 8, or 16 lines constructed from three stimulus dimensions (colour, size, orientation), each with two feature values: big or small, red or green, and horizontal or vertical. Participants responded manually to indicate their *yes/no* decision regarding whether a target line differing in colour, size, or orientation was present among the nontarget (distractor) lines. This was a feature search task in which the distractors were homogeneous, and the target (present on half of the trials) was a singleton that differed from all of the distractors in a single feature value—colour, size, or orientation (see Figure 1). Participants viewed the targets on the computer monitor at a distance of approximately 60 cm, under slightly lower than normal room illumination.

---

[1] We refer to these conditions as feature, dimension, and mixed to characterize the different types of information available for attentional guidance. It is important to note that all three task conditions are a form of feature search, in which the target differs from the distractors on a single feature.

TABLE 1
Participant characteristics

Expt	Variable	M		SD	
		Younger	Older	Younger	Older
1	Age[c]	21.9	67.2[a]	3.2	5.3
	Education[c]	14.2	15.6[a]	1.8	2.4
	Vocabulary[d]	12.0	13.6	5.0	6.1
	Acuity[b]	17.7	19.8	2.9	4.5
	Digit symbol RT[e]	1,319.0	1,950.0[a]	180.8	400.0
	Digit symbol accuracy[f]	96.3	94.9	2.6	3.8
2 & 3	Age[c]	19.6	68.4[a]	1.7	5.0
	Education[c]	13.6	16.3[a]	1.8	2.5
	Vocabulary[d]	63.5	63.8	3.0	4.5
	Acuity[b]	16.7	23.5[a]	4.3	11.0
	Digit symbol RT[e]	1,355.0	2,034.0[a]	249.1	354.1
	Digit symbol accuracy[f]	98.0	97.4	1.8	2.0

Note: RT = reaction time. $n = 24$ per age group.
[a]Age group comparison reliable at $p < .05$. [b]Denominator of the Snellen fraction for corrected near vision. [c]In years. [d]No. correct; max. = 20. [e]In ms. [f]% correct.

Display items were presented against a black background. The red lines (RGB 255, 0, 0) and green lines (RGB 0, 164, 0) were matched for luminance. Big lines were $1.8° \times 0.57°$, and small lines were $1.34° \times 0.19°$ as viewed at a distance of 60 cm. Participants responded using the "Z" and "/" keys on the computer keyboard, resting the index finger of each hand on the two response buttons during testing. The assignment of *yes/no* responses to the two keys was counterbalanced across participants.

In constructing the displays, the 16 possible locations were arranged in a 4×4 cell grid spanning approximately $13.5° \times 13.5°$. For display sizes of four items, all four lines were presented in one of the four-cell quadrants of the grid (see Figure 1). In display sizes of eight, four lines were presented in one quadrant, and the other four lines were presented in the diagonally opposite quadrant. For display sizes of 16, the lines were divided equally among the four quadrants. This design maintained a comparable density of the items across the display sizes, thus minimizing changes in lateral interference

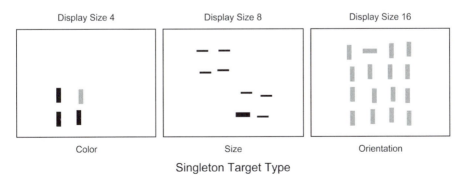

Figure 1.   Display configurations for display size and singleton types in Experiment 1.

effects as a function of display size. Within each quadrant, the position of each of the four lines was jittered randomly up to 0.56° both horizontally and vertically from the centre of its cell.

Design

Each participant performed a total of 1,080 search trials. Two 1,080 display sets (each of an opposing colour) were created and balanced across participants so that singleton target type would not be confounded with colour. Three search conditions (feature, dimension, and mixed) each contained 360 trials. Within each colour set, there were four possible singleton targets (see Table 2) that were all used in each of the three search conditions. What varied across the task conditions was the feature distinguishing the target from the distractors (which defines the type of singleton target in the display) and the predictability of a particular type of target (which defines top–down attentional control). The task conditions were distributed across 17 blocks of trials, each of which contained an equal number of trials for each combination of the three display sizes and two response types (yes/no). These trials were ordered randomly within trial blocks, with the constraint that the same response type did not occur on more than five consecutive trials. On the target-present (yes response) trials, each type of singleton target (colour, size, orientation) appeared in each of the 16 display cell locations equally often within each search condition.

The feature condition contained six blocks of 60 trials, two blocks for each of the three target types (colour, size, and orientation). Participants were informed of the individual feature that would identify the singleton target (e.g., red) at the beginning of each of these trial blocks, and this particular feature remained constant throughout the block (see Table 2). Within each block there were 10 trials for each combination of display size and response type, yielding 20 target-present trials (across the two blocks) for each response type within each of the target types (colour, size, and orientation). Within each feature condition block, the irrelevant features varied across trials (e.g., the orientation and size of lines—when the relevant dimension was colour). However, within a display, the features of all of the distractors were identical, and thus the target differed from the distractors on only one feature.

In the dimension condition, participants were informed at the beginning of each trial block that the target would differ from the distractors along a particular dimension, but the specific feature value distinguishing the target varied across trials (e.g., in the colour dimension trial blocks, the target feature

TABLE 2
Target–distractor pairs during feature search for each singleton type by colour set
and block in Experiment 1

| Colour set | Block | Singleton type | | |
		Colour	Size	Orientation
A	1	BRV–BGV, SRH–SGH	BRV–SRV, BGH–SGH	BRV–BRH, SGV–SGH
	2	SGV–SRV, BGH–BRH	SRH–BRH, SGV–BGV	BGV–BGV, SRH–SRV
B	1	BGV–BRV, SGH–SRH	SGH–BGH, SRV–BRV	SGH–SGV, BRH–BRV
	2	SRV–SGV, BRH–BGH	BRH–SRH, BGV–SGV	BGV–BGH, SRV–SRH

Note: B = big, S = small, V = vertical, H = horizontal, R = red, G = green. For each pair of three letters, the first set of three letters represents the target, and the second set of three letters represents the distractors, with the singleton feature presented in bold (e.g., BRV–BGV represents a big, red, vertical target among big, green, vertical distractors). Data are presented for target-present trials only. Within each trial block, the displays on target-absent trials would be represented by the second set of three letters of each pair.

varied randomly between red and green across trials). As in the feature condition, the irrelevant features varied across trials. There were six trial blocks in this condition. For each target type (colour, size, and orientation), participants performed one block of 48 trials and one block of 72 trials. (Counterbalancing required the number of trials in each block to be a multiple of 24.) This design yielded 20 trials for each combination of response type and display size, per target type.

In the mixed condition, participants were informed at the beginning of each trial block that the target could differ from the distractors on colour, size, or orientation. Participants performed five blocks of 72 trials, yielding 20 target-present trials per display size for each target type and 60 target-absent trials per display size. (In the mixed condition, target type is undefined on target-absent trials.) As in the other search conditions, the distractors within each display in the mixed condition were homogeneous (though varying across trials), and the target differed from the distractors on only one feature. Unlike the other conditions, however, the mixed condition did not enable participants to predict the type of singleton that would occur in an upcoming display.

Procedure

Each block of trials began with an instruction screen that contained information about the characteristics of the target within that block, as described in the previous section (Design). Participants pressed a button to start the first trial. Participants performed a practice block of 36 trials of the mixed search condition before testing began; this practice block was repeated if necessary. The 17 trial blocks used to comprise the feature, dimension, and mixed conditions were counterbalanced across participants with respect to presentation order.

Displays remained on the screen until the participant's key-press response for the target present/absent (yes/no) decision, up to a maximum of 5 s. Reaction times were measured from display onset. After a correct response, the next trial immediately appeared on the screen. After an incorrect response, the computer displayed the word "Error" on the screen for 1.5 s and sounded a tone, before continuing to the next trial.

Results and discussion

Error rate.   For all three experiments, error rates were low for both age groups, and *t* tests revealed no age differences in error rate in any of the three experiments (see Table 3). We recorded failures to respond separately from errors, and response failures did not exceed 0.2% of the trials for either age group in any experiment.

TABLE 3
Proportional error rates by age group and experiment

| | Misses | | | | False alarms | | | |
| | Younger | | Older | | Younger | | Older | |
Experiment	M	SD	M	SD	M	SD	M	SD
1	.025	.014	.028	.019	.020	.018	.018	.013
2	.030	.025	.017	.012	.010	.011	.013	.011
3	.023	.022	.012	.009	.015	.013	.014	.020

Note: Using a Bonferroni corrected alpha level of .025 for each experiment, no age differences in either misses or false alarms were observed for any of the three experiments.

Target-present RT.   The dependent variable in the RT analyses was each participant's median RT in each task condition. Because the differences among the singleton types were undefined for target-absent trials in the mixed condition, we analysed target-present trials and target-absent trials separately. Thus, for the target-present trials in Experiment 1, the resulting design was an Age Group (younger, older) × Search Condition (feature, dimension, mixed) × Singleton Type (colour, size, orientation) × Display Size (4, 8, 16) factorial design. With the exception of age group, all variables were manipulated *within* subjects.

Figure 2 displays the means of the median RTs for correct responses on target-present trials. We analysed these data with a split-plot analysis of variance (ANOVA), averaging across the two blocks of the same singleton type (e.g., red and green) within each search condition. All of the main effects were significant: Reaction time decreased across the mixed, dimension, and feature conditions, $F(2, 92) = 140.7$, $p < .001$. Further, singleton type also affected RT, $F(2, 92) = 85.62$, $p < .001$, with RT decreasing across the size, orientation, and colour singletons. Reaction time also decreased with increasing display size, $F(2, 92) = 30.19$, $p < .001$. Finally, older adults exhibited RTs that were 169 ms higher than those of younger adults, $F(1, 46) = 33.9$, $p < .001$; no interaction involving age group, however, was significant.

The significant Display Size × Singleton Type interaction, $F(4, 184) \times 12.73$, $p < .001$, occurred as the result of a decrease in RT as a function of increasing display size for colour and orientation singletons, both $Fs(2, 94) > 33.2$, $p < .001$, but not for size singletons. The negative display size effect represents the degree of suppression among distractor features, a bottom–up process (Bravo & Nakayama, 1992; Duncan & Humphreys, 1989; Kastner & Ungerleider, 2000). The present variation in the negative display size effect suggests that suppression among distractor features is more effective for colour and orientation than for size.

The Search Condition × Singleton Type interaction, $F(4, 184) = 4.61$, $p = .001$, represents changes in top–down effects across the singleton target features. Bonferroni comparisons

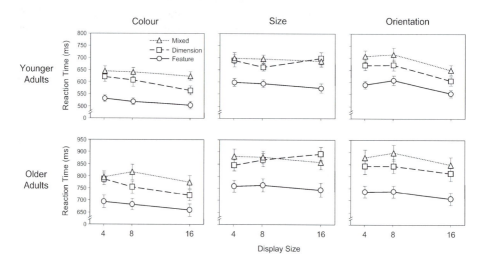

Figure 2.   Mean reaction time (± SE) on target-present trials as a function of display size, singleton type, and age group in Experiment 1.

revealed that for both colour and orientation singletons, responses were significantly faster during the dimension condition than during the mixed condition, and were in addition faster during the feature condition than during the dimension condition, all $t(92)$s > 2.40, $p < .05$. For size singletons, however, although responses were significantly faster in the feature condition than in either the dimension or the mixed condition, $t(92)$s > 2.40, $p < .05$, these last two conditions did not differ significantly. That is, both feature-guided and dimension-guided forms of top–down control were effective for colour and orientation singletons, whereas only feature-guided top–down control was effective for size singletons.

The above pattern was modified by a Search Condition $\times$ Singleton Type $\times$ Display Size interaction, $F(8, 368) = 4.10$, $p < .001$. This effect occurred because there was one exception to the RT benefit provided by both feature and dimension conditions, relative to the mixed condition, for colour and orientation singletons. This exception was colour singletons in four-item displays; there was a substantial benefit for the feature condition relative to the mixed condition, $t(94) > 2.44$, $p < .05$, but the advantage in the dimension condition was not significant.

Target-absent RT.   Given that the variable of singleton target type is undefined for target-absent trials in the mixed condition, median target-absent RTs were collapsed across singleton type. Overall, target absent RTs were only 16 ms slower than target present RTs. As with previous analyses, older adults' RT (823 ms) was slower than that of the younger adults' (630 ms), $F(1, 46) = 35.67$, $p < .001$, and display size effects were slightly negative (22-ms difference between 4- and 16-item displays), $F(2, 92) = 27.61$, $p < .001$. Furthermore, an effect of search condition, $F(2, 92) = 90.52$, $p < .001$, reflects reliable increases in target-absent RT from the feature (664 ms) to the dimension condition (732 ms), and from the latter condition to the mixed condition (784 ms), all $t(92)$s > 2.44, $p < .05$. A Search Condition $\times$ Display Size interaction revealed relatively greater effects of top–down processing for larger display sizes, $F(4, 92) = 5.53$, $p < .001$.

In summary, the effects of search condition in Experiment 1 indicate that colour, size, and orientation were able to effectively support top–down attentional guidance in a highly efficient form of search, singleton detection. That is, as target features became increasingly predictable (i.e., from mixed, to dimension, to feature conditions), responses became reliably faster, as was reported by Wolfe et al. (2003) for target-present trials. In addition, Experiment 1 demonstrated that the top–down effect was present for target-absent trials as well as for target-present trials, which suggests that the top–down attentional guidance influences the decision and response selection processes involved in terminating search (Chun & Wolfe, 1996; Cohen & Magen, 1999), as well as target identification.

The general benefit of top–down guidance was present for all singleton target types, though colour and orientation singletons showed top–down benefits even in the dimension condition, whereas size singletons did not. These results demonstrate that top–down search processes are moderated, in part, by the visual characteristics of the stimulus. That is, top–down and bottom–up attentional processes are not entirely independent but instead interact (Hodsoll & Humphreys, 2001; Krummenacher et al., 2001).

Despite the fact that older adults' responses were generally slower than those of younger adults, the two age groups were similar in the bottom–up processing expressed by the negative display size slopes (i.e., distractor suppression) on both the target-present and the target-absent trials. More critically, younger and older adults did not differ in their ability to engage top–down processing capabilities to facilitate target detection. This result is consistent with the age-related preservation of top–down attentional guidance that has been observed in conjunction search tasks (Humphrey & Kramer, 1997; Madden et al., 1996, 2004). In contrast, Folk and Lincourt (1996) and Watson and Maylor (2002) did report an age-related decline in top–down control in the presence of moving distractors, which may reflect age differences in motion perception specifically. In fact, both Watson and Maylor, and Kramer and Atchley (2000) found that top–down inhibition of distractors, in a visual marking paradigm, was comparable for younger and older adults when the distractors were stationary.

EXPERIMENT 2

Although in Experiment 1 each target singleton differed from the distractors on a single feature, the target features varied in their susceptibility to top–down control, which suggests that top–down and bottom–up processes interact to determine search efficiency. Such effects, however, were similar for younger and older adults. In Experiment 2 we investigated this interaction further. Specifically, we were interested in whether RT changes associated with the degree of target–distractor similarity (a bottom–up process) would vary as a function of top–down control, and whether this interaction varied further in relation to age. We again manipulated the amount of top–down control available by employing both feature- and mixed-search conditions (dimension search was not used). As in Experiment 1, we used size and orientation target types (colour was not manipulated) and homogeneous distractors (see Table 4).[2] We included an additional type of singleton, which differed from the distractors in both size and orientation (e.g., a big vertical target among small horizontal distractors), and participants were aware of this fact. Thus, the difference between the double- and single-feature trials in the

TABLE 4

Target–distractor pairs during feature and mixed search for each target type by colour set and block in Experiment 2

Colour set	Block	Search	Target–distractor pairs		
A		Mixed	BV–SH, **SH–BV**, BV–BH, SH–SV, BH–SH, SV–BV		
B		Mixed	BH–SV, **SV–BH**, BV–BH, SH–SV, BH–SH, SV–BV		
			Double	*Orientation*	*Size*
A	1	Feature	**BV–SH**	BV–BH	BV–SV
	2	Feature	**SH–BV**	SH–SV	SH–BH
B	1	Feature	**BH–SV**	BH–BV	BH–SH
	2	Feature	**SV–BH**	SV–SH	SV–BV

Note: Letter pairs represent display features, as described in the legend to Table 2. In this experiment the colour of all display items was alternated randomly between red and green across trials. For mixed search each colour set block was repeated five times.

---

[2]Colour was not relevant in this task. To maintain similarity to the size and orientation singletons in Experiment 1, all of the items in each display were the same colour, either red or green, and display colour was alternated randomly across trials within each trial block.

mixed condition (which allowed target features to vary) reflects the influence of bottom–up processing (decreasing target–distractor similarity) in the absence of top–down control. Similarly, this single- versus double-feature difference in the feature condition represents the additional contribution of bottom–up processing when top–down control is available.

Using similar manipulations, Krummenacher et al. (2001) and Wolfe et al. (2003) have found an RT advantage for younger adults when targets differed from distractors on two features as opposed to one, indicating a bottom–up effect of target–distractor similarity. These previous investigations differ, however, with regard to the influence of top–down control on this similarity effect. In the Krummenacher et al. study, the advantage for two features (colour and orientation), relative to one, was present for mean RT in both mixed and feature conditions. Only in the feature condition, however, was there additional evidence, from RT distribution analyses (tests of violations of the race model inequality; Miller, 1982), of a particular interaction between top–down and bottom–up effects: The parallel-coactive processing of the colour and orientation dimensions was evident only in the presence of top–down control, when the target feature was blocked. In the Wolfe et al. investigation, in contrast, the double-feature RT advantage was evident only during a mixed condition and not during a feature condition, which suggests that top–down control may be sufficient to preclude further improvement from bottom–up processing.

In view of the age-related decline in efficiency of visual processing at the sensory level (Schneider & Pichora-Fuller, 2000), we predicted that additional support from bottom–up attentional processes, expressed as the RT benefit for double-feature targets relative to single-feature targets, may differentially benefit older adults, especially in the mixed condition where bottom–up processes predominate. If, in addition, older adults are less efficient than younger adults in modifying bottom–up processing by means of top–down control, then the variation in the effect of target–distractor similarity, across feature and mixed search conditions, should be relatively less pronounced for older adults.

Method

Participants

A total of 24 younger adults between 18 and 24 years of age ($M = 19.6$ years) and 24 older adults between 62 and 78 years of age ($M = 68.4$ years) participated in Experiment 2. None of these individuals had participated in Experiment 1, and there were 12 women in each age group. All of these participants were recruited at the Duke University Medical Center, using the same screening criteria as used in Experiment 1, and participants completed the same psychometric measures as those in Experiment 1 (Table 1).

Apparatus and stimuli

All of the testing was conducted with a Pentium 4 processor microcomputer using a 19-in. flat-panel LCD monitor positioned at a viewing distance of 60 cm. The same software as that used to control stimulus presentation in Experiment 1 was also used in Experiment 2. The size and RGB values of the display items were the same as those in Experiment 1. The CIE values of display items on this monitor were measured with the OptiCAL 3.7 system (http://www.colorvision.com). The CIE values were $x = 0.640$, $y = 0.345$, for the red items, and $x = .282$, $y = 0.602$, for the green items. Luminance of red and green display items was $37.0\,\text{cd/m}^2$ and $31.2\,\text{cd/m}^2$, respectively, against a black background.

Design and procedure

The two search conditions, feature and mixed, each comprised 360 trials (see Table 4 for possible singleton target types). The feature condition contained six blocks of 60 trials, with two blocks for each single-feature target (size, orientation) and two blocks for the double-feature target (size plus orientation). The order in which these six blocks were performed across the testing session was counterbalanced using a Latin square design with one of five mixed blocks occurring between each feature block. In each feature condition block, there were 10 single-feature singletons for each display size, yielding a total of 20 trials per response type across both feature condition blocks for size, orientation, and double-feature targets.

The mixed condition contained five blocks of 72 trials, comprising 36 trials per response type. The target-present trials in each block contained (per display size) four targets for each singleton target type (double, size, and orientation) totaling 20 target-present trials for each singleton target type across the five blocks. Each of the mixed blocks also contained 12 target-absent trials per display size. As with the previous experiment, we counterbalanced two colour sets of target–distractor features across participants (see Table 4 for target–distractor pairs).

As in Experiment 1, participants viewed instructions regarding the singleton target at the beginning of each trial block, the displays remained on the screen until the *yes/no* response, and we counterbalanced response hand assignment across participants within each age group. In the double-feature blocks the instructions specified both features of the target (e.g., "target will always be a big, vertical line"), whereas the single-feature and mixed-condition instructions were identical to those in Experiment 1.

Results and discussion

Target-present RT.   As in Experiment 1, we analysed the two response types in separate factorial ANOVAs including age group as a between-subjects variable. On the target-present trials, the within-subjects variables were search condition (feature, mixed), singleton type (size, orientation, double), and display size (4, 8, 16). The means of participants' median RT, for correct responses on target-present trials, are presented in Figure 3.

As with the previous experiment, the main effect of age group, $F(1, 46) = 36.1$, $p < .001$, was the result of responses for older adults that were 236 ms slower than those for younger adults, but no interaction involving age group was significant. The main effect of search condition, $F(1, 46) = 182.6$, $p < .001$, represented the decrease in RT for the feature condition relative to the mixed condition. The singleton type effect, $F(1, 92) = 19.6$, $p < .001$, was significant because mean RT (averaged over search condition) was higher for orientation singletons (804 ms) than for both the size (775 ms) and double-feature (759 ms) singletons. The main effect of display size was also significant, $F(1, 92) = 10.0$, $p < .001$, because mean RTs were higher for 8-item displays (796 ms) than for 4-item (767 ms) or 16-item (774 ms) displays, replicating the negative display size effect observed in Experiment 1.

The Search Condition × Singleton Type interaction, $F(2, 92) = 11.9$, $p < .001$, demonstrated an important difference between the two search conditions. During the mixed condition, even though there was an effect of target type, representing faster responses to size targets (836 ms) than to orientation targets (889 ms), $t(94) > 2.44$, $p < .05$, mean RT for double-feature targets (820 ms) was slightly, but not significantly, lower than that associated with the most discriminable single-feature target (size). During the feature condition, in contrast, mean RT was comparable for size targets (708 ms) and orientation targets (703 ms).

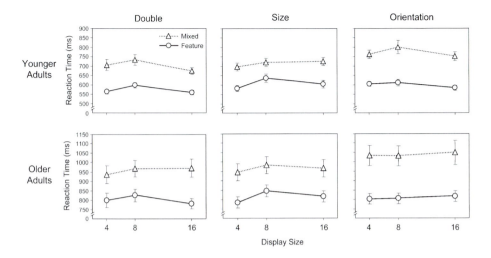

Figure 3.   Mean reaction time (± SE) on target-present trials as a function of display size, singleton type, and age group in Experiment 2.

Responses to the double-feature targets (678 ms), in the feature condition, were significantly lower than those to both types of single-feature target, $t(94) > 2.44$, $p < .05$.

Target-absent RT.   Again, target-absent responses were on average 15 ms slower than target-present responses. Effects were similar to the target-present data, with RT increasing between younger (670 ms) and older adults (919 ms), $F(1, 46) = 28.19$, $p < .001$. Averaged across search condition, there was a 12-ms increase from 4- to 16-item displays, $F(1, 46) = 15.06$, $p < .001$. Responses were faster in the feature (720 ms) than in the mixed condition (869 ms), $F(1, 46) = 91.87$, $p < .001$. (Singleton type is, of course, undefined on the target-absent trials.) The only interaction was a Search Condition × Display Size effect, $F(2, 92) × 13.40$, $p < .001$, which occurred because the positive display size effect was more pronounced in the mixed condition than in the feature condition.

The results of Experiment 2 were in many respects similar to those of Experiment 1. Again, the benefits of top-down processing in the feature condition relative to the mixed condition were present for all three singleton target types (size, orientation, and size plus orientation), and these benefits were comparable for younger and older adults. One difference between the experiments is that the negative display size effect, representing the bottom-up suppression of distractor features at larger display sizes, was present only for target-present trials in Experiment 2, but had been evident for both target-present and target-absent trials in Experiment 1. This pattern may have occurred because target-absent RT receives a relatively greater influence from top-down decision and response selection processes (Chun & Wolfe, 1996), thus reducing the bottom-up effect of distractor suppression.

The primary manipulation in the present experiment was the inclusion of a double-feature singleton target (size plus orientation). We were interested in whether the additional bottom-up information provided by double-feature target would be differentially effective depending on the availability of top–down control. The most intriguing finding involving this manipulation was the presence of the Search Condition × Singleton Target type interaction for target-present trials, which did not interact with age group. In the feature condition, responses to double-feature targets were significantly faster than to both single-feature targets, whereas in the mixed condition there was a nonsignificant RT advantage for the double-feature targets. This result indicates that, for both age groups, the availability of top– down control in the feature condition facilitated the use of additional bottom-up information.

Using a similar manipulation of target–distractor similarity in singleton detection, Wolfe et al. (2003) reported the opposite effect, with double-feature targets showing an RT advantage only in the mixed conditions, whereas Krummenacher et al. (2001) observed faster RTs for double-feature targets than for single-feature targets, in both feature and mixed conditions. Krummenacher et al. also demonstrated, through RT distribution analyses, that the parallel-coactive processing of colour and orientation was evident only in a blocked condition that allowed top–down control. Krummenacher et al. proposed that their results support a dimension-weighting model of search, in which the bottom-up saliency of relevant dimensions is weighted by a top–down mechanism at a detection stage prior to object identification (Found & Müller, 1996; Krummenacher et al., 2002; Müller et al., 1995). Although the RT advantage for double-feature targets was significant only in the feature condition of Experiment 2, our results are generally consistent with the type of interactive effect reported by Krummenacher et al. The feature condition may have allowed the participants in Experiment 2 to alter a top–down template in preparation for the size plus orientation targets. Additional research with a sufficient number of trials to permit RT distribution analyses would be helpful in testing this type of dimension-weighting account.

EXPERIMENT 3

Experiment 2 revealed that top–down and bottom–up processes interacted during a visual search task, resulting in the facilitation of target detection. The goal of Experiment 3 was to examine whether the interaction of these two search processes might also influence the degree to which a noninformative spatial cue was effective in capturing attention. There is a precedent demonstrating that top–down processing has an effect on attentional capture. In a previous study of younger adults, Peterson and Kramer (2001) found that onset distractors were less effective at increasing search RTs when the configuration of the display was one that had been repeated across trials (presumably allowing top–down guidance), relative to during new configuration displays. This result suggests that top–down processes may reduce attentional capture, perhaps by allowing an inhibitory set (cf. Theeuwes, 1992; Theeuwes & Burger, 1998). Pratt and Bellomo (1999) have shown older adults to be more susceptible (relative to younger adults) to attentional capture by onset cues even though the cue is nonpredictive of the target's location, which may be related to the ability to maintain the appropriate level of top–down inhibition (Kramer et al., 2000).

In Experiment 3 we included a noninformative spatial cue indicating target location. As in the previous experiments, we compared feature and mixed blocks as a measure of top–down control. Each trial in this experiment, however, also included the appearance of a spatial cue 150 ms before display onset (see Figure 4), which on some trials indicated a single display

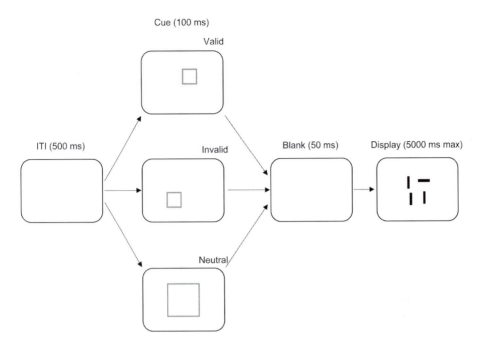

Figure 4.   Display presentation sequence in Experiment 3. ITI = intertrial interval.

location (i.e., an exogenous cue). There were three types of cue trial. On *validly* cued trials, the cue was presented in the same location as that of the singleton target, whereas on *invalid* trials a distractor location was cued. On *neutral* trials a large grey outline box appeared around what would be the entire display. Display size was constant at four items, and cue validity was 25% on target-present trials. The cue was thus noninformative, in that it did not predict the location of the singleton target at a greater than chance level, and participants were instructed to ignore the cue. Any changes in target detection RT associated with the cue should consequently reflect attentional capture: relatively automatic attentional shifts associated with the onset of an exogenous cue. Our question was whether this automatic shift of attention interacts with top–down control.

In Experiment 2 we found that providing additional information that facilitated the distinction between targets and distractors (double-feature singletons) resulted in more efficient search, but only when top–down processing was engaged (i.e., during feature search). In Experiment 3, however, the bottom–up information (the cue) was more frequently unhelpful to target detection (i.e., invalid) than helpful, and thus the best strategy would be to avoid attending to the cue. Thus, participants should be more successful at ignoring the cue when top–down control is available (feature blocks) than when bottom–up processing predominates (mixed blocks). If ageing decreases the ability to avoid attentional capture (Kramer et al., 2000; Pratt & Bellomo, 1999), then this interaction between top–down and bottom–up processing should be more clearly evident for younger adults than for older adults.

Method

Participants, apparatus, and stimuli

The same individuals who participated in Experiment 2 also participated in Experiment 3. The microcomputer and software used in Experiment 2 were also used in Experiment 3, and participants completed both experiments in a single testing session. The task was search for either a colour or orientation singleton line, among homogeneous distractor lines. Two changes were introduced in Experiment 3. First, as noted previously, a valid, invalid, or neutral cue regarding singleton location was presented 150 ms before display onset. Second, both display size (four items) and the size of the lines ($1.8° \times 0.38°$ at a distance of 60 cm) remained constant across all trials. Further, each display of four lines was centred on the screen (see Figure 4) as opposed to being presented in one of four quadrants as in the previous two experiments (see Figure 1).

Design

The order in which participants completed Experiment 2 and Experiment 3 was counterbalanced across participants within each age group. Participants in Experiment 3 performed 960 trials, divided equally between the two search conditions, feature and mixed. As in the previous experiments, age group was a between-subjects variable. On the target-present trials (50% of trials), the within-subjects variables were search condition (feature, mixed), cue type (valid, invalid, neutral), and singleton type (colour, orientation), which were varied orthogonally. The target singleton feature either was repeated across all trials in a block (feature condition) or varied from trial to trial (mixed condition) as in the previous experiments.

The feature condition consisted of eight blocks of 60 trials, comprising four blocks for each singleton target type (colour and orientation). Table 5 displays the target–distractor pairings for each block. Within each block there were 30 trials per response type. For the 30 target-present trials, 5 of the trials were validly cued (with each display location being cued at least once), 15 were invalidly cued (with each location being cued at least three times), and 10 were neutral trials. The occurrence of the different types of cued trial was random within the block. The mixed condition contained 10 blocks of 48 trials each (24 per response type), with the type of singleton feature varying across trials between the four types of target–distractor pairs listed in Table 5. These blocks also maintained the 25% cue validity for target-present trials. The 24 target-present trials in each block contained 4 validly cued

TABLE 5
Target–distractor pairs during feature and mixed
search for each target type by block in Experiment 3

Block	Search	Target–distractor pairs	
1	Mixed	RV–RH, GH–GV, **RH–GH**, **GV–RV**	
2	Mixed	GV–GH, RH–RV, **GH–RH**, **RV–GV**	
		Colour	*Orientation*
1	Feature	**RV–GV**	RV–RH
2	Feature	**RH–GH**	RH–RV
3	Feature	GV–RV	GV–GH
4	Feature	GH–RH	GH–GV

Note: Letter pairs represent display features, as described in the legend to Table 2. Each mixed block was repeated five times.

trials (1 per display location), 12 invalidly cued trials (3 per display location), and 8 neutral trials. The singleton features were also counterbalanced within blocks (though not independently of cue type). Thus, across the 10 blocks in the mixed condition, there was the same representation of target features as in the feature condition, for each of the colour and orientation singletons, on the target-present trials. Similarly, for the target-absent trials, across the 10 mixed blocks there was a total of 80 invalidly cued and 40 neutral trials per singleton dimension. Two types of mixed blocks were created, each using two display types from the colour and orientation features (see Table 5). The order in which the eight colour and orientation feature condition blocks were presented followed an "ABBA" design with mixed blocks positioned in between each feature block. Two slightly different order variations were used as a counterbalancing measure across participants.

Procedure

Practice trials and instructions for the mixed and feature blocks were similar to those in the previous experiments. Further, participants were explicitly instructed that the spatial cue only predicted the target position at chance levels and that they should try to ignore the cue as best they could. All trials began with a 500-ms blank screen. The spatial cue was then presented for 100 ms, followed by a 50-ms blank screen, after which the search display was presented. The search display was terminated by the participant's response, up to a maximum of 5 s. Auditory and visual feedback were given when an error was made, as in the previous experiments.

Results and discussion

Target-present RT. The means of participants' median RT, for correct responses on target-present trials, are presented in Figure 5. As with the previous two experiments, there were reliable effects of age group, $F(1, 46) = 59.16$, $p < .001$ and search condition, $F(1, 46) = 259.76$, $p < .001$, representing a 181-ms age-related slowing and 133-ms top–down control effects (i.e., faster responses in the feature condition than in the mixed condition). Several significant effects involving the singleton type variable were also obtained. The singleton type main effect reflected faster responses to colour targets than to orientation targets, $F(1, 46) = 120.18$, $p < .001$. The Search Condition × Singleton Type interaction, $F(1, 46) = 26.91$, $p < .001$, occurred because although the top–down effect (i.e., RT advantage for the feature condition relative to the mixed condition) was significant for both types of singleton target, the effect was greater in magnitude for colour singletons than for orientation singletons.

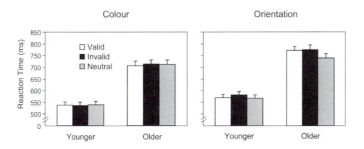

Figure 5.   Mean reaction time (+ SE) on target-present trials as a function of cue type, age group, and singleton type in Experiment 3.

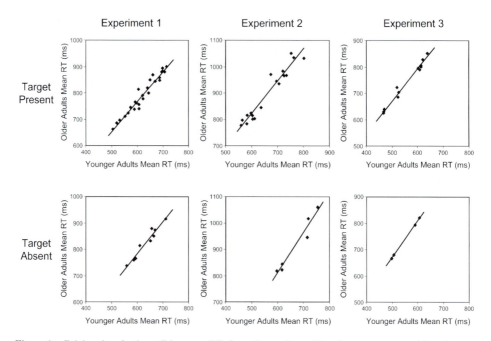

Figure 6.   Brinley plot of task condition mean RTs for each experiment. Data for target-present trials and target-absent trials are presented separately.

An Age Group × Singleton Type interaction, $F(1, 46) = 4.13$, $p < .05$, indicated that age differences in RT were more pronounced during the orientation trials than during the colour trials, but were significant for both types of singleton. To determine whether the Age Group × Singleton Type interaction was a generalized age-related slowing effect, we created Brinley plots of younger and older adults' mean RT for each cell mean in the ANOVA design (see Figure 6). We then used the resulting slope and intercept from the linear regression of the target-present task condition means ($r^2 = .98$) to transform younger adults' RTs (Madden, Pierce, & Allen, 1992). Following this transformation, the age interaction was no longer significant, indicating an effect attributable to generalized slowing.

The remaining effects all involved cue type, in which RTs were generally lower in response to neutral cues than to both valid and invalid cues, $F(2, 92) = 9.17$, $p < .001$. The Singleton Type × Cue Type interaction, $F(2, 92) = 10.46$, $p < .001$, occurred because the cueing effects were present only for orientation targets, and this effect was modified further by the three-way interaction of Search Condition × Singleton Type × Cue Type, $F(2, 92) = 7.43$, $p = .001$. Although the cueing effect for orientation targets was significant for both search conditions, $F(2, 94) > 4.0$, $p < .05$, in each case, the differences among the RT means were more pronounced in the mixed condition than in the feature condition.

An Age Group × Cue Type interaction, $F(2, 92) = 4.20$, $p < .05$, occurred because the cueing effect was significant for older adults, $F(2, 23) = 8.98$, $p < .001$, but not for younger adults. This latter interaction was further modulated by an Age Group × Singleton Type × Cue Type interaction, $F(2, 92) = 4.42$, $p < .05$, that limited the Age × Cue Type effect to the orientation singletons, $F(2, 92) = 7.03$, $p = .001$ (see Figure 5). Tests of simple effects revealed that, for orientation targets, the cueing effect was significant within each age group, $F(2, 46) > 5.0$, $p < .01$, but the pattern of cueing effects varied with age. For the older adults, RTs for both valid and invalid cues were higher than those for neutral cues, both $ts(23) > 2.48$, $p < .05$, whereas for younger adults, RT in response to invalid cues was higher than that for both neutral and valid cues, both $ts(23) > 2.48$, $p < .05$, and these latter two conditions did not differ. Further, these age interactions remained significant, with $F(2, 92) > 3.39$, $p < .05$, in each case, after the younger adults' RTs were transformed by the Brinley plot function ($r^2 = .98$), to account for linear slowing effects.

Target-absent RT. Overall RTs were the same as those for target-present trials (less than 1 ms difference). Replicating the two previous experiments, responses were faster for younger (549 ms) than for older adults (741 ms), $F(1, 46) = 56.5$, $p < .001$, faster during the feature condition (587 ms) than during the mixed (703 ms) condition, $F(1, 46) = 281.8$, $p < .001$, and slower for invalidly cued trials (653 ms) than for neutral trials (637 ms), $F(1, 46) = 31.3$, $p < .001$. (Note that there are only two possible types of cue for the target-absent data.)

A Search Condition × Cue Type interaction, $F(1, 46) = 7.29$, $p < .01$, indicated that although the cueing effect was significant in both search conditions, $Fs(1, 47) > 15.0$, $p < .001$, the cueing effect was larger in magnitude during the mixed condition than during the feature condition. An Age Group × Search Condition effect, $F(1, 46) = 6.32$, $p < .05$, showed that whereas both younger and older adults responded most rapidly during the feature condition, $F(1, 23) > 98.0$, $p < .001$, the effect was larger in magnitude for older adults than for younger adults. When, however, the younger adults' data were transformed by the Brinley plot function for the target-absent mean RTs ($r^2 = .99$), the Age Group × Search Condition interaction was no longer significant.

The results of Experiment 3 support the previous two experiments demonstrating that both younger and older adults are capable of efficiently using top–down processing to guide visual search to the target, in terms of the decrease in RT in the feature condition relative to the mixed condition. Unlike in Experiments 1 and 2, however, an additional task goal was to minimize attentional capture from an irrelevant spatial cue. The effects of spatial cueing on RTs were limited primarily to displays in which targets differed in orientation from distractors, which probably reflects the fact that orientation discrimination is a more spatially dependent process than colour discrimination. Consistent with previous findings with younger adults (Peterson & Kramer, 2001; Theeuwes & Burger, 1998), the Search Condition × Singleton Type × Cue Type interaction for the target-present trials indicated that this cueing effect was more pronounced in the mixed condition than in the feature condition, confirming our prediction of an ability of top–down control to override attentional capture. The target-absent trials also exhibited greater attentional capture in the mixed condition than in the feature condition. Both Experiments 2 and 3 demonstrate that, for both younger and older adults, top–down and bottom–up processes have an interactive role in aiding target detection even when search is highly efficient.

Averaged across the search conditions, the presence of spatial cues overall had a greater impact on RT for older adults than for younger adults. In particular, for orientation targets, both *valid* and *invalid* cues disrupted older adults' search performance relative to the neutral cue condition. For the younger adults, in contrast, only the invalid cues led to a significant increase in RT. This Age Group × Singleton Type × Cue Type interaction in addition survived the transformation controlling for a generalized slowing effect. These results are consistent with findings by Pratt and Bellomo (1999) and Kramer et al. (2000) indicating that under some conditions older adults are more vulnerable to attentional capture than are younger adults. This form of attentional capture is involuntary in that participants are not capable of ignoring the cue even though they know that it is noninformative, but the age difference is independent of the top–down versus bottom–up dimension defined by the difference between the mixed and feature conditions. It would be important to determine whether other forms of top–down control would be able to eliminate entirely the age-related increase in attentional capture expressed in the cueing effects.

GENERAL DISCUSSION

Top–down guidance in singleton detection

The primary purpose of these three experiments was to assess younger and older adults' ability to use top–down attentional guidance during highly efficient forms of visual search. We were also interested in potential top–down effects beyond the level of target activation, the potential interaction between top–down and bottom–up attentional mechanisms, and the ability of top–down control to reduce attentional capture. To these ends, we used a singleton detection paradigm (Wolfe et al., 2003) in which a target differed from a set of homogeneous distractors on one feature (colour, size, or orientation). We manipulated the amount of top–down control available during search by varying the consistency of target and distractor features across trials within a block. In this design, the featural composition of individual displays is comparable across conditions, and decreases in RT for the feature conditions (when target and distractor features remain constant) relative to the mixed conditions (when the features vary unpredictably) thus demonstrate the ability of top–down, a priori knowledge to successfully guide attention during search.

Our data are largely consistent with the recent findings of Wolfe et al. (2003), who demonstrated that singleton detection in both the mixed and feature conditions is very efficient, with flat (if not negative) display size slopes. As in the Wolfe et al. experiments, we found in Experiment 1 that top–down knowledge regarding individual target features (e.g., red, small, or horizontal) is capable of leading to further improvement in singleton detection. Our Experiment 1 data also replicate those of Wolfe et al. in demonstrating that attentional guidance does not require a specific feature value and can be effective at a relatively abstract level of feature dimension, such as colour or orientation, although guidance by size was less reliable at this higher level.

The present findings extend those of Wolfe et al. by documenting top–down effects on target-absent trials. Wolfe et al. focused primarily on the process of target detection and did not include detailed analyses of target-absent data. In all three experiments we obtained an RT advantage for feature conditions, relative to mixed conditions, on target-absent trials as well as on target-present trials. Krummenacher et al. (2001) also reported a significant top–down (feature vs. mixed) effect on target-absent trials in singleton detection. Top–down attentional guidance during singleton detection is thus not limited to target identification processes but also includes the decision and selection processes involved in terminating search when a target is not located (Chun & Wolfe, 1996). This type of result does not necessarily imply that the top–down effect is entirely a response-level effect (cf. Cohen & Magen, 1999), but rather that the attentional guidance influences stages beyond the activation of target features, most likely the setting of a response deadline.

Though it is convenient to conceptualize top–down and bottom–up processes as operating in isolation, the present results agree with other data highlighting the interactive nature of these different attentional processes. The frequently observed fact, confirmed by Experiment 1, that some features are more effective than others, as a basis for top–down control, is a simple illustration of the interactive relation between top–down and bottom–up processing. Hodsoll and Humphreys (2001) reported a more elegant exploration of this issue, in which they demonstrated that top–down guidance for a size singleton is more effective when the target is linearly separable from the distractors (e.g., a small circle target among medium and large circle distractors), relative to when the target is not linearly separable (e.g., a medium target among small and large distractors).

Several other findings from the present experiment are relevant to the issue of the interaction of top–down and bottom–up effects. In particular, Experiment 2 indicated that top–down guidance amplified the RT advantage for double-feature targets relative to single-feature targets. To explore this particular finding further it would be useful to increase the number of trials sufficiently to permit analyses of the RT distribution, which would in turn be informative regarding how target dimensions are weighted in the master map of activations (Found & Müller, 1996; Krummenacher et al., 2001, 2002; Müller et al., 1995). The negative slope of the RT × Display Size function in Experiments 1 and 2 is evidence for a specific bottom–up process, the mutual suppression among homogeneous distractors (Duncan & Humphreys, 1989; Kastner & Ungerleider, 2000). This suppression was evident for target-present trials in both Experiments 1 and 2 but only for target-absent trials in Experiment 1, suggesting that additional decision processes associated with search termination (in the absence of target activation) may either obscure or eliminate the bottom–up suppression. Finally, Experiment 3 exhibited another interaction between top–down and bottom–up processing. For orientation targets, noninformative spatial cues led to greater RT costs (attentional capture) during mixed conditions than during feature conditions. These findings confirm that top–down attention can reduce the effects of attentional capture (Peterson & Kramer, 2001; Theeuwes & Burger, 1998).

Effects of age on top–down guidance

In all three of our experiments we found that the RT benefit of top–down processing during the feature condition relative to the mixed condition was similar for both age groups, on both target-present trials and target-absent trials. Thus, in this context of highly efficient search, we find no evidence of an age-related impairment in top–down attentional control, either for target detection or for the decision processes associated with terminating search. In Experiment 1 we found that the ability to use specific target features (colour, size, and orientation) as a basis for top–down attentional control was similar for younger and older adults. The use of a more abstract level of representation for top–down control (the dimension condition in Experiment 1) was also similar for the two age groups. Increasing the amount of bottom–up information via increased target salience (Experiment 2) led to additional improvement in target detection, when top–down processes predominated (feature condition), and this RT benefit was present for both younger and older adults. Though older adults were more vulnerable to attentional capture from a noninformative spatial cue (Experiment 3), this age difference was independent of the reduction in attentional capture associated with the feature condition relative to the mixed condition.

The age constancy in top–down attentional control for this highly efficient (singleton detection) task is consistent with the age-related preservation of top-down effects reported by Humphrey and Kramer (1997) and Madden et al. (1996, 2004) for a less efficient (conjunction search) task. In contrast, both Folk and Lincourt (1996) and Watson and Maylor (2002) concluded that their results were indicative of an age-related decline in top–down attention. One characteristic of both the latter two studies was the use of displays containing moving targets and distractors. It may consequently be some aspect of motion perception that is differentially difficult for older adults (Kramer & Atchley, 2000; Watson & Maylor, 2002). Interestingly, recent evidence has shown fairly robust age-related deficits in priming for motion stimuli (Jiang, Luo, & Parasuraman, 2002) suggesting that top–down control in older adults may be more sensitive to motion-related features than to colour, size, and orientation (but cf. Kramer, Martin-Emerson, Larish, & Andersen, 1996).

As noted in the Introduction, top–down attentional guidance comprises both an explicit component representing the observer's expectations and an implicit component representing the accumulation of priming effects from repeated targets and distractors (Maljkovic & Nakayama, 1994; Wolfe et al., 2003). The present experiments were concerned primarily with explicit top–down control and were not designed to address the priming issue. Post hoc analyses of priming effects across pairs of adjacent trials in Experiment 1 did not reveal a substantial effect of repetition priming.[3] In other contexts, changes in choice RT associated with repetition priming appear to be largely similar for younger and older adults (Howard & Howard, 1992; Schmitter-Edgecombe & Nissley, 2002). Whether the specific form of implicit top–down control supporting singleton detection varies with age is unknown, but it appears that, at minimum, there is a considerable degree of preservation of top–down attentional guidance during later adulthood. Given that incoming "featural" signals experience decay with age for virtually all of the senses (Madden & Whiting, 2004; Schneider & Pichora-Fuller, 2000), any mechanism that could compensate for such declines would presumably be of considerable benefit in maintaining cognitive performance. The flexibility of knowledge-driven (top–down) processes thus may aide bottom–up processes that rely exclusively on a declining and less flexible sensory system.

Our conclusion that top–down attentional guidance is preserved for older adults is to some extent dependent on the absence of an effect (an age group difference), even though we demonstrated the presence of significant differences between the feature and mixed conditions within each age group. We acknowledge that age differences in top–down control during visual search may exist but were not detected due to lack of statistical power. To investigate this possibility, we conducted post hoc power analyses to calculate the number of participants required to detect the Age × Search condition interaction in Experiment 1,

---

[3]Details of these analyses are available from the corresponding author.

which represented the test of age differences in the use of top–down control during search. The calculated effect size f (Cohen, 1988) of our Age × Search Condition effect was 0.03, indicating a very small effect. Given our alpha level of .05 and numerator $df = 2$, over 1,000 participants in each age group would be necessary to detect this interaction with a power of 0.80. The lack of age effects in this study thus appear to be more the result of very small effects rather than small sample sizes.

In conclusion, across three experiments we consistently found evidence for an age-related preservation of top–down guidance during visual search. Specifically, when top–down control was made available, both younger and older adults showed similar reductions in RT relative to conditions in which search was driven instead by bottom–up processes (Experiment 1). Furthermore, increasing bottom–up saliency between targets and distractors (Experiment 2) further reduced RTs for both age groups when top–down control was engaged. Similarly, including an irrelevant onset cue that induced involuntary attentional capture (Experiment 3), did result in larger capture effects during mixed conditions (relative to feature conditions) for orientation targets. Although older adults were more vulnerable overall to this attentional capture effect, the top–down reduction in the capture effect in the feature condition did not vary with age. The results not only demonstrate a form of top–down attentional control that is preserved with age, they also underscore that top–down and bottom–up search processes operate interactively rather than independently. Singleton detection is a highly efficient form of search, however, and in further research it will be important to determine whether increasing particular types of task demands lead to age-related changes in top–down attentional guidance.

REFERENCES

Bravo, M. J., & Nakayama, K. (1992). The role of attention in different visual search tasks. *Perception & Psychophysics, 51*, 465–472.

Chun, M. M., & Wolfe, J. M. (1996). Just say no: How are visual searches terminated when there is no target present? *Cognitive Psychology, 30*, 39–78.

Cohen, A., & Magen, H. (1999). Intra- and cross-dimensional visual search for single-feature targets. *Perception & Psychophysics, 61*, 291–307.

Cohen, J. (1988). *Statistical power analyses for the behavioral sciences* (2nd ed.). Hillsdale, NJ: Lawrence Erlbaum Associates, Inc.

Colcombe, A. M., Kramer, A. F., Irwin, D. E., Peterson, M. S., Colcombe, S., & Hahn, S. (2003). Age-related effects of attentional and oculomotor capture by onsets and color singletons as a function of experience. *Acta Psychologica, 113*, 205–225.

Duncan, J., & Humphreys, G. W. (1989). Visual search and stimulus similarity. *Psychological Review, 96*, 433–458.

Folk, C. L., & Lincourt, A. E. (1996). The effects of age on guided conjunction search. *Experimental Aging Research, 22*, 99–118.

Found, A. P., & Müller, H. J. (1996). Searching for unknown feature targets on more than one dimension: Investigating a "dimension-weighting" account. *Perception & Psychophysics, 58*, 88–101.

Hodsoll, J., & Humphreys, G. W. (2001). Driving attention with the top down: The relative contribution of target templates to the linear separability effect in the size dimension. *Perception & Psychophysics, 63*, 918–926.

Howard, D. V., & Howard, J. H. (1992). Adult age differences in the rate of learning serial patterns: Evidence from direct and indirect tests. *Psychology and Aging, 7*, 232–241.

Humphrey, D. G., & Kramer, A. F. (1997). Age differences in visual search for feature, conjunction, and triple-conjunction targets. *Psychology and Aging, 12*, 704–717.

Jiang, Y., Luo, Y.-J., & Parasuraman, R. (2002). Priming of two-dimensional visual motion is reduced in older adults. *Neuropsychology, 16*, 140–145.

Kastner, S., & Ungerleider, L. G. (2000). Mechanisms of visual attention in the human cortex. *Annual Review of Neuroscience, 23*, 315–341.

Kramer, A. F., & Atchley, P. (2000). Age-related effects in the marking of old objects in visual search. *Psychology and Aging, 15*, 286–296.

Kramer, A. F., Hahn, S., Irwin, D. E., & Theeuwes, J. (2000). Age differences in the control of looking behavior: Do you know where your eyes have been? *Psychological Science, 11*, 210–217.

Kramer, A. F., Martin-Emerson, R., Larish, J. F., & Andersen, G. J. (1996). Aging and filtering by movement in visual search. *Journal of Gerontology: Psychological Sciences, 51B*, P201–P216.

Krummenacher, J., Müller, H. J., & Heller, D. (2001). Visual search for dimensionally redundant pop-out targets: Evidence for parallel-coactive processing of dimensions. *Perception & Psychophysics, 63*, 901–917.

Krummenacher, J., Müller, H. J., & Heller, D. (2002). Visual search for dimensionally redundant pop-out targets: Parallel-coactive processing of dimensions is location specific. *Journal of Experimental Psychology: Human Perception and Performance, 28*, 1303–1322.

Logan, G. D. (2004). Cumulative progress in formal theories of attention. *Annual Review of Psychology, 55*, 207–234.

Madden, D. J., Pierce, T. W., & Allen, P. A. (1992). Adult age differences in attentional allocation during memory search. *Psychology and Aging, 7*, 594–601.

Madden, D. J., Pierce, T. W., & Allen, P. A. (1996). Adult age differences in the use of distractor homogeneity during visual search. *Psychology and Aging, 11*, 454–474.

Madden, D. J., & Plude, D. J. (1993). Selective preservation of selective attention. In J. Cerella, J. Rybash, W. Hoyer, & M. L. Commons (Eds.), *Adult information processing: Limits on loss* (pp. 273–300). San Diego: Academic Press.

Madden, D. J., & Whiting, W. L. (2004). Age-related changes in visual attention. In P. T. Costa & I. C. Siegler (Eds.), *Recent advances in psychology and aging* (pp. 41–88). Amsterdam: Elsevier.

Madden, D. J., Whiting, W. L., Cabeza, R., & Huettel, S. A. (2004). Age-related preservation of top-down attentional guidance during visual search. *Psychology and Aging, 19*, 304–309.

Maljkovic, V., & Nakayama, K. (1994). Priming of pop-out: I. Role of features. *Memory & Cognition, 22*, 657–672.

McDowd, J. M., & Shaw, R. J. (2000). Attention and aging: A functional perspective. In F. I. M. Craik & T. A. Salthouse (Eds.), *Handbook of aging and cognition* (2nd ed., pp. 221–292). Mahwah, NJ: Lawrence Erlbaum Associates, Inc.

Miller, J. (1982). Divided attention: Evidence for coactivation with redundant signals. *Cognitive Psychology, 14*, 247–279.

Müller, H. J., Heller, D., & Ziegler, J. (1995). Visual search for singleton feature targets within and across feature dimensions. *Perception & Psychophysics, 57*, 1–17.

Peterson, M. S., & Kramer, A. F. (2001). Contextual cueing reduces interference from task-irrelevant onset distractors. *Visual Cognition, 8*, 843–859.

Pratt, J., & Bellomo, C. N. (1999). Attentional capture in younger and older adults. *Aging, Neuropsychology, and Cognition, 6*, 19–31.

Quinlan, P. T. (2003). Visual feature integration theory: Past, present, and future. *Psychological Bulletin, 129*, 643–673.

Salthouse, T. A. (1992). What do adult age differences in the digit symbol substitution test reflect? *Journal of Gerontology: Psychological Sciences, 47*, P121–P128.

Salthouse, T. A. (1993). Speed and knowledge as determinants of adult age differences in verbal tasks. *Journal of Gerontology: Psychological Sciences, 48*, P29–36.

Schmitter-Edgecombe, M., & Nissley, H. M. (2002). Effects of aging on implicit covariation learning. *Aging, Neuropsychology, and Cognition, 9*, 61–75.

Schneider, B. A., & Pichora-Fuller, M. K. (2000). Implication of perceptual deterioration for cognitive aging research. In F. I. M. Craik & T. A. Salthouse (Eds.), *The handbook of aging and cognition* (2nd ed., pp. 155–219). Mahwah, NJ: Lawrence Erlbaum Associates, Inc.

Theeuwes, J. (1992). Perceptual selectivity for color and form. *Perception & Psychophysics, 51*, 599–606.

Theeuwes, J., & Burger, R. (1998). Attentional control during visual search: The effect of irrelevant singletons. *Journal of Experimental Psychology: Human Perception and Performance, 24*, 1342–1353.

Treisman, A. (1988). Features and objects: The fourteenth Bartlett memorial lecture. *Quarterly Journal of Experimental Psychology, 40A*, 201–237.

Watson, D. G., & Maylor, E. A. (2002). Aging and visual marking: Selective deficits for moving stimuli. *Psychology and Aging, 17*, 321–339.

Wolfe, J. M. (1994). Guided search 2.0: A revised model of visual search. *Psychonomic Bulletin & Review, 1*, 202–238.

Wolfe, J. M. (1998). Visual search. In H. A. Pashler (Ed.), *Attention* (pp. 13–73). Hove, UK: Psychology Press.

Wolfe, J. M. (2003). Moving towards solutions to some enduring controversies in visual search. *Trends in Cognitive Sciences, 7*, 70–76.

Wolfe, J. M., Butcher, S. J., Lee, C., & Hyle, M. (2003). Changing your mind: On the contributions of top-down and bottom-up guidance in visual search for feature singletons. *Journal of Experimental Psychology: Human Perception and Performance, 29*, 483–502.

Yantis, S. (1998). Control of visual attention. In H. A. Pashler (Ed.), *Attention* (pp. 223–256). Hove, UK: Psychology Press.

PrEview proof published online 7 July 2004

THE QUARTERLY JOURNAL OF EXPERIMENTAL PSYCHOLOGY
2005, 58A (1), 98–119

Ψ Psychology Press
Taylor & Francis Group

Age-related deficits in free recall:
The role of rehearsal

Geoff Ward

University of Essex, Colchester, UK

Elizabeth A. Maylor

University of Warwick, Coventry, UK

Age-related deficits have been consistently observed in free recall. Recent accounts of episodic memory suggest that these deficits could result from differential patterns of rehearsal. In the present study, 20 young and 20 older adults (mean ages 21 and 72 years, respectively) were presented with lists of 20 words for immediate free recall using the overt rehearsal methodology. The young outperformed the older adults at all serial positions. There were significant age-related differences in the patterns of overt rehearsals: Young adults rehearsed a greater number of different words than did older adults, they rehearsed words to more recent serial positions, and their rehearsals were more widely distributed throughout the list. Consistent with a recency-based account of episodic memory, age deficits in free recall are largely attributable to age differences in the recency, frequency, and distribution of rehearsals.

Immediate free recall is a standard laboratory method in which participants are presented with a series of stimuli (usually words), one at a time, and are then required to recall as many of the words in the list as they can remember, in any order that they like. The data are normally presented in serial position curves, which plot the proportion of items that are recalled by the position of the items in the experimenter's list. A U-shaped serial position curve is usually obtained, illustrating that there is a recall advantage for the first and last items in the list—advantages known as the primacy and recency effects, respectively.

The results of free recall are traditionally explained in terms of dual-store models of memory (e.g., Atkinson & Shiffrin, 1968) in which the most recent words from the lists are retrieved from a short-term memory store (STS) of limited capacity. The words recalled from

Correspondence should be addressed to Geoff Ward, Department of Psychology, University of Essex, Wivenhoe Park, Colchester, CO4 3SQ, UK, or to Elizabeth A. Maylor, Department of Psychology, University of Warwick, Coventry, CV4 7AL, UK. Email: gdward@essex.ac.uk or elizabeth.maylor@warwick.ac.uk

This study was presented as a poster at the Ninth Cognitive Aging Conference, Atlanta, Georgia, April 2002.

We are grateful to Jodie Barden and Helen Palmer for collecting and scoring the data, and to Ursula Richards and Jessica Leech for assistance in data checking.

http://www.tandf.co.uk/journals/pp/02724987.html   DOI:10.1080/02724980443000223

all earlier serial positions are assumed to be the result of a search through the long-term memory store (LTS), with the chance of success proportional to the relative strength of each item in the list (e.g., Shiffrin, 1970). In support of this position, Rundus (1971) showed that the first words in a list are rehearsed many more times than later words. He used the overt rehearsal methodology (Rundus & Atkinson, 1970) in which participants say out loud everything that comes to mind during the presentation of the stimuli, such that the number of rehearsals of each item can be counted. The extra rehearsals afforded to the first items can be assumed to increase the strength of association of these items in LTS and hence can account for the standard primacy effects.

Glanzer (1972) provided further evidence for the dual-store explanation of free recall. He argued that free recall could be considered to be a two-component task: The STS underpins the recency effect, but the LTS underpins all earlier serial positions. In line with this position, Glanzer listed factors that affected the STS component of free recall (STS factors) but had no effect on the early and middle list items. STS factors included the modality of the stimuli and the introduction of a filled delay in which post-list rehearsal was prevented. Factors that affected the LTS component of the serial position curve but had no effect on the recency portion of the serial position curve (LTS factors) were also described. LTS factors included the presentation rate, word frequency, list length, the intelligence and, importantly for this article, the age of the participants.

Evidence that the effectiveness of recall from LTS and not STS is affected with increased age comes from early studies by Craik (1968a, 1968b) and Raymond (1971). Craik (1968a, Exp. V) examined the free recall of younger and older participants on lists of digits, county names, animal names, and unrelated words varying in length from 5 to 20 items. He found an age by list length interaction: Both groups recalled approximately 4–5 words from each list, but as the list length increased, so the young started to outperform the older participants. Craik used a number of different formulae to derive the STS and LTS components and found that the STS component (also known as primary memory, following James, 1890) was reasonably independent of age and material used and was 8–9 syllables in capacity. However, the efficiency of the search from LTS (or secondary memory, James, 1890) declined with increased age and stimulus vocabulary size. A similar conclusion was reached by Raymond (1971), who examined a group of older participants on lists of 12 high-frequency words, at a very slow presentation rate of 8s per item. She found that there was a modest primacy effect and a large and significant recency effect. She then compared her data with those from young participants obtained from other published studies. Although these studies differed in the presentation rate, list length, and type of word, it appeared that the older participants' performance on the last two items was approximately equivalent to that by the young in previous studies, but the older participants' performance on the first two items and middle items was considerably poorer. Raymond concluded that the decrease in free recall with age was not a result of an overall decline in memory, but was due to the selective decline in performance from LTS.

Further support for a selective impairment in LTS comes from evidence from participants' memory spans in the immediate serial recall task. In this quintessential STS task, memory spans have been shown to decrease only slightly with age (e.g., Parkinson, 1982; see Kausler, 1994, and Maylor, Vousden, & Brown, 1999, for reviews), particularly when the stimuli are digits and not words (Salthouse & Babcock, 1991). Although there are differences between recency and memory span in their theoretical interpretation (e.g., Atkinson &

Shiffrin, 1968; Baddeley, 1986; Baddeley & Hitch, 1974; Della Sala, Logie, Trivelli, Cubelli, & Marchetti, 1998; Ward, 2001), there are historical links between both span and recency to STS, and the evidence is provided here for completeness.

Data obtained by Sanders, Murphy, Schmitt, and Walsh (1980) can also be interpreted within a dual-store framework. They tested young and older participants on free recall of lists of 16 words using both normal covert free recall and also the overt rehearsal method used earlier by Rundus (1971). They found that the young greatly outperformed the older participants at all serial positions, with the exception of performance on the very last items in the overt rehearsal conditions where recall was almost equivalent. Importantly, they showed that the young participants rehearsed the early and middle items far more frequently than did the older participants, and this could be argued to indicate that the young had more successfully strengthened the memory traces of the primacy and middle items in LTS. In fact, Sanders et al. focused in their discussion on the difference in rehearsal strategies that the two groups used: The older participants rehearsed serially, and recall performance was similar under covert and overt rehearsal, whereas the young participants rehearsed more strategically, clustering words of the same categories, and showed a 10% decline in recall with overt rehearsal.

However, there are at least three lines of evidence against a dual-store account of ageing effects in free recall. First, there are oft-cited difficulties with the dual-store accounts of rehearsal and recency in free recall. Although the strength of an item in LTS is assumed to be affected by the numbers of rehearsals in free recall, it is found that sometimes increased rehearsal aids recall (e.g., Modigliani & Hedges, 1987; Rundus, 1971) but sometimes it does not (e.g., Craik & Watkins, 1973). Moreover, recency in free recall occurs when the STS is filled with distractor material, such as in the continuous distractor task in which a filled delay is inserted after every item in the list including the final item (e.g., Baddeley & Hitch, 1974; Bjork & Whitten, 1974; Watkins, Neath, & Sechler, 1989). Recency also occurs in everyday situations over the long term, such as recalling the names of opposing rugby teams (Baddeley & Hitch, 1977), recalling where one parked one's car (Pinto & Baddeley, 1991), or recalling movies at the cinema (Hitch & Ferguson, 1991). Clearly, the time scales of these recency effects rule out an interpretation in terms of a limited-capacity STS. Indeed, the magnitude of these recency effects are well fitted by the empirical law known as the ratio rule (Bjork & Whitten, 1974; Crowder, 1976, 1993; Glenberg et al., 1980), which predicts that the magnitude of recency effects will be proportional to the ratio $(\Delta t/T)$ of the interpresentation interval (Δt) to the retention interval (T). One way of explaining the ratio rule is to assume that episodic memory is a continuum, with no distinction made between STS and LTS. Recent items are simply more accessible due to short retention intervals, which result in higher values of the ratio $(\Delta t/T)$. However, the ratio rule in its traditional form cannot be a full account of free recall as it predicts solely recency and no primacy. It should also be noted that although these weaknesses have been acknowledged, there is still considerable support for the dual-store accounts (e.g., Bemelmans, Wolters, Zwinderman, ten Berge, & Goekoop, 2002; Healy & McNamara, 1996; Raaijmakers, 1993; Shiffrin, 1999).

Second, more recent studies of free recall have shown that the age decrement in free recall occurs consistently throughout the serial position curve (e.g., Arenberg, 1976; Capitani, Della Sala, Logie, & Spinnler, 1992; Parkinson, Lindholm, & Inman, 1982; Salthouse, 1980; Wright, 1982). There is little or no evidence in these studies that the recency effect is selectively preserved, nor that the age-related decrement resides solely in the early and middle portions of the serial position curve. One alternative account that predicts a consistent age-related decrement throughout free recall explains age-related differences in free recall in terms of reduced processing speed with age (Bryan & Luszcz, 1996; Salthouse, 1980, 1991, 1992). Salthouse (1980) proposed that age-related differences in free recall could be accounted for by differential rehearsal rates between young and older adults. He proposed that each additional rehearsal made by the participants incremented the strength of an item in the list, and that each item decayed with time. An accumulation of trace strength throughout the list was assumed to occur if the rate of rehearsal was at a rate greater than that needed to overcome the loss due to decay. Salthouse, working with Wright (as described in Salthouse, 1980), manipulated the word length (one- and three-syllable words) and age in a free recall study of 12-word lists. They found the standard primacy and recency effects in the serial position curve. Importantly, there were effects of both age and word length throughout the entire list, but there were no interactions between these three variables, suggesting that differences in age and in word length had similar effects on the serial position curves. They also showed that, in a separate test of rehearsal rate, the older participants took longer to rehearse the items than did the young participants. Furthermore, a replication and extension of this experiment by Bryan and Luszcz (1996) showed that an independent measure of processing speed (performance on the Digit Symbol Substitution Test, DSST; Wechsler, 1981) accounted for all the age-related variance in free recall performance. This rehearsal-based explanation of cognitive ageing, mediated by a general reduction in processing speed with increasing age, obviates the need for the distinction between STS and LTS.

Finally, Tan and Ward (2000) have recently attempted to extend the ratio rule to account for both the primacy and the recency portions of the serial position curve. They expanded on earlier empirical work by Brodie and his colleagues (Brodie, 1975; Brodie & Murdock, 1977; Brodie & Prytulak, 1975) and tested only young participants using the overt rehearsal methodology. Their hypothesis was that recall performance may be affected by far more than simply the number of rehearsals. If the first items in the list were rehearsed most frequently in free recall, then some of these rehearsals may be toward the very end of the list. If the ratio rule account of recency was extended to include the rehearsals of the words as well as the presentation of list items, then a recency-based retrieval mechanism such as gives rise to the ratio rule may be able to account for the full serial position curve. An analysis of the schedules of rehearsals showed that early list items were indeed rehearsed toward the end of their lists. When the U-shaped serial position curves were replotted by when each word was last rehearsed, extended recency effects were obtained, showing little or no primacy. In addition, LTS factors such as presentation rate and word frequency (Tan & Ward, 2000; Ward, Woodward, Stevens, & Stinson, 2003), and also list length (Ward, 2002), were shown to affect the number of early and middle items that participants continued to rehearse until the end of the list presentation. Subsequent analyses and additional experiments showed that the greater the number, the recency and the distribution of the rehearsals, the greater was the free recall performance. Interestingly, these factors may also separate earlier studies showing a positive effect of number of rehearsals in free recall (e.g., recent and distributed rehearsals in Rundus, 1971; and Modigliani & Hedges, 1987) from those that showed no effect (e.g., massed rehearsals in Craik & Watkins, 1973).

The present study attempted to replicate and extend the Tan and Ward (2000) findings by examining free recall with young and older participants using overt free rehearsal. The rationale of the study was twofold. First, as discussed earlier, old age has been considered by some authors to be an LTS variable (Glanzer, 1972). A reconsideration of the effect of age in free recall using the overt rehearsal methodology essentially continues the theme started by Tan and Ward (2000) and Ward (2002) of attempting to reinterpret LTS variables in terms of differential effects on rehearsal and subjective recency.

Second, an analysis of the rehearsal schedules generated from the overt rehearsal methodology of free recall might provide further evidence as to the locus of age-related deficits in free recall. Following from Tan and Ward's (2000) analysis, age-related differences might be explained by age differences in the number of rehearsals, the distribution of rehearsals, or the recency with which the words are last rehearsed, or some combination of these. The studies by Bryan and Luszcz (1996), Salthouse (1980), and Sanders et al. (1980) predict that young participants will be able to rehearse words more frequently than will older participants. However, these earlier studies concentrated solely on the frequency or rate of rehearsal and did not consider possible age-related differences in the recency and distribution of these rehearsals in free recall. Indeed, in both Salthouse's and Bryan and Luszcz's studies, the rehearsal order in free recall was fixed, whereas in Sanders et al.'s study, the relevant post hoc analyses relating to recency and distribution were not performed. In addition, there may be a residual difference in the slope of the recency functions when the data are equated for the number, distribution, and recency of when the words are last rehearsed. Older participants may suffer from more trace decay, interference, or difficulty in temporal discrimination than young participants, resulting in steeper forgetting curves. Although a possibility, we might expect that this would be unlikely given that the forgetting curves appear to be no steeper in the Brown–Peterson paradigm for older than for young participants (Schonfield, 1969, reported in Kausler, 1994) and the release from proactive interference in this task is of equivalent magnitude (Elias & Hirasuna, 1976). Finally, Tan and Ward (2000) have argued that understanding which words were rehearsed at different points throughout the list may provide interesting insights into the development of the serial position curve. Similar analyses in this study may provide on-line measures of age-related differences at different points throughout presentation of the study list.

In summary, young and healthy older participants were presented with six lists of 20 words at a rate of 1 word every 4 s. Participants were instructed to say out loud each word as it appeared on the screen, and were also requested to say out loud any word that came to mind during the list. Participants recalled the words at the end of the list out loud, all responses were recorded using a tape recorder, and the recalls and rehearsals were transcribed. Finally, independent measures of processing speed (DSST) and vocabulary were taken to determine whether age-related differences in free recall might themselves be mediated by processing speed.

Method

Participants

There were 20 young participants (15 women; 5 men) and 20 older participants (14 women; 6 men). The young participants were undergraduate students from the University of Warwick and were aged between 19 and 28 years ($M = 21.3$; $SD = 1.9$). The older participants were aged between 64 and

79 years (M = 72.2; SD = 4.2) and were members of a panel of volunteers who had been recruited to take part in studies of memory and ageing at the University of Warwick. The older participants had previously travelled to the university for a group testing session during which background data were collected. Because the University of Warwick is a campus university situated a few miles from the nearest town, the volunteer panel probably represents a relatively able and active sample of older people. For the young group, the background tests were administered immediately after completing the free recall task.

Vocabulary was measured by the first part of the Mill Hill Vocabulary Test (Raven, Raven, & Court, 1988) in which participants select the best synonym for a target word from a set of six alternatives (maximum score = 33). The mean scores for the young and older groups were 18.4 (SD = 1.9) and 24.7 (SD = 3.4), respectively, and these differed significantly, $t(38)$ = 7.22, $p < .0001$. Speed was measured by the Digit Symbol Substitution Test of the Wechsler Adult Intelligence Scale–Revised (Wechsler, 1981).[1] The mean scores for the young and older groups were 72.4 (SD = 7.4) and 48.0 (SD = 11.4), respectively, and these differed significantly, $t(37)$ = 7.88, $p < .0001$.[2] This pattern of superior vocabulary but inferior speed for older adults in comparison with young adults is typical in the ageing literature (e.g., Salthouse, 1991, 1992).

Self-rated measures of participants' current state of health, eyesight (with glasses, if worn), and hearing (with aids, if worn) were available for the older group only. On a 5-point scale (1 = *very poor*, 2 = *poor*, 3 = *fair*, 4 = *good*, 5 = *very good*), the mean ratings were 4.0 (SD = 0.7) for health, 4.1 (SD = 0.6) for eyesight, and 3.9 (SD = 0.7) for hearing. Because of the demanding nature of the present experiment, the following exclusion criteria were used when selecting older participants: a score below 15 on the vocabulary test, a score below 30 on the speed test, or a self-rating below 3.

Materials and apparatus

A set of 140 words was selected from the Oxford Psycholinguistic Database (Quinlan, 1992). The words were predominantly monosyllables that were between three and seven letters in length and had an occurrence greater than 100 counts per million (Kucera & Francis, 1967). Examples include "COURSE", "RANGE", and "SQUARE". The words were randomly assigned to six experimental lists of 20 words and a practice list of 10 words, with 10 words not used; thus, no participant received the same word twice throughout the experiment. Twenty different random orders were produced, with each order being assigned to one young and one older participant. The materials were presented using the application Hypercard on an Apple Macintosh laptop computer.

Design

In the basic design there was one between–subjects factor, age, with two levels (young and older adult participants), and there was one within-subjects factor, serial position, with five levels (serial positions 1–4, 5–8, 9–12, 13–16, 17–20). The proportion of words recalled and the number of rehearsals made after each word throughout the study phase were recorded, and additional analyses based on these measures were also performed.

---

[1]Due to an administrative error, the young participants were allowed only 60 s, rather than 90 s, to perform the task. Their scores were therefore adjusted by multiplying by 1.5.

[2]One young participant misunderstood the instructions for this test; his data were therefore excluded from this comparison and also from the correlational and regression analyses presented in the Results section.

Procedure

The young participants and older adults were tested individually seated at a table in a quiet room free from distractions. All participants were told that they would see a list of words presented one at a time in the centre of the computer screen. At the start of the list was a warning tone, and the words were presented in upper case, 64-point Times font, for 1 s followed by a 3-s interstimulus interval in which the screen was blank. The participants were instructed to repeat each word loudly and clearly as it appeared, and they were also instructed to use the interval between words to rehearse aloud any words that they were currently thinking of as they were studying the list. A series of three beeps sounded 3 s after the last word was presented, signalling the beginning of the 60-s recall period, in which the participants recalled out loud as many words as they could remember from the just-presented list, in any order that they wished. Throughout the experiment, all the participants' rehearsals and responses were tape-recorded. Participants were given six experimental lists of 20 words, preceded by a shorter practice list of 10 words. Participants were free to rest between lists at their discretion. Following the free recall task, the young participants were asked to complete the DSST and Mill Hill Vocabulary Test (which took approximately 5 minutes). These background scores were already available for the older participants from the University of Warwick panel database. The participants were then debriefed.

Results

Initial analysis

The data were initially submitted to four analyses. Recall performance for each group was first analysed as a function of the *nominal serial position* (SP)—that is, the position of the words on the experimenter's list. This is the standard analysis that provides the characteristic U-shaped serial position curve in free recall.

The second analysis replots these data by the *functional serial position* (fSP) of each word (Brodie, 1975; Brodie & Murdock, 1977; Brodie & Prytulak, 1975). In this analysis, the patterns of presentations and overt rehearsals provide a rank ordering of the list items for each participant and each list from the most recently experienced word (fSP 20) to the least recently experienced word (fSP 1). An example will help clarify the term, fSP. Imagine that during list presentation, a participant says out loud the following utterance, "...**14**, *1*, *2*, *3*, **15**, *1*, *2*, *3*, **16**, *15*, *1*, *3*, **17**, *7*, *1*, *3*, **18**, *14*, *1*, *3*, **19**, *1*, **20**, *17*, *1*, *3*", in which the bold numbers refer to the nominal serial positions of the words that the participant says out loud as they are presented, and the italicized numbers refer to the nominal serial positions of earlier list items that they overtly rehearse. An examination of the utterance can provide the rank ordering of words, from least recently rehearsed to most recently rehearsed, that determine each word's fSP. Thus in the example above, the words presented at nominal serial positions 2, 16, 15, 7, 18, 14, 19, 20, 17, 1, and 3 correspond to fSPs 10 to 20. Note that there is an even distribution of data across the fSP curve, because for every participant and every list there is exactly one occurrence for each fSP. Note also that in the analysis in this paper, the measure of fSP is a strict rank ordering rather than a close approximation used in some earlier papers (Tan & Ward, 2000; Ward, 2002; Ward, Woodward, Stevens, & Stinson, 2003).

The third analysis replots the same data as a function of the *rehearsal set* (RS) to which the words were last rehearsed (the "last RS", Rundus, 1971). The RS refers to the 4 s (1-s presentation and 3-s interstimulus interval) following the onset of each word. Using the illustrative schedule of presentations and rehearsals presented in the previous paragraph, the words from nominal serial positions 14 to 20 are last rehearsed in the following distribution of occurrences: Last RS 14: no words; Last RS 15: 2; Last RS 16: 15, 16; Last RS 17: 7; Last RS 18: 14, 18; Last RS 19: 19; Last RS 20: 1, 3, 17, 20. Note that the distribution of data points across the values of last RS is uneven; there may be some last RSs in each list with no words, and there may be some last RSs with more than one word. Considering the data from an entire experiment, it is typically found that many words are rehearsed to later last RSs (and hence there are many occurrences contributing to later last RS values), and there are relatively few words that were presented early in the list that remain unrehearsed (and so there are fewer occurrences contributing to early last RS values). Like fSPs, this analysis provides a recency-based measure of subjective experience that takes into account both the presentations and the rehearsals of the list items. Unlike fSPs, last RS can additionally provide an accurate measure of the retention interval between when a word was last experienced and the beginning of the recall period. Its main drawback is the uneven distribution of the data, which makes data analysis difficult.

The fourth analysis considers the number of positions that each word is moved through rehearsal toward the end of the list. The number of positions moved is calculated by subtracting the nominal SP of each word in each list from the RS to which that word was last rehearsed. Thus, the word presented in nominal SP 1 in our example above moved 19 positions, nominal SP 2 moved 13 positions, and so on. This provides a measure of the distance toward the end of the list that words from different nominal SPs are typically rehearsed.

Nominal serial position.   The proportion of words recalled at each SP for the young and older participants is shown in Figure 1A. A 2×5 mixed-design analysis of variance (ANOVA) with age (young and older participants) as a between-subjects factor, and nominal SP (5 levels: 1–4, 5–8, 9–12, 13–16, 17–20) as a within-subjects factor revealed a significant main effect of age, $F(1, 38) = 13.69$, $MSE = 0.033$, $p < .001$, a significant main effect of serial position, $F(4, 152) = 52.91$, $MSE = 0.019$, $p < .0001$, and a nonsignificant interaction, $F < 1$. Newman–Keuls pairwise comparisons of the main effect of serial position showed that recall performance at SP 1–4 and SP 17–20 was significantly different from that at all other SPs, $p < .01$, indicating significant primacy and recency effects, respectively. The significant main effect of age and the lack of a significant interaction demonstrate that the young ($M = .414$) outperformed the older participants ($M = .319$) in all parts of the SP curve. The overall difference in the proportion of words correctly recalled by the two age groups was .095, which represents a 22.9% age-related reduction in recall performance.

Functional serial position.   The proportion of words recalled at each functional serial position for the young and older participants is shown in Figure 1B. A 2×5 mixed-design ANOVA with age (young and older participants) as a between-subjects factor, and functional serial position (fSP 1–4, 5–8, 9–12, 13–16, 17–20) as a within-subjects factor revealed a significant main effect of age, $F(1, 38) = 13.76$, $MSE = 0.033$, $p < .001$, a significant main effect of serial position, $F(4, 152) = 129.30$, $MSE = 0.017$, $p < .0001$, and an interaction that approached significance, $F(4, 152) = 2.37$, $MSE = 0.017$, $p < .06$. Newman–Keuls pairwise comparisons of the main effect of serial position showed that recall performance at all fSPs was significantly different from all other fSPs, $p < .01$ (with the sole exception of the comparison between fSPs 1–4 and fSPs 5–8, which failed to reach significance). An analysis of the simple main effects

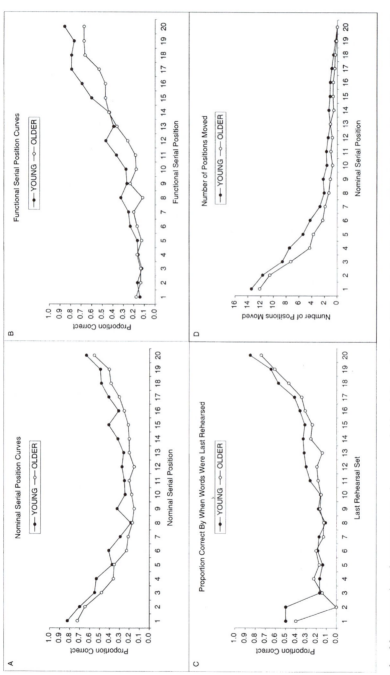

Figure 1. Mean proportion of correct responses by young and older adults as a function of (A) nominal serial position, (B) functional serial position, and (C) last rehearsal set to which an item was rehearsed. (D) plots the mean number of rehearsal sets moved by the nominal serial position of the list items for both young and older adults.

revealed that the near-significant interaction was largely attributable to the fact that there was a significant age difference (p at least $<.05$) at all fSPs except the earliest, fSPs 1–4. Thus, when the data are replotted in terms of the subjective rank ordering of the list items, there was a clear and extended recall advantage for words that were experienced more recently. The significant main effect of age and the near-significant interaction demonstrate that the young outperformed the older participants at all fSPs, with perhaps the exception of the very earliest fSPs.

Last RS.   The proportion of words recalled at each last RS for the young and older participants is shown in Figure 1C. Table 1 shows the number of correct responses and the number of occurrences that are averaged to provide the values in Figure 1C. As predicted, there are relatively large numbers of words that are rehearsed to late RSs and relatively few words that are presented early in the list that remain unrehearsed. In this case, a 2 × 9 mixed-design ANOVA was conducted with age (young and older participants) as a between-subjects factor, and last RS (9 levels: 1–6, 7–8, 9–10, 11–12, 13–14, 15–16, 17–18, 19, and 20) as a within-subjects factor. This revealed a near-significant main effect of age, $F(1, 38) = 3.83$, $MSE = 0.081$, $p < .06$, a highly significant main effect of serial position, $F(8, 304) = 79.50$, $MSE = 0.025$, $p < .0001$, and a nonsignificant interaction, $F(8, 304) = 1.40$, $MSE = 0.025$, $p > .05$. Newman–Keuls pairwise comparisons of the main effect of serial position showed that recall performance of the three most recent last RSs (17–18, 19, and 20) was significantly different from that of all other last RSs, $p < .01$, and that the recall performance of the last RSs 13–14 and 15–16 was significantly different from that of the earliest last RSs (1–6 and 7–8; and RSs 1–6, 7–8 and 9–10, respectively). The overall difference in the proportion of words correctly recalled by the two age groups was .059 (cf. .095 earlier). These results suggest that the age differences have been somewhat reduced when the data are replotted by last RS, and they again demonstrate extended recency effects with little primacy for both groups.

Number of RSs moved.   Figure 1D shows the number of RSs moved toward the end of the list at each serial position for the young and older participants. A 2 × 5 mixed-design ANOVA with age (young and older participants) as a between-subjects factor, and nominal SP (1–4, 5–8, 9–12, 13–16, 17–20) as a within-subjects factor revealed a significant main effect of age, $F(1, 38) = 10.54$, $MSE = 3.788$, $p < .01$, a significant main effect of SP, $F(4, 152) = 191.98$, $MSE = 2.915$, $p < .0001$, and a nonsignificant interaction, $F(4, 152) = 1.26$, $MSE = 2.915$, $p > .05$. Newman–Keuls pairwise comparisons of the main effect of SP showed significant differences between all pairwise comparisons ($p < .01$) with the exceptions of comparisons between the two latest neighbouring pairs (13–16 vs. 17–20). These results show that the young participants rehearsed the list items to more recent list positions than did the older participants and that words from earlier nominal SPs were moved a greater number of RSs toward the end of the list than words from later nominal SPs.

The results from this initial set of four analyses reveal that (a) there is clear evidence for an age-related deficit across all nominal SPs in free recall, (b) the traditional U-shaped serial position curve can be replotted as large and extended recency effects for both age groups when the subjective order of the rehearsals as well as the experimenter's presentations are taken into account, (c) young adults rehearse the words to later RSs than those for older participants, and

TABLE 1

Number of words recalled, total number of words, and proportion recalled that were last rehearsed at each rehearsal set for young and older participants

Measure	Last rehearsal set																			
	1	2	3	4	5	6	7	8	9	10	11	12	13	14	15	16	17	18	19	20
Young																				
Number of words recalled	1	1	1	4	9	18	19	13	20	21	30	44	45	46	43	46	60	106	150	315
Total number of words	2	2	6	24	66	97	109	117	110	132	115	146	140	139	137	127	144	185	232	370
Proportion	.50	.50	.17	.17	.14	.19	.17	.11	.18	.16	.26	.30	.32	.33	.31	.36	.42	.57	.65	.85
Older																				
Number of words recalled	2	0	3	11	17	29	15	16	21	18	25	25	16	35	30	42	56	78	127	191
Total number of words	5	8	21	49	100	143	115	126	129	116	137	128	112	137	125	135	163	165	209	257
Proportion	.40	.00	.14	.22	.17	.20	.13	.13	.16	.16	.18	.20	.14	.26	.24	.31	.34	.47	.61	.74

(d) the age-related deficit is reduced, but still borders on significance, when recall performance is compared across age groups for words that have received the same recency of last rehearsals.

Analysis of rehearsal schedules

A further series of four analyses examined the differing rehearsal schedules of young and older participants to determine more clearly why young adults rehearse words to later positions than those for older participants. In this series, two analyses examined the absolute quantity of rehearsals that were made by both the young and older participants, and two analyses examined the distribution of rehearsals throughout the study period.

Number of rehearsals made to each word.   Figure 2A shows the mean number of rehearsals that were made to words from each nominal SP for the young and older participants. A 2×5 mixed-design ANOVA with age (young and older participants) as a between-subjects factor, and nominal SP (1–4, 5–8, 9–12, 13–16, 17–20) as a within-subjects factor revealed a non-significant main effect of age, $F(1, 38) = 2.69$, $MSE = 5.80$, $p > .05$, a significant main effect of serial position, $F(4, 152) = 127.61$, $MSE = 3.59$, $p < .0001$, and a nonsignificant interaction, $F < 1$. This analysis shows that the total quantity of rehearsals afforded to words from different list positions did not vary significantly between the young and older adults. In addition, both groups rehearsed early list items more frequently than words that occurred later in the list. Newman–Keuls pairwise comparisons of the main effect of SP confirmed that the number of rehearsals received by words at SPs 1–4 and SPs 5–8 were significantly different from the number of rehearsals received by words at all other SPs, $p < .05$.

Number of different RSs in which each word was rehearsed.   Figure 2B shows the mean number of different RSs in which each word was rehearsed as a function of the nominal SP of the words for both young and older participants. This analysis provides a measure of the dispersion or the distribution of the rehearsals, rather than simply the quantity of the rehearsals that each word received. A 2×5 mixed-design ANOVA with age (young and older participants) as a between-subjects factor, and nominal SP (1–4, 5–8, 9–12, 13–16, 17–20) as a within-subjects factor revealed a significant main effect of age, $F(1, 38) = 8.82$, $MSE = 2.87$, $p < .01$, a significant main effect of SP, $F(4, 152) = 124.62$, $MSE = 2.09$, $p < .0001$, and a non-significant interaction, $F(4, 152) = 1.87$, $MSE = 2.09$, $p > .05$. Newman–Keuls pairwise comparisons of the main effect of SP showed that the number of different RSs in which words at SPs 1–4 and SPs 5–8 were rehearsed was significantly different from that for all other SPs, $p < .05$, indicating that words that were presented early in the list received more widely distributed rehearsals than later list items. Although the previous analysis showed that the absolute number of rehearsals made by the young and older participants to each word did not differ significantly, this analysis revealed that those rehearsals made by the young participants were more widely distributed than those made by the older adults.

Total number of rehearsals made at each RS.   Figure 2C shows the mean total number of rehearsals that were made in the RS following each nominal SP for the young and older participants. A 2×5 mixed-design ANOVA with age (young and older participants) as a between-subjects factor, and RS (1–4, 5–8, 9–12, 13–16, 17–20) as a within-subjects factor revealed

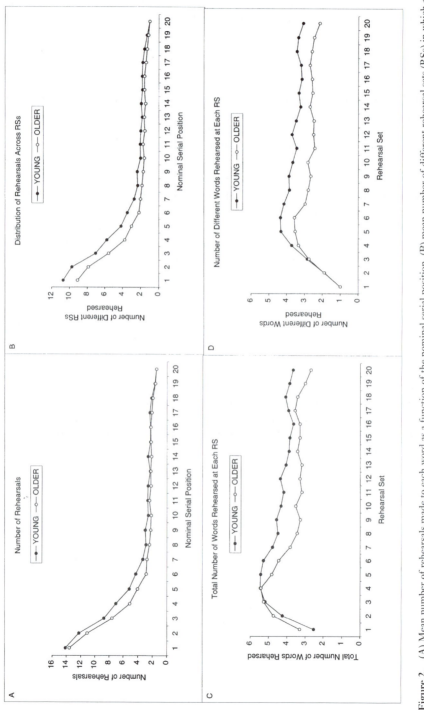

Figure 2. (A) Mean number of rehearsals made to each word as a function of the nominal serial position, (B) mean number of different rehearsal sets (RSs) in which a word was rehearsed, as a function of the nominal serial position, (C) mean total number of words rehearsed at each rehearsal set (RS), and (D) mean number of different words rehearsed at each rehearsal set, for both young and older adults.

a nonsignificant main effect of age, $F(1, 38) = 2.69$, $MSE = 5.80$, $p > .05$, a significant main effect of RS, $F(4, 152) = 36.74$, $MSE = 0.278$, $p < .0001$, and a significant interaction, $F(4, 152) = 10.27$, $MSE = 0.278$, $p < .0001$. An analysis of the simple main effects revealed that there was no significant difference between the number of rehearsals made by the young and older participants in RSs 1–4 (in fact, the older participants produced numerically more rehearsals in this period), but that young participants made significantly more rehearsals than older adults at later RSs (specifically, RSs 5–8 and 9–12), and nonsignificantly more rehearsals at later RSs.

Number of different words rehearsed at each RS.   Figure 2D shows the mean number of different words rehearsed at each RS for both the young and the older participants. A 2×5 mixed-design ANOVA with age (young and older participants) as a between-subjects factor, and RS (1–4, 5–8, 9–12, 13–16, 17–20) as a within-subjects factor revealed a significant main effect of age, $F(1, 38) = 9.02$, $MSE = 2.89$, $p < .01$, a significant main effect of RS, $F(4, 152) = 54.85$, $MSE = 0.184$, $p < .0001$, and a significant interaction, $F(4, 152) = 7.37$, $MSE = 0.184$, $p < .0001$. An analysis of the simple main effects revealed that there was no significant difference between the number of different words that were rehearsed by the young and older participants in RSs 1–4 but that young participants rehearsed significantly more different words than did older adults at all later RSs. Note that there is an important difference between the number of rehearsals made at each RS and the number of different words rehearsed at each RS. As can be seen in Figure 2C, there is very little age-related difference in the maximum articulation rate: The maximum articulation rate reached for both groups is at RS 4 where the young made 5.45 rehearsals compared with the older participants' 5.41 rehearsals. By contrast, in Figure 2D, there is a large age-related difference in the maximum number of different words that are rehearsed. This occurs for both groups at RS 6 where the young rehearsed on average 4.34 different words compared with 3.57 different words rehearsed by the older participants.

Together, these four analyses on the overall patterns of rehearsals show that the older participants make approximately the same number of rehearsals as do the young adults early in the list, and the maximum rehearsal rate reaches a comparable rate at RS 4. However, the young adults maintain a greater number of rehearsals at later RSs than do older participants and, in particular, rehearse a greater number of different words, throughout a wider number of different RSs. The greater variety of words rehearsed at any given time is largely responsible for the words of young adults being rehearsed to more recent list positions than those of older participants.

Examination of the full schedule of rehearsals

The tables in the Appendix show the proportions of words from each nominal SP that were rehearsed at least once during each RS. A consideration of these values allows us to examine the development of the U-shaped SP curve and the development of the age-related deficits. The values on the leading diagonal for each age group have the value of 1.00, reflecting the fact that all the participants from both age groups were obeying our instructions to repeat the words out loud as they were presented. The bold values represent the proportion of words from each nominal SP that are rehearsed at least once during RSs 4, 7, and 20—three informative time periods at encoding. At RS 4, all three earlier words are equally well rehearsed, and the age-related decrement approaches significance at RS 4, $t(38) = 2.01$, $p = .05$. At RS 7, there is clear extended primacy with 1- or 2-item recency, and a significant age-related deficit, $t(38) = 3.26$, $p < .01$. At RS 20, the classic U-shaped SP curve in free recall is apparent in the pattern of rehearsals, and there is a significant age-related deficit, $t(38) = 2.93$, $p < .01$.

The effect of both number and recency of rehearsals on free recall

Finally, and most importantly, we examined the extent to which age-related differences in the proportion of correct responses can be accounted for by some of these age-related differences in the patterns of rehearsals. Figure 3 shows the mean proportion of correct responses for the two age groups as a function of both the number of rehearsals and the recency to which the words were last rehearsed.

It can be seen that there are clear recall advantages in both rehearsing words many times and in rehearsing words toward the end of the list, for both young and older participants. In addition, if one averages the values across all 25 data points, one finds that that the average performance for older participants (.34) is approximately equal to (indeed is marginally greater than) the average performance for young participants (.33). However, it should be noted that not all participants contributed to all the cells, making some data points more reliable than others and statistical analyses difficult. If we consider only the 11 most reliable data points (those that average over at least 100 different occurrences in each of the young and older participants' data) we find that the average performance for older participants (.30) is slightly lower than that for the young participants (.35). Nevertheless, given that the overall age difference is .095 in the nominal SP curves, this fine-grain analysis reveals that the age-related decline in performance is reduced, if not eliminated, if one equates for the number and recency of the rehearsals.

Processing speed and free recall

As expected, there were significant correlations between participants' exact ages and proportion correct in free recall, $r(37) = -.55$, between free recall and processing speed as measured by the DSST, $r(37) = .53$, and between processing speed and age, $r(37) = -.79$ (all $ps < .0005$). Regression analyses as described by Salthouse (1992) revealed that the R^2 associated with age in the prediction of free recall was reduced from a highly significant .299 to a nonsignificant .041 after controlling for speed. This corresponds to an attenuation of the age–recall relation of 86.3% $[(.299 - .041)/.299]$, which provides an estimate of the age-related variance in free recall that is shared with a measure of processing speed (see Bryan & Luszcz, 1996; Dunlosky & Salthouse, 1996; Salthouse, 1996, for similar findings).

Discussion

Young participants recalled on average 8.28 words from the 20-word list, whereas the older participants recalled on average 6.38 words. Consistent with recent analyses, this 22.9% age-related decrement in performance was constant throughout the U-shaped nominal SP

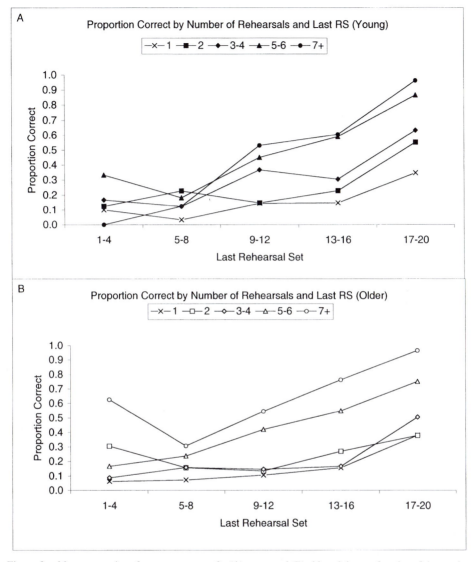

Figure 3.   Mean proportion of correct responses for (A) young and (B) older adults as a function of the number of rehearsals (1, 2, 3–4, 5–6, 7+) and the recency of the last rehearsal set (RS) to which each word was rehearsed.

curves (e.g., Arenberg, 1976; Capitani et al., 1992; Kahana, Howard, Zaromb, & Wingfield, 2002; Kausler, 1994; Parkinson, Lindholm, & Inman, 1982; Salthouse, 1980; Wright, 1982). This finding contradicts Glanzer's (1972) analysis of the SP curve in which primacy but not recency was selectively impaired in older adults.

  Overall, there was no significant difference in the overall number of rehearsals made by young and older adults. However, young participants rehearsed significantly more *different* words than older participants. The rate was relatively constant and near ceiling performance over the first three RSs, but a one-word difference emerged as the number of different words that were rehearsed reached its peak at RSs 5 and 6 for both groups, and this age difference was maintained as the rate declined at later RSs. In both groups of participants, the early words in the list were rehearsed more often, the rehearsals were more widely distributed throughout the list, and the words were rehearsed to more recent list positions, than were later list items. However, because the young participants maintained their rehearsal rates at a higher value and rehearsed more different words than older adults, the young rehearsed words more often, more widely, and more recently than did older participants.

In line with Tan and Ward's (2000) findings, both the number and the recency of rehearsals are important variables in predicting free recall performance. When the U-shaped nominal serial position curves for both age groups were replotted by functional serial position and by when the words were last rehearsed, these serial position curves showed extended recency effects with little or no primacy, although there was still a significant age-related deficit. However, when the data were equated for both the number of rehearsals and the recency of the most recent rehearsal, the age-related deficit was reduced, if not eliminated. This latter finding suggests that there is little difference in the slope of the recency functions when the data are equated for the number and recency of rehearsals, and it supports the findings of Schonfield (1969), among others, who observed that the forgetting curves were no steeper in the Brown–Peterson task for older than for young participants (see Salthouse, 1991, for a summary).

A tentative conclusion from this study therefore is that the older participants differ from the young in the recency and frequency of rehearsals and that taking these together into account, much of the age-related deficit in free recall is removed. Further, since the young have also been shown here to distribute their rehearsals more widely than the older partici-pants, this third factor (also identified by Tan & Ward, 2000) could be responsible for the remaining age deficit. We appeal to Glenberg's contextual retrieval hypothesis (Glenberg, 1984, 1987; Glenberg et al., 1980) in explaining how these variables might affect recall per-formance. It is assumed that all presented (and rehearsed) items are experienced in terms of an experimental context that fluctuates throughout the study list. In addition, we assume that retrieving a study word relies, at least in part, on retrieving the context in which that item was experienced. At test, there will be greater overlap between recent study list con-texts and the test context, and so retrieving the more recent list items (via their study con-texts) will be far easier than retrieving earlier list items. Repeated words will be associated with multiple study contexts, and thus there will be multiple ways of accessing them, and the more widely distributed the repetitions, so the greater the probability that any retrieved study context will be able to act as an effective cue for that item.

Interestingly, age-related differences can be observed early in each trial. When only four words have been presented, there is already a marginal age-related difference in the propor-tion of words that have been rehearsed at least once, and a clear significant difference emerges in RS 7, where the "serial position curves" resemble those typically found in the immediate serial recall task. Intuitively, there is something similar between the process of rehearsing the early items in the list in free recall and attempts to encode the entire list in immediate serial recall (when the presentation rate is slow). Age-related differences in imme-diate serial recall have been found, particularly at supraspan list lengths (Friedman, 1966;

Maylor et al., 1999), and age-related decrements in memory span have at least in part been linked to differences in speech rates (Multhaup, Balota, & Cowan, 1996). These similarities could reflect the use of common memory mechanisms between immediate serial recall and free recall (Ward, 2001). Finally, age-related deficits and U-shaped patterns of rehearsals are found in the pattern of rehearsals at RS 20, and these are subsequently mirrored in recall.

It is important to emphasize that our study has examined age-related differences in free recall of unrelated list items using the overt rehearsal methodology. We have said little about possible age-related differences in the use of organizational strategies in free recall of categorically related list items that are randomly distributed throughout the same list (cf. Sanders et al., 1980; Schmitt, Murphy, & Sanders, 1981; Wingfield, Lindfield, & Kahana, 1998). This is not because we disregard their existence, as there appears to be convincing evidence that these factors are important in understanding the age-related decrements in strategic organization and interitem associations in categorized free recall (e.g., see Verhaeghen, Marcoen, & Goossens, 1993). Rather, we believe that the overt rehearsal methodology that we used will tend to reduce the effects of these strategies (cf. Sanders et al., 1980), and the unrelated nature of the list items will reduce the incentive and necessity to make new inter-item associations (Naveh-Benjamin, 2000; though see also Ward et al., 2003, for evidence of some residual effects of inter-item associations in free recall). Nevertheless, we remain open-minded that some of the age-related differences in the schedules of rehearsals and subsequent recalls that we have observed may be the result of differences between young and older adults in forming and using interitem associations.

REFERENCES

Arenberg, D. (1976). The effects of input condition on free recall in young and old adults. *Journal of Gerontology*, *31*, 551–555.

Atkinson, R. C., & Shiffrin, R. M. (1968). Human memory: A proposed system and its control processes. In K. W. Spence & J. T. Spence (Eds.), *The psychology of learning and motivation* (Vol. 2, pp. 89–195). New York: Academic Press.

Baddeley, A. D. (1986). *Working memory*. Oxford, UK: Clarendon Press.

Baddeley, A. D., & Hitch, G. J. (1974). Working memory. In G. Bower (Ed.), *Recent advances in learning and motivation* (Vol. VIII, pp. 47–90). London: Academic Press.

Baddeley, A. D., & Hitch, G. J. (1977). Recency re-examined. In S. Dornic (Ed.), *Attention and performance VI* (pp. 647–667). Hillsdale, NJ: Lawrence Erlbaum Associates, Inc.

Bemelmans, K. J., Wolters, G., Zwinderman, K., ten Berge, J. M. F., & Goekoop, J. G. (2002). Evidence for two processes underlying the serial position curve of single- and multi-trial free recall in a heterogeneous group of psychiatric patients: A confirmatory factor analytic study. *Memory*, *10*, 151–160.

Bjork, R. A., & Whitten, W. B. (1974). Recency-sensitive retrieval processes in long-term free recall. *Cognitive Psychology*, *6*, 173–189.

Brodie, D. A. (1975). Free recall measures of short-term store: Are rehearsal and order of recall data necessary? *Memory & Cognition*, *3*, 653–662.

Brodie, D. A., & Murdock, B. B. (1977). Effect of presentation time on nominal and functional serial-position curves of free recall. *Journal of Verbal Learning and Verbal Behavior*, *16*, 185–200.

Brodie, D. A., & Prytulak, L. S. (1975). Free recall curves: Nothing but rehearsing some items more or recalling them sooner? *Journal of Verbal Learning and Verbal Behavior*, *14*, 549–563.

Bryan, J., & Luszcz, M. A. (1996). Speed of information processing as a mediator between age and free-recall performance. *Psychology and Aging*, *11*, 3–9.

Capitani, E., Della Sala, S., Logie, R. H., & Spinnler, H. (1992). Recency, primacy, and memory: Reappraising and standardising the serial position curve. *Cortex*, *28*, 315–342.

Craik, F. I. M. (1968a). Short-term memory and the aging process. In G. A. Talland (Ed.), *Human aging and behavior* (pp. 131–168). New York: Academic Press.

Craik, F. I. M. (1968b). Two components in free recall. *Journal of Verbal Learning and Verbal Behavior, 7*, 996–1004.

Craik, F. I. M., & Watkins, M. J. (1973). The role of rehearsal in short-term memory. *Journal of Verbal Learning and Verbal Behavior, 12*, 599–607.

Crowder, R. G. (1976). *Principles of learning and memory.* Hillsdale, NJ: Lawrence Erlbaum Associates, Inc.

Crowder, R. G. (1993). Short-term memory: Where do we stand? *Memory & Cognition, 21*, 142–145.

Della Sala, S., Logie, R. H., Trivelli, C., Cubelli, R., & Marchetti, C. (1998). Dissociation between recency and span: Neuropsychological and experimental evidence. *Neuropsychology, 12*, 533–545.

Dunlosky, J., & Salthouse, T. A. (1996). A decomposition of age-related differences in multitrial free recall. *Aging, Neuropsychology, and Cognition, 3*, 2–14.

Elias, C. S., & Hirasuna, N. (1976). Age and semantic and phonological encoding. *Developmental Psychology, 12*, 497–503

Friedman, H. (1966). Memory organization in the aged. *Journal of Genetic Psychology, 109*, 3–8.

Glanzer, M. (1972). Storage mechanisms in recall. In G. H. Bower (Ed.), *The psychology of learning and motivation: Advances in research and theory* (Vol. V, pp. 129–193). New York: Academic Press.

Glenberg, A. M. (1984). A retrieval account of the long-term modality effect. *Journal of Experimental Psychology: Learning, Memory, and Cognition, 10*, 16–31.

Glenberg, A. M. (1987). Temporal context and recency. In D. S. Gorfein & R. R. Hoffman (Eds.), *Memory and learning: The Ebbinghaus Centennial Conference.* Hillsdale, NJ: Lawrence Erlbaum Associates, Inc.

Glenberg, A. M., Bradley, M. M., Stevenson, J. A., Kraus, T. A., Tkachuk, M. J., Gretz, A. L., Fish, J. H., & Turpin, B. M. (1980). A two-process account of long-term serial position effects. *Journal of Experimental Psychology: Human Learning and Memory, 6*, 355–369.

Healy, A. F., & McNamara, D. S. (1996). Verbal learning and memory: Does the modal model still work? *Annual Review of Psychology, 47*, 143–172.

Hitch, G. J., & Ferguson, J. (1991). Prospective memory for future intentions: Some comparisons with memory for past events. *European Journal of Cognitive Psychology, 3*, 285–295.

James, W. (1890). *Principles of psychology.* New York: Henry Holt.

Kahana, M. J., Howard, M. W., Zaromb, F., & Wingfield, A. (2002). Age dissociates recency and lag recency effects in free recall. *Journal of Experimental Psychology: Learning, Memory, and Cognition, 28*, 530–540.

Kausler, D. H. (1994). *Learning and memory in normal aging.* London: Academic Press.

Kucera, H., & Francis, V. W. (1967). *Computational analysis of present-day American English.* Providence, RI: Brown University Press.

Maylor, E. A., Vousden, J. I., & Brown, G. D. A. (1999). Adult age differences in short-term memory for serial order: Data and a model. *Psychology and Aging, 14*, 572–594.

Modigliani, V., & Hedges, D. G. (1987). Distributed rehearsals and the primacy effect in single-trial free recall. *Journal of Experimental Psychology: Learning, Memory, and Cognition, 13*, 426–436.

Multhaup, K. S., Balota, D. A., & Cowan, N. (1996). Implications of aging, lexicality, and item length for the mechanisms underlying memory span. *Psychonomic Bulletin & Review, 3*, 112–120.

Naveh-Benjamin, M. (2000). Adult-age differences in memory performance: Tests of an associative deficit hypothesis. *Journal of Experimental Psychology: Learning, Memory, and Cognition, 26*, 1170–1187.

Parkinson, S. R. (1982). Performance deficits in short-term memory tasks: A comparison of amnesiac Korsakoff patients and the aged. In L. S. Cermak (Ed.), *Human memory and amnesia* (pp. 77–96). Hillsdale, NJ: Lawrence Erlbaum Associates, Inc.

Parkinson, S. R., Lindholm, J. M., & Inman, V. W. (1982). An analysis of age differences in immediate recall. *Journal of Gerontology, 37*, 425–431.

Pinto, A. C., & Baddeley, A. D. (1991). Where did you park your car? Analysis of a naturalistic long-term recency effect. *European Journal of Cognitive Psychology, 3*, 297–313.

Quinlan, P. T. (1992). *The Oxford Psycholinguistic Database.* Oxford, UK: Oxford Electronic Publishing, Oxford University Press.

Raaijmakers, J. G. W. (1993). The story of the two-store model of memory: Past criticisms, current status, and future directions. In D. E. Meyer & S. Kornblum (Eds.), *Attention and performance, XIV* (pp. 467–480). Cambridge, MA: MIT Press.

Raven, J. C., Raven, J., & Court, J. H. (1988). *The Mill Hill Vocabulary Scale.* London: H. K. Lewis.

Raymond, B. J. (1971). Free recall among the aged. *Psychological Reports, 29*, 1179–1182.

Rundus, D. (1971). Analysis of rehearsal processes in free recall. *Journal of Experimental Psychology, 89*, 63–77.

Rundus, D., & Atkinson, R. C. (1970). Rehearsal processes in free recall: A procedure for direct observation. *Journal of Verbal Learning and Verbal Behavior, 9*, 99–105.

Salthouse, T. A. (1980). Age and memory: Strategies for localizing the loss. In L. W. Poon, J. L. Fozard, L. S. Cermak, D. Arenberg, & L. W. Thompson (Eds.), *New directions in memory and aging: Proceedings of the George A. Talland Memorial Conference* (pp. 47–65). Hillsdale, NJ: Lawrence Erlbaum Associates, Inc.

Salthouse, T. A. (1991). *Theoretical perspectives on cognitive aging.* Hillsdale, NJ: Lawrence Erlbaum Associates, Inc.

Salthouse, T. A. (1992). *Mechanisms of age-cognition relations in adulthood.* Hillsdale, NJ: Lawrence Erlbaum Associates, Inc.

Salthouse, T. A. (1996). The processing-speed theory of adult age differences in cognition. *Psychological Review, 103*, 403–428.

Salthouse, T. A., & Babcock, R. L. (1991). Decomposing adult age differences in working memory. *Developmental Psychology, 27*, 763–776.

Sanders, R. E., Murphy, M. D., Schmitt, F. A., & Walsh, K. K. (1980). Age differences in free recall rehearsal strategies. *Journal of Gerontology, 35*, 550–558.

Schmitt, F. A., Murphy, M. D., & Sanders, R. E. (1981). Training older adult free recall rehearsal strategies. *Journal of Gerontology, 36*, 329–337.

Schonfield, A. E. D. (1969). Age and remembering. In, *Duke University Council on Aging and Human Development, Proceedings of Seminars.* Durham, NC: Duke University.

Shiffrin, R. M. (1970). Memory search. In D. A. Norman (Ed.), *Models of memory* (pp. 375–447). New York: Academic Press.

Shiffrin, R. M. (1999). 30 years of memory. In C. Izawa (Ed.), *On human memory: Evolution, progress and reflections on the 30th Anniversary of the Atkinson–Shiffrin model* (pp. 17–34). Hove, UK: Lawrence Erlbaum Associates Ltd.

Tan, L., & Ward, G. (2000). A recency-based account of primacy effects in free recall. *Journal of Experimental Psychology: Learning, Memory, and Cognition, 26*, 1589–1625.

Verhaeghen, P., Marcoen, A., & Goossens, L. (1993). Facts and fictions about memory aging: A quantitative integration of research findings. *Journal of Gerontology: Psychological Sciences, 48*, P157–P171.

Ward, G. (2001). A critique of the working memory model. In J. Andrade (Ed.), *Working memory in perspective* (pp. 219–239). Hove, UK: Psychology Press.

Ward, G. (2002). A recency-based account of the list length effect in free recall. *Memory & Cognition, 30*, 885–892.

Ward, G., Woodward, G., Stevens, A., & Stinson, C. (2003). Using overt rehearsals to explain word frequency effects in free recall. *Journal of Experimental Psychology: Learning, Memory, and Cognition, 29*, 186–210.

Watkins, M. J., Neath, I., & Sechler, E. S. (1989). Recency effect in recall of a word list when an immediate memory task is performed after each word presentation. *American Journal of Psychology, 102*, 265–270.

Wechsler, D. (1981). *Manual for the Wechsler Adult Intelligence Scale–Revised.* New York: Psychological Corporation.

Wingfield, A., Lindfield, K. C., & Kahana, M. J. (1998). Adult age differences in the temporal characteristics of category free recall. *Psychology and Aging, 13*, 256–266.

Wright, R. E. (1982). Adult age similarities in free recall output order and strategies. *Journal of Gerontology, 37*, 76–79.

PrEview proof published online 6 August 2004

APPENDIX

TABLE A1

Mean proportion of words that were rehearsed at least once at each rehearsal set and each nominal serial position by young participants

RS	*Nominal serial position*																			
	1	2	3	4	5	6	7	8	9	10	11	12	13	14	15	16	17	18	19	20
1	1.00																			
2	.88	1.00																		
3	.91	.93	1.00																	
4	**.88**	**.93**	**.92**	**1.00**																
5	.83	.85	.83	.83	1.00															
6	.70	.72	.68	.66	.58	1.00														
7	**.58**	**.62**	**.50**	**.50**	**.39**	.56	1.00													
8	.49	.52	.38	.38	.34	.32	.42	1.00												
9	.48	.48	.32	.32	.37	.24	.27	.40	1.00											
10	.45	.46	.28	.24	.22	.21	.19	.20	.42	1.00										
11	.43	.41	.27	.26	.18	.11	.15	.16	.23	.25	1.00									
12	.45	.43	.31	.27	.19	.13	.10	.13	.16	.19	.36	1.00								
13	.44	.40	.21	.23	.10	.14	.13	.07	.12	.13	.16	.35	1.00							
14	.36	.28	.22	.19	.09	.10	.09	.08	.09	.08	.15	.18	.32	1.00						
15	.35	.33	.20	.17	.15	.11	.06	.05	.07	.10	.11	.13	.18	.33	1.00					
16	.31	.32	.23	.15	.11	.10	.07	.04	.08	.08	.07	.10	.08	.18	.28	1.00				
17	.34	.29	.21	.13	.13	.11	.05	.05	.04	.05	.03	.06	.07	.13	.18	.34	1.00			
18	.29	.28	.19	.20	.11	.14	.08	.05	.06	.06	.04	.08	.07	.11	.16	.19	.33	1.00		
19	.28	.26	.15	.11	.10	.10	.03	.06	.08	.04	.06	.05	.07	.11	.08	.13	.26	.38	1.00	
20	.28	.24	.16	.14	.10	.09	.04	.03	.01	.03	.05	.03	.03	.04	.08	.13	.15	.18	.27	1.00

Note: RS = rehearsal set.

TABLE A2

Mean proportion of words that were rehearsed at least once at each rehearsal set and each nominal serial position by older participants

Nominal serial position

RS	1	2	3	4	5	6	7	8	9	10	11	12	13	14	15	16	17	18	19	20
1	1.00																			
2	.88	1.00																		
3	.88	.87	1.00																	
4	**.77**	**.83**	.77	**1.00**																
5	.58	.63	.65	.68	1.00															
6	.60	.59	.43	.48	.48	1.00														
7	**.44**	**.42**	**.33**	**.27**	**.20**	**.31**	1.00													
8	.41	.33	.26	.18	.17	.17	.29	1.00												
9	.33	.35	.19	.12	.11	.11	.18	.26	1.00											
10	.39	.36	.27	.13	.12	.11	.10	.13	.24	1.00										
11	.26	.23	.16	.10	.08	.07	.06	.09	.13	.28	1.00									
12	.24	.27	.21	.08	.09	.05	.06	.04	.10	.10	.27	1.00								
13	.33	.28	.18	.08	.10	.05	.04	.04	.02	.03	.11	.24	1.00							
14	.33	.31	.19	.13	.06	.05	.03	.04	.06	.06	.11	.10	.23	1.00						
15	.30	.24	.19	.10	.13	.04	.04	.04	.03	.02	.08	.04	.10	.18	1.00					
16	.30	.24	.17	.08	.09	.03	.04	.03	.05	.04	.02	.05	.08	.11	.25	1.00				
17	.28	.26	.16	.11	.11	.06	.04	.03	.01	.02	.04	.03	.07	.08	.14	.28	1.00			
18	.27	.28	.15	.08	.09	.03	.04	.03	.03	.02	.03	.02	.02	.06	.10	.13	.21	1.00		
19	.28	.19	.14	.06	.06	.05	.05	.03	.02	.02	.03	.01	.04	.01	.04	.09	.13	.22	1.00	
20	**.20**	**.20**	**.12**	**.07**	**.10**	**.02**	**.02**	**.05**	**.02**	**.00**	**.02**	**.02**	**.06**	**.00**	**.02**	**.03**	**.03**	**.07**	**.13**	**1.00**

Note: RS = rehearsal set.

THE QUARTERLY JOURNAL OF EXPERIMENTAL PSYCHOLOGY
2005, 58A (1), 120–133

Ψ Psychology Press
Taylor & Francis Group

The attraction effect in decision making: Superior performance by older adults

Sunghan Kim

University of Toronto, Toronto, Canada

Lynn Hasher

University of Toronto, Toronto, Canada, and
Baycrest Centre, Rotman Research Institute, Toronto, Canada

Previous work showed that older adults' choice performance can be wiser than that of younger adults (Tentori, Osherson, Hasher, & May, 2001). We contrasted two possible interpretations: a general expertise/wisdom view that suggests that older adults are generally more skilled at making decisions than younger adults and a domain-specific expertise view that suggests that older adults are more skilled decision makers only in domains in which they have greater knowledge. These hypotheses were contrasted using attraction effect tasks in two different domains: earning extra credit in a course and grocery shopping, domains presumed to be of different levels of knowledge to younger and older adults. Older adults showed consistent choice for both domains; younger adults showed consistent choice only for the extra credit problem. Several explanations of these findings are considered, including Damasio's somatic marker theory and age differences in reliance on heuristic versus analytic styles.

Although older adults often perform more poorly than younger adults on laboratory problem-solving tasks (e.g., Denney, 1982; Giambra & Arenberg, 1980; Rabbitt, 1977), their performance on everyday, practical problem-solving tasks can be as good as that of younger adults (e.g., Denney & Palmer, 1981; Denney & Pearce, 1989; Hartley, 1989; Marsiske & Willis, 1995) and occasionally even better (Cornelius & Caspi, 1987). Decision making can be regarded as a type of problem solving and, in fact, has been argued to be more relevant to everyday problem solving than are many traditional laboratory problem-solving tasks (Hartley, 1989). However, there has not been much age-comparative research on decision making (see Peters, Finucane,

Correspondence should be addressed to Sunghan Kim, Department of Psychology, University of Toronto, 100 St. George Street, Toronto, Ontario M5S 3G3, Canada. Email: shkim@psych.utoronto.ca

This research was supported by a grant from the National Institute on Aging (R37 AGO4306). We thank all the people who helped us in the data collection process of this project, including Cynthia May, Cindy Lustig, Carrick Williams, Jason Blevins, Stephanie Davis, Rachelle Ta-Min, and Sudipa Bhattacharyya. We also extend thanks to John Payne, James Bettman, David Rubin, Amy Needham, Matt Serra, Andrew Mitchell, and David Goldstein for advice at various stages of this project.

http://www.tandf.co.uk/journals/pp/02724987.html   DOI:10.1080/0272498044300160

McGregor, & Slovic, 2000; Sanfey & Hastie, 2000; Yates & Patalano, 1999, for reviews). In this paper, we demonstrate that decision-making performance by older adults can be at least as good as that of younger adults and, in one instance, even better.

In rational choice theories of decision making, the consistency of choice across contexts or variants of a problem is an important construct for maximization of utility (e.g., Tversky & Kahneman, 1986; Tversky, Sattath, & Slovic, 1988). Inconsistency across similar problems can, for example, result in very great costs to a decision maker, as the work of Lichtenstein and Slovic (1971, 1973) has shown with both undergraduate students and adult gamblers. It is widely thought that inconsistencies arise in the absence of well-established or preexisting preferences that then allow people to construct them on each occasion. As a result, minor changes in wording of a problem or in alternatives to select from can lead to differences in preferences and so inconsistencies in choice across variants of the same problem (e.g., Payne, Bettman, & Johnson, 1993; Slovic, 1995). As an example, individuals' preferences are known to vary within the exact same set of options when they make a *choice* (e.g., between Gamble A, 10% chance of earning $ 90, and Gamble B, 90% chance of earning $10), compared to when they make a *judgement* (e.g., how much would you pay for each of these gambles?). People in the choice condition are likely to choose Gamble B whereas people in the judgement condition are likely to value Gamble A more highly (e.g., Lichtenstein & Slovic, 1971; Slovic, 1995). This phenomenon, called preference reversal, is one example of inconsistency in decision making.

Another widely cited example of inconsistency associated with small changes in the decision context is found in the *asymmetric dominance effect*, or more generally, the *attraction effect*. The attraction effect refers to a phenomenon in which adding an irrelevant alternative into an existing choice set increases the proportion of people choosing an alternative from the original set. This phenomenon violates a fundamental assumption of many rational choice models, the *principle of regularity*, by which the probability of choosing one option from an initial choice set cannot be increased by adding a new alternative (e.g., Huber, Payne, & Puto, 1982).

The top portion of Figure 1 presents an example of a decision problem that has the potential to show the attraction effect. Here there are two brands, and each has both a quality and a price associated with it. Brands A and B are competitive to each other because Brand A (termed the competitor) is weaker on the quality dimension and stronger on the price dimension, while the reverse is the case for Brand B (termed the target). In the problem depicted in the bottom part of Figure 1, the identical brands are available, with the same values for quality and for price, but now there is a change in the problem's context because a third brand (termed the decoy) has been added (see Wedell & Pettibone, 1996, for a summary of decoy types).

Across a number of attraction effect tasks, there is widespread evidence of inconsistency shown by young adults ranging in age from the late teens into the thirties (e.g., Ariely & Wallsten, 1995; Dahr & Glazer, 1996; Heath & Chatterjee, 1995; Huber et al., 1982; Huber & Puto, 1983; Mishra, Umesh, & Stem, Jr., 1993; Pan & Lehmann, 1993; Ratneshwar, Shocker, & Stewart, 1987; Sen, 1998; Simonson, 1989; Simonson & Tversky, 1992; Tversky & Simonson, 1993; Wedell, 1991; Wedell & Pettibone, 1996). In addition to being seen across a wide range of participants, inconsistency in choice has also been reported across a wide range of decision contexts including consumer, job, political, and partner choices (Doyle, O'Connor, Reynolds, & Bottomley, 1999; Highhouse, 1996; Pan, O'Curry, & Pitts, 1995; Sedikides, Ariely, & Olsen, 1999).

```
Two-choice version:

    Brand   Quality (out of 100)   Price       Terms

      A              50            $30      Competitor

      B              70            $40      Target


Three-choice version:

    Brand   Quality (out of 100)   Price       Terms

      A              50            $30      Competitor

      B              70            $40      Target

      C              72            $100     Decoy
```

Figure 1.   A sample attraction effect task in the two-choice version (top) and in the three-choice version (bottom).

Against this substantial literature then, recent work suggesting that older adults are less likely than young adults to show the attraction effect is quite surprising (Tentori, Osherson, Hasher, & May, 2001). By the terms widely used in the decision literature, older adults' choice behaviour would then be viewed as more *reliable*[1] than that of younger adults. Although this interpretation might be consistent with findings on everyday problem solving (e.g., Cornelius & Caspi, 1987), when judged against a large literature showing cognitive declines associated with ageing (see, e.g., Craik & Salthouse, 2000), the Tentori et al. finding is particularly surprising.

We note, however, that the problems used by Tentori et al. (2001) were all variants requiring a decision in the context of shopping for groceries. For the sake of generality, participants in that study came from both the US and Italy, with the same findings across a series of experiments. Nonetheless, this particular context, grocery shopping, permits two different explanations for the apparent superiority of older adults: a general expertise/wisdom interpretation and a domain-specific expertise interpretation. Tentori et al. preferred a general expertise interpretation, citing the similarity between their findings and the work of Baltes and his group (e.g., Baltes & Staudinger, 1993, 2000), findings that suggest that age-related increases in wisdom can compensate for other cognitive problems that increase with age.

However, it is also possible that older adults failed to show greater consistency across two- and three-choice variants because of their greater *specific* expertise relative to that of younger adults. After all, it is likely that older adults have had much more experience than younger adults with grocery shopping. This explanation is analogous to the argument made by Denney and her colleagues (Denney & Pearce, 1989; Denney, Pearce, & Palmer, 1982) that if everyday problem-solving performance is determined by experience alone, each age group

---

[1]Given that invariance or consistency is a basic assumption of rational choice theories (e.g., Tversky & Kahneman, 1986), the term "rational" is also widely used to refer to these decision patterns.

should outperform the other group on the problems with which they are most familiar. In fact, the possibility that greater specific knowledge about grocery shopping reduces susceptibility to the attraction effect is consistent with research in the decision literature (e.g., Coupey, Irwin, & Payne, 1998; Wedell & Boeckenholt, 1990) suggesting that expertise reduces error rates across a number of decision tasks. With respect to the attraction effect, some evidence is consistent with the specific knowledge argument (Sen, 1998), although the data are not entirely straightforward (see, e.g., Mishra et al., 1993; Ratneshwar et al., 1987). Taken together, the Tentori et al. (2001) age superiority effect may be due to the domain-specific expertise that older adults have about grocery shopping relative to that of younger adults, rather than to older adults' general expertise in making decisions in different contexts.

In the present study, we contrasted the specific versus general expertise hypotheses about the source of older adults' previously reported advantage in the attraction effect decision task (Tentori et al., 2001). In doing so, we were also able to address the role of specific expertise in the choice behaviour of younger adults. We did this by using one of the original grocery problems from Tentori et al. along with a new problem in a domain (earning extra credit in a course) about which younger adults could be expected to have more knowledge than older adults. The general expertise view predicts that older adults will show greater consistency than younger adults (or the absence of an attraction effect) in choosing an option across the two- and three-choice versions of both choice problems. The specific expertise view predicts consistency for younger adults in the extra credit problem but not in the grocery problem and, for older adults, in the grocery problem but not in the extra credit problem.

Method

Participants

A total of 689 undergraduate students (age 17 to 27 years) from Duke University, the College of Charleston, Michigan State University, and the University of Toronto and 384 senior citizens (age 60 to 79 years) from the Durham NC, Charleston SC, East Lansing MI, and Toronto ON areas participated in this experiment. Of those, 483 undergraduate students and 220 senior citizens received only one choice problem: either the grocery shopping or the extra credit problem in its two-choice or three-choice version. A subset of 206 undergraduate students and 164 senior citizens did both choice problems[2] and also provided knowledge ratings for each problem. All participants were tested at the times that other work (e.g., Yoon, May, & Hasher, 1999) has shown are generally optimal for each age group: in the morning for older adults and in the afternoon for younger adults. Younger adults received credit for an introductory psychology course in exchange for their participation. Older adults received $10 for their participation.[3] As in many ageing studies, older adults had more education and higher vocabulary score (years of

---

[2]In this research tradition, it is quite common to give multiple problems to the same participants (e.g., Huber et al., 1982), and we also wished to maximize the number of participants. Analyses comparing the participants who received one vs. two problems altered none of the conclusions based on collapsing these participants.

[3]Studies with college students have used both monetary compensation and course credit (e.g., Sedikides et al., 1999; Sen, 1998); participants showed the attraction effect in both instances. Thus, the fact that the two age groups received different compensation for participation should not be a factor for the attraction effect. We note that most studies in cognitive gerontology done in North America use a similar compensation scheme.

education, $M = 15.92$ years, $SD = 3$; vocabulary score, $M = 32.64$, $SD = 9.14$) than younger adults (years of education, $M = 13.4$ years, $SD = 1.79$; vocabulary score, $M = 21.57$, $SD = 8.18$).

Materials

Using the structure of the original grocery shopping problem from Tentori et al. (2001), a new choice task, earning extra credit in a course, was created in a domain that younger adults would have greater experience with than older adults. In the extra credit problem, each of the options was defined on the following two attributes: the amount of extra credit offered and the minimum amount of time required to finish the extra credit task. The extra credit problem started with the same values as the discount attribute from the grocery shopping problem. Based on pilot work to ensure that Option B was more attractive than C, we doubled the values of the minimum required purchase attribute from the grocery shopping problem before we used them as the values of the minimum required time attribute. Both problems can be seen in Figure 2.

The Grocery Shopping Problem

	Discount offered	Minimum purchase required	I would choose:
Card A	15%	$20	
Card B	25%	$45	
Card C	26%	$100	

The Extra Credit Problem

	Extra credit offered	Minimum amount of time required	I would choose:
Option A	15 points	40 minutes	
Option B	25 points	90 minutes	
Option C	26 points	200 minutes	

Figure 2. The grocery shopping and extra credit problems.

As an approximate index of domain-specific expertise, we assessed knowledge about decision domains for a subset of participants using four questions. These were adopted from Mitchell and Dacin (1996; see also Mishra et al., 1993; Ratneshwar et al., 1987; Sen, 1998). The four questions were as follows:

1. "How familiar are you with grocery shopping (earning extra credit for a course)?" (7-point scale anchored by "not familiar at all" and "very familiar").
2. "I know a lot about grocery shopping (earning extra credit for a course)" (7-point scale anchored by "disagree" and "agree").
3. "How would you rate your knowledge about grocery shopping (earning extra credit for a course) relative to the rest of the population?" (7-point scale anchored by "one of the least knowledgeable people" and "one of the most knowledgeable people").
4. "How interested are you in grocery shopping (earning extra credit for a course)?" (7-point scale anchored by "not interested at all" and "very interested").

The index of knowledge in a domain was the mean score on the four questions.

Design and procedure

A total of 160 participants received only the grocery shopping problem, and 543 participants received only the extra credit problem in either their two-choice or their three-choice versions. A total of 370 participants received both problems; for those participants, both problems were presented in either the two- or the three-choice versions. Each problem was presented on a separate sheet of paper with instructions to consider the information that was presented and to choose whichever option they like. Participants given both problems received the subjective knowledge questionnaire after each of the two problems. Otherwise, the procedure was identical to that used for the other participants. At the end of the experimental session, all participants completed the Extended Range Vocabulary Test (ERVT), Version 3 (Educational Testing Service, 1976).

Results

Choice among options

Following Tentori et al. (2001), we report the proportions of people choosing B and not choosing B in each problem for all participants (see Table 1). As can be seen, younger adults showed the attraction effect in the grocery shopping problem, $\chi^2(1, N = 306) = 23.37, p < .01$, with 50% choosing Option B in the two-choice version and 77% choosing it in the three-choice version. By contrast, there was no evidence of a change in the choices made by younger adults across the two versions of the extra credit problem, $\chi^2(1, N = 589) = 0.11$, with 80 and 81% choosing Option B in the two- and three-choice versions, respectively. Older adults did not show the attraction effect for either problem: grocery shopping, $\chi^2(1, N = 224) = 0.28$; extra credit, $\chi^2(1, N = 324) = 1.32$. Moreover, a logistic regression analysis also revealed that the interaction between age group (younger vs. older adults) and choice condition (two- vs. three-choice conditions) on the choice of Option B was statistically significant for the grocery shopping domain, β (regression coefficient) $= -1.04, \chi^2(1, N = 530) = 8.14, p < .01$, but not for the extra credit domain, $\beta = 0.21, \chi^2(1, N = 913) = 0.42$, indicating an age effect for the grocery shopping domain only.

The subset of participants who rated knowledge showed the same choice patterns as the larger group of participants (see Table 2). Again, the younger adults showed the attraction effect only in the grocery shopping problem, $\chi^2(1, N = 206) = 10.46, p < .01$, but not in the

TABLE 1

Numbers and proportions of younger and older adults choosing and not choosing B in the grocery shopping and extra credit domains (entire data set)

	Younger adults								Older adults							
	Chose B		Total		Did not choose B				Chose B		Total		Did not choose B			
					Chose A		Chose C						Chose A		Chose C	
Choice condition	No.	%	No.	%	No.	%	No.	%	No.	%	No.	%	No.	%	No.	%
							Grocery shopping									
2-choice	76	50	76	50					54	49	57	51				
3-choice	118	77	36	23	27	17	9	6	59	52	54	48	42	37	12	11
							Extra credit									
2-choice	235	80	59	20					105	65	56	35				
3-choice	239	81	56	19	31	11	25	8	116	71	47	29	29	18	18	11

TABLE 2

Numbers and proportions of younger and older adults choosing and not choosing B in the grocery shopping and extra credit domains, for participants who received both choice problems and the subjective knowledge questionnaire

	Younger adults								Older adults							
	Chose B		Did not choose B						Chose B		Did not choose B					
			Total		Chose A		Chose C				Total		Chose A		Chose C	
Choice condition	No.	%	No.	%	No.	%	No.	%	No.	%	No.	%	No.	%	No.	%
Grocery shopping																
2-choice	49	48	53	52	25	24	6	6	37	46	44	54	31	38	6	7
3-choice	73	70	31	30	11	10	6	6	46	55	37	45	15	18	6	7
Extra credit																
2-choice	83	81	19	19			9	9	55	68	26	32	15	18	13	16
3-choice	84	81	20	19	11	10	9	9	55	66	28	34	15	18	13	16

extra credit problem, $\chi^2(1, N = 206) = 0.01$, whereas older adults did not show the attraction effect for either problem: grocery shopping, $\chi^2(1, N = 164) = 1.56$; extra credit, $\chi^2(1, N = 164) = 0.05$. These findings support the general expertise hypothesis for older adults, by which their greater experience with decisions makes them less susceptible to changing their choices when an additional, but not terribly attractive, choice is added to a set of alternatives. By contrast, for younger adults, consistency in decisions appears to be tied to specific knowledge.

Knowledge ratings

The knowledge measure had good reliability; Cronbach's α ranged from .83 to .87 across the four combinations of problems and ages. Confirming our ad hoc assumptions, younger adults were more knowledgeable about extra credit than were older adults, $t(368) = 8.46$, $p < .01$, whereas older adults were more knowledgeable about grocery shopping than were younger adults, $t(368) = 6.52$, $p < .01$ (see Table 3). As well, older adults were more knowledgeable about grocery shopping than about extra credit, $t(326) = 13.44$, $p < .01$, while younger adults reported themselves to be equally knowledgeable about both grocery shopping and extra credit, $t(410) = 0.34$.

Thus, the attraction effect patterns shown by younger and older adults do not follow directly from their knowledge scores: Younger adults showed the attraction effect in the grocery shopping domain, but not in the extra credit domain, although their self-rated knowledge about the two domains did not differ; older adults did not show the attraction effect in either domain, although they reported themselves to be more knowledgeable about grocery shopping than about extra credit. Moreover, a logistic regression analysis also showed that the interaction between domain knowledge and choice condition (two- vs. three-choice conditions) on the choice of Option B was not significant for either younger, β (regression coefficient) $= -0.1$, $\chi^2(1, N = 412) = 0.33$, or for older adults, $\beta = .05$, $\chi^2(1, N = 328) = 0.12$. Thus choice behaviour, at least for these particular problems, could not be predicted on the basis of knowledge ratings.

Discussion

Younger adults showed the attraction effect, or evidence of inconsistent decision-making behaviour, in the grocery shopping problem, as they had previously in the Tentori et al.

TABLE 3
Means and standard deviations of knowledge and interest scores for the grocery shopping and extra credit domains for each age group

Age group		Grocery shopping		Extra credit	
		Knowledge	Interest	Knowledge	Interest
Younger adults	Mean	4.94	4.16	4.90	6.02
	SD	1.14	1.56	1.30	1.33
Older adults	Mean	5.70	4.70	3.58	4.94
	SD	1.10	1.86	1.70	2.14

(2001) study. They did not show the effect in the extra credit domain. This pattern of choice is consistent with the idea that it is specific expertise that determines performance in attraction effect tasks. By contrast, older adults appeared to conform to a general expertise view; they failed to show the attraction effect for either the grocery shopping problem or the extra credit problem, thus showing greater consistency in choice than did younger adults.

What accounts for the choice behaviour of these two age groups? Our data suggest that knowledge about a domain is not a particularly helpful construct, at least as it is measured here (and perhaps elsewhere in the decision literature, Ratneshwar et al., 1987). For one thing, younger adults reported themselves to be equally knowledgeable about both grocery shopping and earning extra credit for a course and yet they showed consistent choice on the extra credit problem but not the grocery shopping problem. Hence, with respect to younger adults, our findings add to the pattern of inconsistent findings from previous studies on the effect of knowledge on the attraction effect (Mishra et al., 1993; Ratneshwar et al., 1987; Sen, 1998): Sometimes knowledge matters (Sen, 1998), sometimes it does not (Mishra et al., 1993; Ratneshwar et al., 1987), and the precise determinants of the relation between knowledge and choice are as yet unknown in the attraction effect.

Since Mishra et al. (1993) suggested that interest or motivation also influences the attraction effect, we considered the role that interest might play in the present findings. Our analyses can only be considered suggestive, of course, because there is a one-item scale (Question 4) available to assess interest (see Table 3). Younger adults were more interested in extra credit than in grocery shopping, $t(410) = 13.03$, $p < .01$, and this pattern does coincide with choice behaviour: When interest was higher (extra credit), young adults did not show an attraction effect; when interest was lower (grocery shopping), young adults showed an attraction effect. A logistic regression analysis showed a significant interaction between domain interest and choice condition for younger adults, $\beta = -0.27$, $\chi^2(1, N = 412) = 4.24$, $p < .05$. Our younger adults' data are consistent with Mishra et al.'s suggestion: Interest levels might be a stronger factor than knowledge in reducing the attraction effect.

Older adults were equally interested in both problems, $t(326) = 1.06$, with an interest level that was slightly above indifference on the 7-point scale. Perhaps a moderate level of interest is sufficient to erase the attraction effect for older adults, suggesting that interest also explains their choice behaviour. However, a logistic regression analysis on the level of domain interest and the size of the attraction effect was not significant for older adults, $\beta = -.02$, $\chi^2(1, N = 328) = 0.05$.[4] Of course, these data can only be seen as suggestive, and we note that interest may not succeed in explaining age differences in choice because there are large age differences seen for interest in earning extra credit, with no difference in choice patterns. Nonetheless, within age groups, interest may ultimately prove to play a role in determining the attraction effect. Such a conclusion will require the development of a good measure of interest, along with choice problems that vary greatly on the interest scale for both younger and older adults.[5]

---

[4]A logistic regression analysis on the level of domain interest and the size of the attraction effect collapsed across both ages was not significant, $\beta = -.13$, $\chi^2(1, N = 740) = 2.35$, $p = .13$.

[5]When all data are reanalysed using a three-question knowledge scale (averaged over the first three questions, taking out the last question on interest), no conclusions change except that younger adults' knowledge score for grocery shopping is higher than that for extra credit, which does not match their choice patterns anyway.

An additional explanation for age patterns in choice was also considered in part because of the substantial age-related differences in vocabulary scores. Insofar as vocabulary and crystallized intelligence are related (e.g., Horn, 1982; Horn & Hofer, 1992; Schaie, 1994), it is possible that this factor accounts for the superior decision skills of older adults. However, a logistic regression analysis assessing the interaction between vocabulary scores and choice conditions across both age groups was not significant, $\beta = -.005$, $\chi^2(1, N = 1408) = 0.19$.

A final explanation for the better performance shown here by older adults than by younger adults might lie in older adults' increased propensity to rely on heuristic or intuitive information processing coupled with younger adults' greater reliance on analytic, systematic information processing (e.g., Klaczynski & Robinson, 2000; Peters et al., 2000). For example, Johnson (1990) demonstrated that older adults use heuristic-type decision strategies (i.e., so-called noncompensatory decision strategies) to arrive at the same decision as do young adults who used more analytic strategies. As well, there is some evidence that the engagement of analytic processes may actually *impair* performance on attraction-type tasks (e.g., Simonson, 1989; Wedell & Pettibone, 1996) at least to judge by the increase in the size of the attraction effect seen when participants were asked to provide a justification for their decisions. These findings can also be taken as consistent with views (e.g., Chaiken & Trope, 1999; Epstein, 1994; Kahneman, 2003; Stanovich & West, 2000; Wilson & Schooler, 1991) proposing that an effortless processing system can be more effective and adaptive in solving (some) problems than a more effortful, rational system of the sort that young adults may be more inclined to rely on.

Furthermore, Damasio (1994) in his somatic-marker hypothesis argues that feelings or emotions (called somatic markers) become associated with the positive or negative outcomes of responses to situations through a lifetime of experience. During decision making, positive or negative markers activate pleasant or unpleasant feelings to options, and people can use these markers to eliminate options that could potentially lead to negative outcomes. Thus, it is conceivable that this process could actually help older adults perform as well as or better than younger adults in some situations that require solutions that match their feelings or intuitions formulated throughout their life. Neuropsychological evidence consistent with these speculations comes from findings on a gambling task (Bechara, Damasio, Damasio, & Anderson, 1994) thought to use an age-spared, ventromedial prefrontal system (MacPherson, Phillips, & Della Sala, 2002). Older and younger adults did equally well on this task (MacPherson et al., 2002). By contrast, age-related changes in dorsolateral prefrontal areas may reduce the likelihood of using analytic processes requiring executive control.

Overall, older adults appear to be less irregular and more consistent in decision tasks that assess the attraction effect than are younger adults. Younger adults, by contrast, appear to show consistent decisions in a domain of high interest, although not in a domain of indifferent interest. It is unclear whether this pattern is due to interest levels or to perhaps a somatic-markers explanation (Damasio, 1994). Certainly there is evidence from young adults that following one's feelings/instincts can sometimes result in decisions that are more satisfactory to the person than are decisions based on careful analysis of alternatives (Wilson & Schooler, 1991).

With respect to ageing and decision making, the present data are consistent with conclusions of Tentori et al. (2001) and, in particular, with the wisdom perspective in the ageing literature (e.g., Baltes & Staudinger, 1993, 2000); that is, a lifetime of experience may result in skilled decision making across a range of topic domains, independent of interest level.

Whether or not consistency (or superior decision making) is attributable to spared versus impaired neural pathways, or to an age-related increase in reliance on heuristic decision rules, or to the accumulation of somatic markers, or to some combination of these factors remains to be seen. Nonetheless, the present findings show superior decisions being made by older than by younger adults. As a final note, it is possible that one aspect of wisdom—or of increasing experience with decisions—is that heuristic rules (and their neural underpinnings) are good enough for the vast majority of choices that people make in a day.

REFERENCES

Ariely, D., & Wallsten, T. S. (1995). Seeking subjective dominance in multidimensional space: An explanation of the asymmetric dominance effect. *Organizational Behavior and Human Decision Processes, 63,* 223–232.

Baltes, P. B., & Staudinger, U. M. (1993). The search for a psychology of wisdom. *Current Directions in Psychological Science, 2,* 75–80.

Baltes, P. B., & Staudinger, U. M. (2000). Wisdom: A metaheuristic (pragmatic) to orchestrate mind and virtue toward excellence. *American Psychologist, 55,* 122–136.

Bechara, A., Damasio, A. R., Damasio, H., & Anderson, S. W. (1994). Insensitivity to future consequences following damage to human prefrontal cortex. *Cognition, 50,* 7–15.

Chaiken, S., & Trope, Y. (Eds.). (1999). *Dual-process theories in social psychology.* New York: Guilford Press.

Cornelius, S. W., & Caspi, A. (1987). Everyday problem solving in adulthood and old age. *Psychology and Aging, 2,* 144–153.

Coupey, E., Irwin, J. R., & Payne, J. W. (1998). Product category familiarity and preference construction. *Journal of Consumer Research, 24,* 459–468.

Craik, F. I. M., & Salthouse, T. A. (Eds.). (2000). *The handbook of aging and cognition* (2nd ed.). Mahwah, NJ: Lawrence Erlbaum Associates, Inc.

Dahr, R., & Glazer, R. (1996). Similarity in context: Cognitive representation and violation of preference and perceptual invariance in consumer choice. *Organizational Behavior and Human Decision Processes, 67,* 280–293.

Damasio, A. R. (1994). *Descartes' error: Emotion, reason, and the human brain.* New York: Quill.

Denney, N. W. (1982). Aging and cognitive changes. In B. B. Wolman & G. Stricker (Eds.), *Handbook of developmental psychology* (pp. 807–827). Englewood Cliffs, NJ: Prentice Hall.

Denney, N. W., & Palmer, A. M. (1981). Adult age differences on traditional and practical problem-solving measures. *Journal of Gerontology, 36,* 323–328.

Denney, N. W., & Pearce, K. A. (1989). A developmental study of practical problem solving in adults. *Psychology & Aging, 4,* 438–442.

Denney, N. W., Pearce, K. A., & Palmer, A. M. (1982). A developmental study of adults' performance on traditional and practical problem-solving tasks. *Experimental Aging Research, 8,* 115–118.

Doyle, J. R., O'Connor, D. J., Reynolds, G. M., & Bottomley, P. A. (1999). The robustness of the asymmetrically dominated effect: Buying frames, phantom alternatives, and in-store purchases. *Psychology and Marketing, 16,* 225–243.

Educational Testing Service. (1976). *Kit of factor-referenced cognitive tests.* Princeton, NJ: Author.

Epstein, S. (1994). Integration of the cognitive and the psychodynamic unconscious. *American Psychologist, 49,* 709–724.

Giambra, L. M., & Arenberg, D. (1980). Problem solving, concept learning, and aging. In L. W. Poon (Ed.), *Aging in the 1980s: Selected contemporary issues in the psychology of aging* (pp. 253–259). Washington, DC: American Psychological Association.

Hartley, A. (1989). The cognitive ecology of problem solving. In L. W. Poon, D. C. Rubin, & B. A. Wilson (Eds.), *Everyday cognition in adulthood and late life* (pp. 300–329). New York: Cambridge University Press.

Heath, T. B., & Chatterjee, S. (1995). Asymmetric decoy effects on lower-quality versus higher-quality brands: Meta-analytic and experimental evidence. *Journal of Consumer Research, 22,* 268–284.

Highhouse, S. (1996). Context-dependent selection: The effects of decoy and phantom job candidates. *Organizational Behavior and Human Decision Processes, 65,* 68–76.

Horn, J. L. (1982). The aging of human abilities. In B. B. Wolman (Ed.), *Handbook of developmental psychology* (pp. 847–870). Englewood Cliffs, NJ: Prentice-Hall.

Horn, J. L., & Hofer, S. M. (1992). Major abilities and development in the adult period. In R. J. Sternberg & C. A. Berg (Eds.), *Intellectual development* (pp. 44–99). New York: Cambridge University Press.

Huber, J., Payne, J. W., & Puto, C. (1982). Adding asymmetrically dominated alternatives: Violations of regularity and the similarity hypothesis. *Journal of Consumer Research, 9*, 90–98.

Huber, J., & Puto, C. (1983). Market boundaries and product choice: Illustrating attraction and substitution effects. *Journal of Consumer Research, 10*, 31–44.

Johnson, M. M. S. (1990). Age differences in decision making: A process methodology for examining strategic information processing. *Journal of Gerontology, 45*, 75–78.

Kahneman, D. (2003). A perspective on judgment and choice: Mapping bounded rationality. *American Psychologist, 58*, 697–720.

Klaczynski, P. A., & Robinson, B. (2000). Personal theories, intellectual ability, and epistemological beliefs: Adult age differences in everyday reasoning biases. *Psychology and Aging, 15*, 400–416.

Lichtenstein, S., & Slovic, P. (1971). Reversals of preference between bids and choices in gambling decisions. *Journal of Experimental Psychology, 89*, 46–55.

Lichtenstein, S., & Slovic, P. (1973). Response-induced reversals of preference in gambling: An extended replication in Las Vegas. *Journal of Experimental Psychology, 101*, 16–20.

MacPherson, S. E., Phillips, L. H., & Della Sala, S. (2002). Age, executive function, and social decision making: A dorsolateral prefrontal theory of cognitive aging. *Psychology and Aging, 17*, 598–609.

Marsiske, M., & Willis, S. L. (1995). Dimensionality of everyday problem solving in older adults. *Psychology and Aging, 10*, 269–283.

Mishra, S., Umesh, U. N., & Stem, D. E., Jr. (1993). Antecedents of the attraction effect: An information-processing approach. *Journal of Marketing Research, 30*, 331–349.

Mitchell, A. A., & Dacin, P. A. (1996). The assessment of alternative measures of consumer expertise. *Journal of Consumer Research, 23*, 219–239.

Pan, Y., & Lehmann, D. R. (1993). The influence of new brand entry on subjective brand judgments. *Journal of Consumer Research, 20*, 76–86.

Pan, Y., O'Curry, S., & Pitts, R. (1995). The attraction effect and political choice in two elections. *Journal of Consumer Psychology, 4*, 85–101.

Payne, J. W., Bettman, J. R., & Johnson, E. J. (1993). *The adaptive decision maker.* New York: Cambridge University Press.

Peters, E., Finucane, M. L., McGregor, D. G., & Slovic, P. (2000). The bearable lightness of aging: Judgment and decision processes in older adults. In National Research Council; Committee on Future Directions for Cognitive Research on Aging; P. C. Stern & L. L. Carstensen (Eds.), *The aging mind: Opportunities in cognitive research* (Appendix C, pp. 144–165). Washington, DC: National Academy Press.

Rabbitt, P. (1977). Changes in problem solving ability in old age. In J. E. Birren & K. W. Schaie (Eds.), *Handbook of the psychology of aging* (pp. 606–625). New York: Van Nostrand Reinhold.

Ratneshwar, S., Shocker, A. D., & Stewart, D. W. (1987). Toward understanding the attraction effect: The implications of product stimulus meaningfulness and familiarity. *Journal of Consumer Research, 13*, 520–533.

Sanfey, A. G., & Hastie, R. (2000). Judgment and decision making across the adult life span: A tutorial review of psychological research. In D. Park & N. Schwarz (Eds.), *Cognitive aging: A primer* (pp. 253–273). Philadelphia: Psychology Press.

Schaie, K. W. (1994). The course of adult intellectual development. *American Psychologist, 49*, 304–313.

Sedikides, C., Ariely, D., & Olsen, N. (1999). Contextual and procedural determinants of partner selection: Of asymmetric dominance and prominence. *Social Cognition, 17*, 118–139.

Sen, S. (1998). Knowledge, information mode, and the attraction effect. *Journal of Consumer Research, 25*, 64–77.

Simonson, I. (1989). Choice based on reasons: The case of attraction and compromise effects. *Journal of Consumer Research, 16*, 158–174.

Simonson, I., & Tversky, A. (1992). Choice in context: Tradeoff contrast and extremeness aversion. *Marketing Research, 29*, 281–295.

Slovic, P. (1995). The construction of preference. *American Psychologist, 50*, 364–371.

Stanovich, K. E., & West, R. F. (2000). Individual differences in reasoning: Implications for the rationality debate. *Behavioral and Brain Sciences, 23*, 645–665.

Tentori, K., Osherson, D., Hasher, L., & May, C. (2001). Wisdom and aging: Irrational preferences in college students but not older adults. *Cognition, 81*, B87–B96.

Tversky, A., & Kahneman, D. (1986). Rational choice and the framing of decisions. *Journal of Business, 59*, 251–278.

Tversky, A., Sattath, S., & Slovic, P. (1988). Contingent weighting in judgment and choice. *Psychological Review*, *95*, 371–384.

Tversky, A., & Simonson, I. (1993). Context-dependent preferences. *Management Science*, *39*, 1179–1189.

Wedell, D. H. (1991). Distinguishing among models of contextually induced preference reversals. *Journal of Experimental Psychology: Learning, Memory, and Cognition*, *17*, 767–778.

Wedell, D. H., & Boeckenholt, U. (1990). Moderation of preference reversals in the long run. *Journal of Experimental Psychology: Human Perception and Performance*, *16*, 429–438.

Wedell, D. H., & Pettibone, J. C. (1996). Using judgments to understand decoy effects in choice. *Organizational Behavior and Human Decision Processes*, *67*, 326–344.

Wilson, T. D., & Schooler, J. W. (1991). Thinking too much: Introspection can reduce the quality of preferences and decisions. *Journal of Personality and Social Psychology*, *60*, 181–192.

Yates, J. F., & Patalano, A. L. (1999). Decision making and aging. In D. C. Park, R. W. Morrell, & K. Shifren (Eds.), *Processing of medical information in aging patients: Cognitive and human factors perspectives* (pp. 31–54). Mahwah, NJ: Lawrence Erlbaum Associates, Inc.

Yoon, C., May, C. P., & Hasher, L. (1999). Aging, circadian arousal patterns, and cogition. In N. Schwarz, D. C. Park, B. Knauper, & S. Sudman (Eds.), *Cognition, aging, and self reports* (pp. 117–143). Philadelphia: Psychology Press.

PrEview proof published online 7 July 2004

THE QUARTERLY JOURNAL OF EXPERIMENTAL PSYCHOLOGY
2005, 58A (1), 134–154

Ψ **Psychology Press**
Taylor & Francis Group

Ageing and switching of the focus of attention in working memory: Results from a modified N-Back task

Paul Verhaeghen and Chandramallika Basak

Syracuse University, Syracuse, New York, USA

We conducted two experiments using a modified version of the N-Back task. For younger adults, there was an abrupt increase in reaction time of about 250 ms in passing from $N = 1$ to $N > 1$, indicating a cost associated with switching of the focus of attention within working memory. Response time costs remained constant over the range $N = 2$ to $N = 5$. Accuracy declined steadily over the full range of N (Experiment 1). Focus switch costs did not interact with either working memory updating (Experiment 1), or global task switching (Experiment 2). There were no age differences in RT costs once general slowing was taken into account, but there was a larger focus-switch-related accuracy cost in older adults than in younger adults. No age sensitivity was found for either updating or global task switching. The results suggest (a) that focus switching is a cognitive primitive, distinct from task switching and updating, and (b) that focus switching shows a specific age-related deficit in the accuracy domain.

Adult age differences favouring the young have been demonstrated in a wide variety of cognitive tasks. Such age-sensitive tasks include simple and choice reaction times, working memory tasks, tests of episodic memory, tests of spatial and reasoning abilities, mental rotation, and visual search performance (for exhaustive reviews, see, e.g., Kausler, 1991; Salthouse, 1985, 1991). Given that almost all tasks that depend on fluid mental abilities show age-related decline, it seems likely that a small number of factors may be responsible for these changes. Hence, much of the research on cognitive ageing has focused on the investigation of how age affects so-called cognitive primitives—that is, variables that influence many aspects of the cognitive system without themselves being reducible to other psychological constructs. One such primitive that has been researched extensively is processing speed (Salthouse, 1991, 1996; Verhaeghen & Salthouse, 1997). Salthouse notes that information processing occurs at a given rate, and this rate slows with age. This theory has led to the adoption of age-related slowing as the null hypothesis to explain age-related differences

Correspondence should be addressed to Paul Verhaeghen or Chandramallika Basak, Department of Psychology, 430 Huntington Hall, Syracuse University, Syracuse, New York 13244–2340, USA. Email: pverhaeg@psych.syr.edu or cbasak@mailbox.syr.edu

This research was supported in part by a grant from the National Institute on Aging (AG-16201). We thank John Cerella for his many useful comments. Marc Howard and Kara Bopp provided valuable additional comments.

http://www.tandf.co.uk/journals/pp/02724987.html   DOI:10.1080/0272498044300241

in cognitive tasks (e.g., Cerella, 1990; Faust, Balota, Spieler, & Ferraro, 1999; and Perfect & Maylor, 2000).

More recently, attention has been drawn towards more process-specific accounts of cognitive ageing, particularly focusing on basic executive processes operating in working memory. To date, ageing research has focused on three types of control process (see Miyake, Friedman, Emerson, Witzki, & Howerter, 2000, for an empirically derived classification of control processes). The first is resistance to interference, also known as inhibitory control. This process has been a central explanatory construct in ageing theories since the 1990s (e.g., Hasher & Zacks, 1988; Hasher, Zacks, & May, 1999). The theory states that older adults have more trouble inhibiting intrusive stimuli and intrusive thoughts. This presumed breakdown in resistance to interference will lead to mental clutter in working memory, thereby limiting its functional capacity and perhaps also its speed of operation. However, the finding that two paradigmatic tasks that measure resistance to interference—namely Stroop interference and negative priming—are not age sensitive once the effects of basic age differences in speed are taken into account casts doubt on the viability of this explanation for age-related differences in cognition (for meta-analyses, see Verhaeghen & De Meersman, 1998a, 1998b).

A second suggestion for an age-sensitive control process has been the ability to coordinate distinct tasks or distinct processing streams. One of the paradigms used is dual-task performance (e.g., Hartley & Little, 1999; McDowd & Shaw, 2000), but the concept has also been applied to working memory tasks (e.g., Mayr & Kliegl, 1993; Verhaeghen, Kliegl, & Mayr, 1997). Meta-analysis has supported the view that the age sensitivity of dual-task performance cannot be explained simply in terms of age-related slowing (Verhaeghen, Steitz, Sliwinski, & Cerella, 2003).

During the late 1990s and early 2000s, an emergent third candidate for an age-sensitive control task has been task switching (e.g., Mayr, Spieler, & Kliegl, 2001). Investigators have used two different methods of quantifying costs to performance when switches between tasks occur. First, it is possible to compare mean reaction times (RTs) for blocks of successive responses within tasks given in isolation with mean RTs for blocks of successive responses in the same task when the demand to switch to another is also present. This may be termed the global task-switching cost. It is thought to reflect the difficulty associated with maintaining and scheduling two different mental task sets. A second method is to examine performance within blocks where task switching occurs, comparing mean RT for trials in which task switching was actually required against mean RT for trials in which no switch was demanded. This local task-switching cost is held to reflect the demands of the executive process associated with the actual switching. Meta-analysis (Wasylyshyn, Verhaeghen, & Sliwinski, 2003) has shown that global task-switching costs are age sensitive, but local costs are not.

A bold summary of this all-too-brief review of the literature on ageing and executive control (see also Verhaeghen & Cerella, 2002) might be that age differences are present in tasks that require the simultaneous maintenance of two distinct mental sets—for instance, in dual-task performance and global task switching—but not in tasks that require selection among sets that are already loaded in working memory—for instance, in Stroop performance, in negative priming, and in local task switching. This interpretation of the literature suggests that the age-related deficit may not be located in the control processes per se, but may rather be due to underlying difficulties with efficient maintenance or retrieval of task sets when more than one set is involved.

Focus switching: A new cognitive primitive?

Very recent work in cognitive psychology (Garavan, 1998; McElree, 2001; McElree & Dosher, 1989; Oberauer, 2002) has dealt with exactly these issues: storage in and retrieval from working memory in a single versus multiple item context. The starting point for these efforts is the embedded-process account of working memory, best exemplified by the work of Nelson Cowan. Cowan (1995, 2001) proposed a hierarchical two-tier structure for working memory, distinguishing a zone of immediate access, labelled the focus of attention (typically considered to contain a magical number of 4 ± 1 elements), from a larger, activated portion of long-term memory that holds information that is available but not immediately accessible. The recent challenge to Cowan's model by Garavan (1998), McElree (2001), and Oberauer (2002) is that the focus of attention is much narrower than previously assumed and, in fact, that it can hold no more than a single element at any given time.

Perhaps the most compelling evidence for this narrow-focus view comes from McElree's (2001) work with the identity judgement N-Back task. In this task, the participant is presented with a sequence of digits, one at a time, and is required to press one of two keys to indicate whether the digit presented on the screen is identical or not to the digit presented N positions back in the sequence. McElree found that speed of access was much faster for $N = 1$ than for either $N = 2$ or $N = 3$, but that speeds of access for $N = 2$ and $N = 3$ were identical. The interpretation is that only a single element can be held in the focus of attention at any given time. When $N > 1$, the target must be retrieved from outside this attentional focus and moved into focal attention for processing. This operation (the focus switch) comes at a cost. In the RT domain, the cost associated with focus switching appears to be all-or-none—that is, the increase in reaction time is dependent on the presence of a focus switch, but independent of further increases of the working memory load, otherwise RTs should have increased from $N = 2$ to $N = 3$.

Our experimental paradigm: Focus switching in an identity judgement N-Back task

Given that focus switching appears to be a very fundamental process, implicated in any task that requires the processing of more than a single sequential stream of items, we hypothesized that it may well be the source of the age deficits observed in task switching (and also in dual tasking, although the latter possibility was not investigated here). Two experiments were conducted to investigate this hypothesis. The first was designed to establish the existence or absence of age differences in focus-switching costs. The second was designed to examine whether age deficits in focus switching, if any, give rise to age deficits in other executive processes associated with maintenance and retrieval in working memory. We investigated the relation between focus switching and global task switching, because they seem to be closely related by definition. This comparison is also potentially crucial for cognitive theory. Because age-related dissociations between processes indicate selective influence, such dissociation would provide strong evidence that the two processes are functionally separate (Sternberg, 2001).

We based our task on McElree's (2001) identity judgement N-Back task. McElree's study used a speed–accuracy methodology; we investigate RTs alone. The reason for this change is pragmatic: Response time studies yield stable data in fewer trials. This in turn allows for the inclusion of more conditions (e.g., a wider range of N values in Experiment 1; the introduction of task switching in Experiment 2).

The extension of N beyond 3 is crucial for a thorough test of McElree's assertion that the focus switch cost is all-or-none. His model predicts a step difference in RT from $N = 1$ to $N > 1$ (see Figure 1). That is, it is assumed that the item in the $N = 1$ version of the task has privileged access because, unlike the items in the $N > 1$ versions, no retrieval process is needed prior to the comparison process. Access times are not expected to differ for larger values of N as long as N is smaller than working memory capacity, because items outside the focus of attention are, like items in long-term memory, directly content addressable. Note, however, that McElree (2001) posits no such step in accuracy. In his view, accuracy is supposed to decrease monotonically and smoothly over N (see Figure 1). This is because

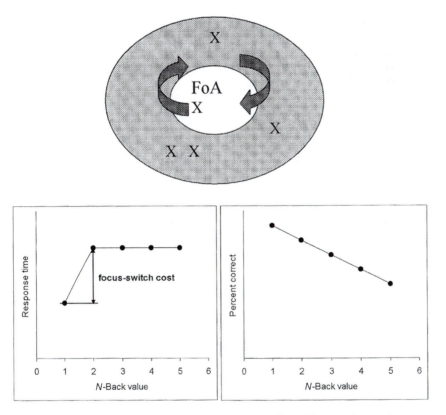

Figure 1. An illustration of the expected effects. The top of the figure illustrates the two-tier structure of working memory (McElree, 2001), with a focus of attention holding only a single item. If more than two items are present in working memory, item swapping becomes necessary before the second element can be processed. The bottom of the figure shows the predictions for our identity judgement N-Back task under this model: a step function in RTs (the size of the step defines the focus-switching effect) and a monotonic decline (not necessary linear) in accuracy over increasing values of N.

accuracy measures the probability that an item is available for processing. It is assumed that this availability is susceptible only to item decay, to the effects of interfering items, or to both. The decline is expected to be monotonic because both storage time and the number of interfering items in working memory are directly related to N. The decline is expected to be smooth because there is no reason to assume that items that are stored outside the focus of attention should lose activation due to decay or interference more rapidly than the item stored inside the focus of attention.

An additional adaptation to the McElree (2001) paradigm, introduced to minimize extraneous control demands, is that we separated presentation of the stimuli by colour and by spatial position in the time series. That is, the stimuli were presented one at a time in N virtual columns, defined by location and colour (see the Methods section for more details). From the participant's point of view, this meant that each item presented had to be compared to the item previously presented in the same column and the same colour. Recently, Hartley (2002) has demonstrated that when relative position of stimuli was defined by location and colour rather than merely by their place in a time sequence, as in traditional N-Back tasks, accuracy of both younger and older adults improved, and, interestingly, age differences disappeared. Like Hartley, we take this to indicate that external spatial and colour cues for the location of an item in the time series removes some demand on processing that is extraneous to the memory component of the task. Therefore, we adopted this modification of the standard layout of the task in our N-Back experiments.

Other control processes in the identity judgement N-Back task

The identity N-Back task obviously involves other basic control processes as well. The most apparent of these is item updating. After the identity judgement has been made, the item currently in the Nth position back will need to be overwritten with the item currently on the screen. This updating process is only necessary when the item presented in the Nth position back is different from the item currently visible (i.e., a "no" answer); no updating is required when the two items are identical (i.e., a "yes" answer). Therefore, we expect that RTs will be longer for "no" items than for "yes" items. Obviously, other processes besides updating might contribute to differences between "no" and "yes" responses. We should note, however, that in working memory access experiments that require no updating, "yes" and "no" responses typically yield identical RTs, provided that the prior probability of each type of response is 50% (Sternberg, 1969). Therefore, we interpret interactions involving the difference in RTs between the "no" and the "yes" condition as primarily due to the updating process. This presupposes that the updating process is completed before the answer key is pressed. We feel this is a reasonable assumption. It makes logical sense to update the item while it is on the screen, rather than to wait until a new item appears, which would then interfere with the element to be updated and would require the formation of an additional temporary memory trace.

A question central to the present study is what the effect of combinations of executive control processes will be on performance and, additionally, whether the associated costs differ between age groups. Our working assumption is that control processes in the N-Back task will not operate in parallel, but rather will be chained in a serial fashion. This seems a reasonable assumption for both updating (Experiments 1 and 2) and task switching (Experiment 2): An item needs to be fully available in the focus of attention before it can be updated, and a focus switch needs to be fully executed before another set of processes can gain access to the item. The expectation for a purely serial system is strict additivity of RTs (Sternberg, 1969, 1998). Underadditivity would be an indication that at least part of the processing can occur in parallel. Overadditivity would indicate an additional cost, associated, for instance, with a strategic scheduling/monitoring component or with the necessity to unlock particular stages needed for both processes. If the pattern of age by condition interaction differs between focus switching and any of the other processes, this would indicate differential sensitivity to ageing and would thereby signal that at least some of the component processes of focus switching are distinct from those present in updating and task switching.

Summary and hypotheses

Our hypotheses concerning general effects with regard to the focus-switching phenomenon are represented in Figure 1. In the RT domain, we expect a step function, with the step occurring between $N = 1$ and $N = 2$. In the accuracy domain, we expect a monotonic (though not necessarily linear) decline. If focus switching is age sensitive, we expect (a) an age by condition interaction in RT evaluated at $N = 1$ and $N = 2$, (b) an age by condition interaction in accuracy evaluated at $N = 1$ and $N = 2$, or (c) both. We also investigate age by condition interactions in the $N > 1$ portion of the curve. Such interactions would suggest an age-related decrease in efficiency of retrieval processes in working memory (indexed by RT), an age-related decrease in working memory storage or availability (indexed by accuracy), or both. Additionally, if the focus-switching process is a true cognitive primitive, we would expect to obtain differential patterns of age by condition interactions between focus switching and any of the other processes.

EXPERIMENT 1

Method

Participants

The sample consisted of 28 younger adults (mean age = 18.79 years; $SD = 0.74$; ranging from 18 to 20 years; 18 females and 10 males), who received course credit for participating in the study, and 27 older adults (mean age = 72.15 years; $SD = 3.91$; ranging from 63 to 80 years; 17 females and 10 males), who received \$15.00 in return for their time and effort. Younger adults averaged 12.61 years of education ($SD = 0.69$); older adults averaged 15.41 years of education ($SD = 2.39$); the difference is significant, $t(53) = -2.80$. Our older adults scored significantly higher on the multiple-choice version of the Mill Hill Vocabulary test (22.11, $SD = 4.80$) than did the younger adults (18.82, $SD = 3.88$), $t(53) = -3.29$. This sample was part of a larger original sample; we discarded data from 2 younger and 5 older participants because they did not meet a preset accuracy criterion of 90% correct in the $N = 1$ condition. This criterion was set to ensure data quality. Because the identity judgement task at $N = 1$ is very easy (comparing a single digit currently projected on the screen with a single digit that was presented just before it), we assume that low accuracy is indicative of a lack of motivation, poor cognitive skills, or both.

Task and procedure

As explained above, the baseline task is an identity judgement task (McElree, 2001). In this task, participants indicate whether the item currently presented on the screen is identical to the item presented N positions back. Figure 2 shows a black-and-white rendition of a sample stimulus set for one trial (in this case $N = 4$), as it would appear on the computer screen if all items remained visible. The digits shown were 6 mm tall, the horizontal separation between columns was 1.3 cm. In practice, only one digit was shown at any time; the order of presentation was the conventional reading pattern for the English language: left-to-right, top-to-bottom. Each column was depicted in a different colour; colour–column assignments remained constant for the whole experiment. For the first row, a new digit was presented every 2,000 ms; from the second row on, participants pressed either of two keys to indicate their answer. The "/" key stood for "yes" (i.e., identical) and was masked with a piece of green tape; the "z" key stood for "no" (i.e., different) and was masked with a piece of red tape. Participants were instructed to be both fast and accurate. As soon as the key was pressed, the next stimulus appeared. Participants were encouraged to choose a comfortable viewing distance from the screen.

Each stimulus set (a "trial") contained a total of 20 to-be-responded-to items. After each trial, the subject received feedback about both total accuracy and average RT over the run of 20 items. A total of 11 trials (yielding a total of 220 RTs) were presented for each value of N (N varied from 1 to 5), distributed as follows: first 6 trials for $N = 1$, then 6 for $N = 2$, 6 for $N = 3$, 6 for $N = 4$, 6 for $N = 5$, 5 for $N = 5$, 5 for $N = 4$, 5 for $N = 3$, 5 for $N = 2$, and 5 for $N = 1$. The first trial for each of the values of N in the first half of the experiment was considered practice and discarded from further analysis. For each trial, half of the stimuli were identical to the item N back, and the other half were not. The exact composition of a trial was determined by an online algorithm that used a random seed. Participants were encouraged to take breaks between blocks. All participants were tested in a single session, typically lasting between 60 and 90 minutes.

3	5	8	1
3	6	7	1
4	5	7	3
4	5	9	3
3	5	9	8
2	5	9	8

Figure 2. An example of a trial in the 4-back version of the task, if all stimuli remained onscreen. In the experiment, stimuli were shown one at a time, in a reading pattern (left to right, then on the next line, etc.); each column was depicted in a different colour. The first row was presented at a 2 s/item pace; presentation of subsequent stimuli was participant paced. The response required was a judgement of whether the digit currently projected was identical to the digit previously shown one row higher in the same column.

Response time analysis

All RT analyses were conducted on correct responses only. For each condition within each individual, RT distributions were truncated at three interquartile ranges above or below the mean as indicated by a box plot analysis; this was done to remove outliers. Additionally, reaction times of 100 ms or less were considered anticipatory and were removed from the data set. In total, 0% of the data points of younger adults and 3.3% of the data points of older adults were discarded after applying this procedure. Response times for the second "row"—that is, when the comparison items were the items initially presented by the experimenter—were also discarded from these analyses. To examine differential age effects in RTs, logarithmic transformation was applied to the data prior to testing for age by condition interactions (e.g., Cerella, 1990; Faust, Balota, Spieler, & Ferraro, 1999). The reason for this is that one of the most pervasive effects of ageing is near-multiplicative slowing—that is, RTs of older adults are typically close to a ratio of RTs of younger adults (e.g., Cerella, 1990). Only age by condition interactions that survive a logarithmic transformation can be considered indicative of effects that go over and beyond the expected multiplicative effect of ageing.

Alpha level for all statistical testing was set at $p < .05$.

Results

Response times as a function of N

The results are presented in Figure 3. An analysis of variance (ANOVA) covering all 5 values of N revealed a significant effect of N, $F(4, 212) = 73.56$, $MSE = 26,847.04$ (larger values of N yield longer RTs), of age group, $F(1, 53) = 74.06$, $MSE = 373,159.10$ (older adults are slower), and of the age by N interaction, $F(4, 212) = 10.10$, $MSE = 26,847.04$. This interaction remained significant after logarithmic transformation, $F(4, 212) = 2.74$, $MSE = 0.011$, and indicates that age differences favouring the young increase with increasing values of N.

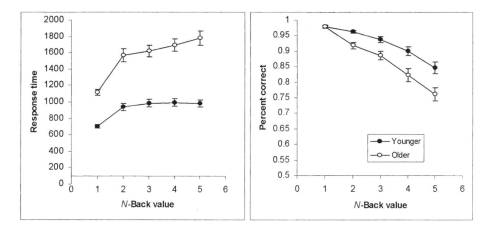

Figure 3. Response time (correct trials) and accuracy data for Experiment 1 as a function of N, separated by age group. Focus switch costs are calculated as the difference in performance between $N = 1$ and $N = 2$. Error bars denote standard errors.

Restricting the analysis to the values of N associated with focus switching—that is, $N = 1$ and $N = 2$—we found significant main effects of N, $F(1, 53) = 94.01$, $MSE = 34,443.77$ ($N = 2$ yields slower responses than $N = 1$), and of age, $F(1, 53) = 77.56$, $MSE = 96,417.53$ (older adults are slower), as well as a significant age by N interaction, $F(1, 53) = 9.03$, $MSE = 34,443.77$. This interaction, however, did not survive logarithmic transformation, $F(1, 53) = 0.85$, $MSE = 0.014$, indicating that the age difference in focus switching is not larger than that expected from general slowing alone.

For the values of N associated with the region outside the focus of attention—that is, from $N = 2$ to $N = 5$—we found significant effects of N, $F(3, 159) = 9.18$, $MSE = 17,783.49$ (larger values of N yield longer RTs), and of age, $F(1, 53) = 64.45$, $MSE = 404,849.76$ (older adults are slower), as well as a significant age by N interaction, $F(3, 159) = 4.89$, $MSE = 17,783.49$. This interaction remained significant even after logarithmic transformation, $F(3, 159) = 3.47$, $MSE = 0.007$. Figure 3 clarifies this interaction. In the young, RT remains flat with increasing N in the region outside the focus of attention; in the old, there is a steady linear increase in RT with N. This was verified by conducting a series of multiple regression analyses, one for each individual, regressing RT on N, for the values of $N > 1$. The average slope of the regression lines for younger adults was 14.77 ms/N, which was not significantly different from zero ($SE = 10.17$); the average slope for the older adults was 71.22 ms/N, which was significantly larger than zero ($SE = 20.30$) and also significantly larger than the average slope for the younger adults, $t(53) = 2.51$. Note that the (nonsignificant) slope for the young is entirely due to an increase in RT from $N = 2$ to $N = 3$.

Accuracy as a function of N

Results are presented in Figure 3. An ANOVA covering all 5 values of N revealed a significant effect of N, $F(4, 212) = 109.18$, $MSE = 0.002$ (accuracy declines over increasing N), and of age group, $F(1, 53) = 11.26$ (older adults are less accurate), $MSE = 0.016$, and a significant age by N interaction, $F(4, 212) = 6.50$, $MSE = 0.002$ (indicating that age differences favouring the young increase with increasing N).

For the values of N associated with focus switching—that is, $N = 1$ and $N = 2$—we found significant main effects of N, $F(1, 53) = 49.78$, $MSE = 0.001$ (performance at $N = 2$ is less accurate), and of age, $F(1, 53) = 9.44$, $MSE = 0.001$ (older adults are less accurate), as well as a significant age by N interaction, $F(1, 53) = 16.31$, $MSE = 0.001$ (age differences favouring the young increase with increasing N).

For the values of N associated with the region outside the focus of attention—that is, $N > 1$—we found significant effects of N, $F(3, 159) = 93.38$, $MSE = 0.002$ (accuracy decreases with increasing values of N), and of age, $F(1, 53) = 12.06$, $MSE = 0.019$ (older adults are less accurate). The age by N interaction was not significant, $F(3, 159) = 2.36$, $MSE = 0.002$.

Response times as a function of trial type

A series of ANOVAs was conducted with trial type ("yes" vs. "no") and N as between-subject and age group as within-subject measures. Figure 4 presents the data. Over the full range of N values, "no" responses were slower than "yes" responses, $F(4, 212) = 132.63$, $MSE = 51,420.74$. Trial type interacted with N, $F(4, 212) = 4.32$, $MSE = 15,717.18$ (the

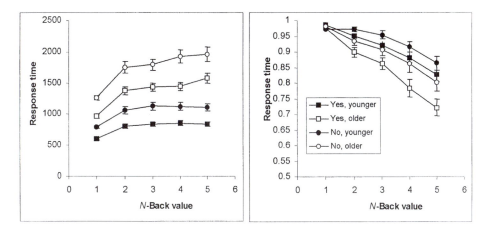

Figure 4.   Response time (correct trials) and accuracy data for Experiment 1, separated by age group and by trial type ("yes" responses vs. "no" responses). Error bars denote standard errors.

source of the interaction is explored in the next two paragraphs), and with age group, $F(1, 53) = 5.19$, $MSE = 103,986.22$. The latter interaction became nonsignificant after logarithmic transformation, $F(1, 53) = 0.49$, $MSE = 0.03$. The three-way interaction between the values of N, age group, and trial type was not significant, $F(4, 212) = 1.31$, $MSE = 15,717.18$.

For focus switching—that is, for $N = 1$ and $N = 2$—the main effect of trial type is significant, $F(1, 53) = 210.47$, $MSE = 66,979.50$ ("no" responses are slower), as well as the interaction with N, $F(1, 53) = 9.73$, $MSE = 8,985.25$ (the time difference between "no" and "yes" responses was larger for $N = 2$), and with age, $F(1, 53) = 8.12$, $MSE = 20,049.22$. The age by trial type interaction did not survive logarithmic transformation, $F(1, 53) = 0.25$, $MSE = 0.01$. The three-way interaction again did not reach significance, $F(1, 53) = 0.06$, $MSE = 8,985.25$.

For items outside the focus of attention—that is, for $N > 1$—the main effect of trial type was significant, $F(1, 53) = 104.71$, $MSE = 119,018.08$ ("no" responses were slower). The interaction with age was marginally significant, $F(1, 53) = 3.96$, $MSE = 471,592.21$, $p = .052$. This interaction was clearly nonsignificant after logarithmic transformation, $F(1, 53 = 0.59$, $MSE = 0.04$. The interaction between N and trial type was not significant, $F(3, 159) = 1.37$, $MSE = 13,111.09$, and neither was the three-way interaction, $F(3, 159) = 1.98$, $MSE = 13,114.09$.

Combined, the last two analyses suggest that the source of the interaction between type of response and N is entirely due to an increase from $N = 1$ to $N = 2$ in the difference between the time needed for "yes" and "no" responses. In other words, the presence of a focus switch slowed down the updating process.

Accuracy as a function of trial type

Analysis of the accuracy of "yes" versus "no" responses (see Figure 4) indicates that "no" responses are more accurate than "yes" responses, $F(1, 53) = 21.68$, $MSE = 0.008$. Trial type interacted with N, $F(4, 212) = 8.24$, $MSE = 0.002$ (larger values of N yield larger differences), but not with age group, $F(1, 53) = 3.01$, $MSE = 0.025$. The three-way interaction was not significant, $F(4, 212) = 0.78$, $MSE = 0.002$.

To further explore the N by type of response interaction, we conducted two ANOVAs, one for $N = 1$ contrasted with $N = 2$, and one for all $N > 1$. For focus switching—that is, for $N = 1$ and $N = 2$—the interaction between N and trial type was significant, $F(1, 53) = 18.74$, $MSE = 0.001$ ($N = 2$ yielded a larger difference between trial types). For items outside the focus of attention, however—that is, for $N > 1$—the interaction between N and trial type was not significant, $F(3, 159) = 2.66$, $MSE = 0.002$.

Discussion

Focus switching and updating in younger adults

Turning our attention first to the data obtained from the younger adults, we find that the results are completely in line with the predictions from the McElree (2001) model (see Figure 1), notwithstanding our change in the methodology from speed–accuracy trade-off to RT and from single-location to columnar presentation. Looking at RTs first, the results are as expected. There is a sharp increase in RT from $N = 1$ to $N = 2$ (from 700 ms to 937 ms, an increase of about 240 ms), followed by a flat curve from $N = 2$ to $N = 5$. This step function in mean RTs suggests, in accordance with McElree's theory, that the focus of attention can accommodate one and only one item at any given time; the other items are stored in working memory outside this focus of attention. The quarter-second delay between $N = 1$ and $N = 2$ indicates the time required for shunting items in and out of the focus—the focus switch cost. The finding that RTs are (almost) flat over the $N = 2$ to $N = 5$ portion of the curve is likewise as expected from McElree's model. The extremely shallow slope (a nonsignificant 15 ms/N) suggests two things. First, the focus switch effect is not a mere artifact of increased memory load. If the effect were dependent on load, RTs would be expected to continue to rise steadily with increasing N even after $N = 2$. Second, the elements contained in the portion of working memory outside the focus of attention are not subject to a Sternberg-like parallel or serial search process, either of which would give rise to increasing RTs with N, with an expected slope of about 40 ms/item (e.g., Ashby, Tein, & Balakrishnan, 1993; Hockley, 1984). Rather, the items outside the focus of attention appear to be directly content addressable, much in the way elements stored in long-term memory are. The present findings show that the area outside the focus of attention that is directly content addressable appears to be rather large—that is, that it can contain at least four items.

Second, our results also confirm McElree's (2001) predictions with regard to accuracy. At $N = 1$, performance is near perfect, indicating perfect retrievability of the item stored in the focus of attention. We also find the expected monotonic decline over N, suggestive of a smooth decrease in item availability. Note that the function we obtained is positively accelerating over N. This form clearly rules out one explanation for the decline in accuracy—namely, the mere compounding of errors over successive values of N. Error compounding is an exponential process. That is, if P is the relative frequency of accurate response obtained for $N = 1$, the predicted value under error compounding over N is P^N. This function is negatively accelerating over N, with a horizontal asymptote at zero. The form does not rule out forgetting due to decay. Although such curves typically yield negatively accelerating functions with a horizontal asymptote (Rubin & Wenzel, 1996), positively accelerating curves are not without precedent. Interference is another likely explanation for the positive acceleration. Atkinson and Shiffrin (1968, Exp. 4) obtained and modeled positive acceleration over short lags due to item interference, asserting that this shape will occur when each of the items presented has a very high probability of entering the temporary memory buffer. Atkinson and Shiffrin manipulated this probability by requesting overt rehearsal. Even though our task did not use overt rehearsal, the N-Back task requirement of an explicit response to each item obviously leads to a high probability that each item will be attended to and stored.

A third outcome, not investigated by McElree (2001), concerns the updating process, examined by comparing "yes" responses, where no further updating of the item is necessary, with "no" responses, where the item has to be updated. "No" responses are about 100 ms slower than "yes" responses for $N = 1$ and about 140 ms slower for subsequent values of N. The 40 ms increase for values of N larger than 1 than for $N = 1$ indicates that the updating and focus-switching processes cannot be executed in a strictly serial fashion without additional cost. One possible explanation is that focus switching and updating rely partially on the same resources or mental structures for their execution. These would then need to be freed or unlocked, respectively, thereby affecting the total duration of the execution of both processes. Another possibility is that the necessity to switch between processes is in itself a control process that needs to be inserted as an additional stage in the processing stream. In accuracy, we note a difference between "no" and "yes" responses only for items residing outside the focus of attention. "No" responses are performed with greater accuracy than "yes" responses for $N > 1$. This result is to be expected when the memory trace is inexact. The reason for this is that "yes" responses can only be answered correctly if the memory trace contains the correct item (e.g., if the target is "7" and the probe is "7", the item will be answered correctly if and only if the trace is "7"), whereas correct "no" responses only require that the memory trace is different from the target (e.g., if the target is "7" and the probe is "5", the item will be answered correctly if the trace is "7", but also if the trace contains any number different from "5"). The interaction between N and type of response then suggests that the memory trace is vulnerable outside the focus of attention, but is virtually exact when the item is stored within the focus of attention.

Age differences in focus switching

Our prime interest in this study was to examine age sensitivity of the control process of focus switching. Looking at the relevant contrast—that is, differences between the $N = 1$ and $N = 2$ conditions—we found that relative to younger adults, older adults have no specific problems with accessing items that reside outside the focus of attention, as measured by RT. In contrast, the relative availability of items residing outside the focus of attention is markedly lower for older adults, as measured by the probability of correct retrieval.

When we investigate the age-associated effects on items outside the focus of attention, two interesting results emerge. First, we find that for the items stored outside the focus of attention, the decrease in accuracy over N is identical for younger and older adults. Thus, we are faced with an age-related dissociation in the accuracy domain. For the item residing in the focus of attention, no age difference is present, but for the items outside the focus of attention, age differences are present, and they remain identical over all values of N. The simplest explanation for this dissociation is that the items stored inside and outside the focus of attention are differentially susceptible to interference. In fact, our result implies that the item that is present in the focus of attention is not at all vulnerable to interference from the items outside the focus. In younger adults, high overall accuracy rates obscured the breaking point in the accuracy by N curve. The differential nature of the two stores, however, becomes apparent in older adults, where focus switching decreases performance sufficiently to make the breaking point visible. This age-related dissociation then indicates that there might be a sharper boundary between the items stored inside and outside the focus of attention than previously thought.

Second, with regard to RTs, we found a significant age by N interaction for the items stored outside the focus of attention, with growing age differences with increasing N. Furthermore, as stated above, whereas the regression line over $N = 2$ to $N = 5$ was flat for younger adults, we found a significant slope (of about $70\,ms/N$) for older adults. We took the flatness of the slope of younger adults as an indication that the items stored outside the focus of attention are directly content addressable. The presence of this ramp in the data of the older adults can mean at least three things: (a) with advancing age, content addressability gets lost over the whole range of the working memory store outside the focus of attention, resulting in an active search of the store; (b) with advancing age, content addressability of the working memory store outside the focus of attention declines with a probability that is proportional to N; or (c) the ramp is an artifact of data averaging over interindividually different step functions (see Basak & Verhaeghen, 2003, for a similar effect concerning enumeration speed). At present, unfortunately, none of these alternatives can be ruled out.

Age differences in updating and in the combination of updating and switching

Once general slowing effects were taken into account by logarithmic transformation of the data, no age differences were apparent in the updating process as indexed by the difference between "yes" and "no" responses in either RT or accuracy. This was unexpected, because age differences in the updating process have been observed in earlier research (Hartman, Dumas, & Nielsen, 2001; Van der Linden, Brédart, & Beerten, 1994). As stated above, updating and focus switching interacted in an overadditive fashion, suggesting either a reliance on shared resources or the existence of a metacontrol process. The joint effects of focus switching and updating were not larger for older adults than for younger adults, indicating no specific age difference in resource sharing or metacontrol.

EXPERIMENT 2

In Experiment 2, we compare focus switching with (global) task switching, to investigate whether these two processes can be reduced to a single underlying requirement, namely that of switching.

Method

Participants

The sample consisted of 30 younger adults (mean age = 18.77 years; SD = 0.81; ranging from 18 to 21 years of age), who received course credit for participating, and 27 older adults (mean age = 70.63 years; SD = 5.30; ranging from 62 to 80 years of age) who received $20.00 for participating; none of these volunteers had participated in Experiment 1. The average years of education of younger adults was 12.7 (SD = 0.99), and that of older adults was 15.07 (SD = 2.72); the difference is significant, $t(55)$ = −2.37. The older adults also scored higher on the multiple-choice version of the Mill Hill Vocabulary test (mean score = 22.63; SD = 5.05) than the younger adults (mean score = 17.90; SD = 3.30), $t(55)$ = −4.73. This sample was a subset of a larger sample, from which three older adults were deleted because they did not meet our preset accuracy criterion of 90% correct on the identity judgement task at N = 1.

Tasks and procedure

We used a 1-Back and a 2-Back task, under three conditions. In all tasks, the nature and presentation format of the stimuli were identical. Stimuli were presented in blocks of 20, which appeared as either one (for N = 1) or two (for N = 2) virtual columns (with a 1.3-cm horizontal separation) of 20 (for N = 1) or 10 (for N = 2) items each. The stimuli were shown in alternating yellow and blue, on a black background. For N = 1, this implies that the stimuli appeared in blue and yellow alternately within one column, whereas for N = 2, one column consisted of yellow stimuli and the other of blue stimuli. The digits shown were 6 mm tall, and the horizontal separation between columns was 1.3 cm. In practice, only one digit was shown at any time; the order of presentation was a reading pattern: left-to-right, top-to-bottom. For the first row, a new digit was presented every 2,000 ms; from the second row on, participants pressed either of two keys to indicate their answer. The "/" key stood for "yes" (i.e., identical, or larger) and was masked with a piece of green tape; the "z" key stood for "no" (i.e., different, or smaller) and was masked with a piece of red tape. Participants were instructed to be both fast and accurate. As soon as the key was pressed, the next stimulus appeared.

In the identity condition, the subject decided whether the stimulus currently on screen and the stimulus immediately preceding it in the same column were identical. In the size comparison condition, the decision was whether the numerical value of the stimulus currently onscreen was larger than the numerical value of the stimulus immediately preceding it in the same column. In the task-switching condition, the tasks alternated on an ABAB . . . schedule, starting with the identity task. Even though the scheduling was predictable, tasks were additionally colour coded, with a yellow stimulus indicating the identity judgement task and a blue stimulus the relative size judgement task. For N = 2, the scheduling implied that the participants made identity judgements for the right-hand column and size judgements for the left-hand column. At all times, a word indicating the task (i.e., "identical?", and "larger?", respectively), printed in the relevant colour, was shown at the top of the screen. The first row of stimuli of each block did not require a response, and each item in that row was presented for 2,000 ms each. Presentation after the first row was terminated by the subject's response, which also initiated presentation of the next stimulus. After each block, the subject received feedback about both accuracy and reaction time. All participants were tested in a single session, typically lasting between 90 and 120 minutes, in the order: identity judgement, size judgement, task switching, and then again identity judgement, size judgement, and task switching. Within each condition, 11 trials of 20 stimuli each were presented; the first trial was discarded as practice. Half of the participants started the first half of the experiment performing first the N = 1 version within each condition, and then the N = 2 version; during the second half, $N = 2$ trials were presented first and then $N = 1$ trials. For the other half of the participants, the order was reversed. Participants were encouraged to take breaks between blocks.

Alpha level for all statistical testing was set at $p < .05$.

Results

Response times as a function of N

All RT analyses were conducted on correct responses only, and after removing RTs within each condition within each individual that occurred 3 interquartile ranges above or below the mean. Additionally, reaction times of 100 ms or less were considered anticipatory and were removed from the data set. In total, 1.6% of the data points of younger adults and 1.4% of the data points of older adults were discarded by applying this procedure.

Contrasting task switch conditions with the average of the two nonswitch conditions (see Figure 5) in a 2 (task switch vs. non-task-switch) by 2 (N) by 2 (younger vs. older) ANOVA yielded the following results (see Figure 5). Task switch trials took longer to complete than nonswitch trials, $F(1, 55) = 345.30$, $MSE = 18,494.85$. $N = 1$ yielded faster responses than $N = 2$, $F(1, 55) = 170.62$, $MSE = 35,536.00$. Task switching and N interacted in an under-additive fashion, such that switch costs were higher at $N = 1$ than at $N = 2$, $F(1, 55) = 26.07$, $MSE = 22,181.60$. Older adults were slower than younger adults, $F(1, 55) = 35.79$, $MSE = 271,652.58$. Switch trials yielded larger age differences than nonswitch trials, $F(1, 55) = 10.68$, $MSE = 18,494.85$, but this interaction disappeared after logarithmic transformation, $F(1, 55) = 0.10$, $MSE = 0.011$. Age differences were larger for $N = 2$ than for $N = 1$, $F(1, 55) = 17.17$, $MSE = 35,536.00$, and this interaction survived logarithmic transformation, $F(1, 55) = 7.29$, $MSE = 0.015$. This result was due to task switch trials only, as confirmed in a follow-up analysis. For single tasks only, the N by age interaction was nonsignificant, $F(1, 55) = 2.14$, $MSE = 0.014$; for the task switch condition, however, the

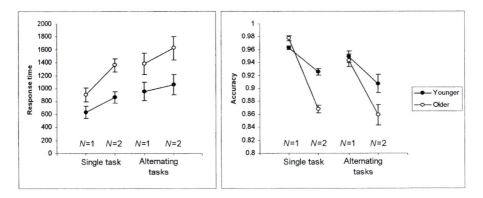

Figure 5.   Response time (correct trials) and accuracy data for Experiment 2 as a function of N and task-switching condition (single vs. alternating), separated by age group. Focus switch costs are indicated by performance differences between $N = 1$ and $N = 2$, task switch costs by differences between alternating tasks and single tasks. Error bars denote standard errors.

interaction was reliable, $F(1, 55) = 7.80$, $MSE = 0.012$. Despite this finding, the three-way interaction was not significant, $F(91, 55) = 0.62$, $MSE = 22,181.60$.

Accuracy as a function of N

Contrasting task switch conditions with the average of the two nonswitch conditions (see Figure 5) in a 2 (task switch vs. non-task-switch) by 2 (N) by 2 (younger vs. older) ANOVA, we found the following results. Task switch trials yielded lower accuracies than nonswitch trials, $F(1, 55) = 21.25$, $MSE = 0.001$, and $N = 2$ yielded lower accuracies than $N = 1$, $F(1, 55) = 267.53$, $MSE = 0.002$. Type of task and N did not interact significantly, $F(1, 55) = 2.74$, $MSE = 0.001$. Older adults performed more poorly than younger adults, $F(1, 55) = 4.40$, $MSE = 0.007$. Age differences were larger for $N = 2$ than for $N = 1$, $F(1, 55) = 13.08$, $MSE = 0.002$. The switching requirement did not influence age differences, $F(1, 55) = 2.66$, $MSE = 0.001$, nor was the three-way interaction significant, $F(1, 55) = 0.15$, $MSE = 0.001$.

Response times and accuracy in the identity judgement condition as a function of trial type

In the relative size judgement task, both trial types (i.e., "yes" or "no" trials) entail item updating. Therefore, the effects of updating can be examined only for the identity judgement condition. With regard to RT, the results mainly replicated those of Experiment 1. For focus switching—that is, for the contrast between $N = 1$ and $N = 2$—the main effect of trial type is significant, $F(1, 55) = 74.77$, $MSE = 29,021.18$ ("no" responses were slower), as well as the interaction between trial type and age, $F(1, 55) = 5.46$, $MSE = 29,021.18$. This age by trial type interaction did not survive logarithmic transformation, $F(1, 55) = 0.67$, $MSE = 0.02$. The three-way interaction again did not reach significance, $F(1, 55) = 1.05$, $MSE = 39,528.47$. A result that differed from that of Experiment 1 was that the interaction between trial type and N was not significant, $F(1, 55) = 0.49$, $MSE = 39,528.47$.

Analysis of the accuracy of "yes" versus "no" responses in the identity judgement condition yielded a direct replication of the effects obtained in Experiment 1. "No" responses were answered more accurately than "yes" responses, $F(1, 55) = 47.98$, $MSE = 0.004$. Trial type interacted with N, $F(1, 55) = 17.84$, $MSE = 0.003$ ($N = 2$ yielded larger trial type differences), but not with age group, $F(1, 55) = 0.03$, $MSE = 0.003$. The three-way interaction was likewise not significant, $F(1, 55) = 1.42$, $MSE = 0.003$.

Discussion

Focus switching, task switching, and updating in younger adults

As expected, each of the three executive control processes examined in the present experiment—focus switching, task switching, and updating—led to costs in both reaction time and accuracy. The results for focus switching replicated those of Experiment 1: Response time increased from $N = 1$ to $N = 2$, and accuracy decreased. We note one important exception: We failed to replicate the focus switching by updating interaction obtained for RTs in Experiment 1. The source of this discrepancy between Experiment 1 and Experiment 2 is unclear. The overadditive interaction obtained in accuracy in Experiment 1, however, did replicate in the present experiment.

The processes of focus switching and of task switching did not chain in a serial fashion, as indicated by an N by task switching interaction in RTs. The interaction was underadditive—that is, the focus switch cost was smaller in task-switching trials than in nonswitching trials. This indicates that the focus-switching and task-switching processes are not queued in a strictly sequential manner, but that some substages of these processes can proceed in parallel.

Age differences

With regard to age differences, the RT and accuracy data for the single tasks replicate the results obtained for focus switching from the identity N-Back task in Experiment 1: (a) A focus-switching cost is present in both RT and accuracy in older adults; (b) there is no age effect in the RT focus-switching cost; but (c) there is a larger focus-switching cost in accuracy in older adults than in younger adults, suggesting a higher frequency of item loss in older adults' working memory due to the focus-switching operation. The latter interaction takes the same form as that in Experiment 1: There are no age differences for $N = 1$, but reliable age differences in $N = 2$.

Adding the task-switching requirement did not differentially affect older adults' accuracy or RTs (after taking general slowing into account). This is an unexpected result, because previous research has shown that global task switching is age sensitive (for a review, see Verhaeghen & Cerella, 2002). However, recent research, published after we collected our data, has shown that predictability of task switches, especially in the presence of external cues, may eliminate age differences in global switch costs (Kray, Li, & Lindenberger, 2002). It should be noted that if predictability is the source of the absence of age effects in task switching, this makes the results with regard to age differences in focus switching (an eminently predictable and a clearly externally cued process) all the more remarkable.

The three-way age by focus by task switching interaction on (log-transformed) RTs was not significant. However, when we examined single task and task-switching conditions separately, we found a nonsignificant age by focus switching interaction in the single task condition and a reliable interaction in the task-switching condition. The conservative conclusion derived from the overall ANOVA would be that older adults are as proficient as younger adults in dealing with the requirements of the combined tasks. The analyses separated by the absence or presence of a task-switching requirement, however, would lead to the conclusion that the combination of focus switching and task switching does lead to larger age differences. Despite this controversial result, one conclusion is certain—namely, that there is an age-related dissociation between task switching and focus switching. The former is age insensitive, at least under the conditions of our experiment; the latter is age sensitive. This strongly suggests that these two processes are not identical and should be considered as at least partially independent.

Age differences in the updating process were not found to be age sensitive. The updating process did not take disproportionately longer in older adults than in younger adults, nor did it lead to a larger decrease in accuracy in older adults than in younger adults. This result is in complete accordance with the findings from Experiment 1.

GENERAL DISCUSSION

Age differences in executive processes have often proven to be elusive. Previous research has clearly shown that not all executive control processes are sensitive to age (e.g., Kramer, Humphrey, Larish, Logan, & Strayer, 1994; Verhaeghen & Cerella, 2002). The present study's main aim was to examine age differences in a process that has only recently been identified— namely, focus switching within working memory. We also investigated how this process and its age effects interact with task switching and with memory updating.

The focus switch process

Before we summarize the results regarding age differences, we review some of the characteristics of the focus-switching process as evidenced in our two experiments. First, focus switching leads to cost in both RT and accuracy. For young adults, the focus-switching process slowed RTs by about 240 ms. Our results indicate that this is truly an effect of focus switching, and not an artifact of increased working memory load. This was found in Experiment 1, in which the load was varied from 1 to 5 items. After the focus switch occurred (i.e., when the load increased from 1 to 2), additional load (from 2 to 3, etc.) did not result in an additional effect on the RTs of younger adults. The focus-switching process and memory-updating processes appear to queue in a serial fashion, as evidenced by pure additivity (Experiment 2) or overadditivity (Experiment 1). The latter finding indicates that the concatenation of processes might invoke a metaprocess or that shared resources need to be unlocked before updating can follow focus switching. Contrary to the results concerning updating, focus switching shows an underadditive interaction with task switching. We interpret this finding as indicating that task switching and focus switching can be executed partially in a parallel fashion.

Age differences in focus switching

How does performance of older adults compare to that of younger adults on the control process of focus switching? First and foremost, there is age stability in at least one important aspect of focus switching—namely, access times for items residing outside the focus. Response time costs, measured as the RT difference between $N = 1$ and $N = 2$, are not larger for older adults than for younger adults once general slowing is taken into account.

Some aspects of focus switching, however, do show clear age deficits. First, focus switching induces a differential cost in the availability of items. No age differences were found in accuracy for the item held in the focus of attention, but a clear age deficit emerged for the items residing outside the focus of attention. The effect appears to be tied to the focus switching process per se, because age differences in accuracy did not further increase reliably over $N = 2$ to $N = 5$. Second, the RT by N function for the items outside the focus of attention in older adults is not flat as in younger adults, but has a significant slope of about 70 ms/N, at least as seen in the group data.

These findings may have far-reaching implications for ageing theory. Many complex cognitive tasks must implicate some form of focus switching, and, therefore, the age difference observed in focus switching may be the root of age differences seen in other complex tasks, such as dual-task performance (for a meta-analysis, see Verhaeghen & Cerella, 2002; Verhaeghen et al., 2003), or in tasks requiring the coordination of multiple steps of processing (Mayr & Kliegl, 1993; Verhaeghen, Kliegl, & Mayr, 1997).

Age-related dissociations between control processes in working memory

The process of item updating was age invariant in both experiments. In the second experiment, global task switching also was found to be age invariant. As explained above, it is possible that the latter result is due to the predictable nature of task switching in our experiment (see also Kray et al., 2002). Additionally, no age differences were evident in the effects of combining updating and focus switching. This indicates that if a metaprocess (such as monitoring or scheduling) is involved when focus switching and updating are combined, this metaprocess itself is age insensitive. It remains, however, possible (see Experiment 2) that compounding task switching and focus switching leads to larger age effects than those present in each of the processes separately. The dissociations found here—focus switching is age sensitive, task switching and working-memory updating are not—strongly suggest that focus switching is a process in its own right and not simply a different manifestation of a general switching ability. It is also not simply a different manifestation of memory overwriting and updating. Therefore, focus switching may well be a cognitive primitive, not reducible to any other control process.

REFERENCES

Ashby, F. G., Tein, J. Y., & Balakrishnan, J. D. (1993). Response time distributions in memory scanning. *Journal of Mathematical Psychology*, *37*, 526–555.

Atkinson, R. C., & Shiffrin, R. M. (1968). Human memory: A proposed system and its control process. In K. W. Spence & J. T. Spence (Eds.), *The psychology of learning and motivation* (Vol. 2, pp. 89–195). New York: Academic Press.

Basak, C., & Verhaeghen, P. (2003). Subitizing speed, subitizing range, counting speed, the Stroop effect, and aging: Capacity differences, speed equivalence. *Psychology and Aging*, *18*, 240–249.

Cerella, J. (1990). Aging and information processing rate. In J. E. Birren & K. W. Schaie (Eds.), *Handbook of the psychology of aging* (3rd ed., pp. 201–221). San Diego, CA: Academic Press.

Cowan, N. (1995). *Attention and memory: An integrated framework*. New York: Oxford University Press.

Cowan, N. (2001). The magical number 4 in short-term memory: A reconsideration of mental storage capacity. *Behavioral and Brain Sciences*, *24*, 87–185.

Faust, M. E., Balota, D. A., Spieler, D. H., & Ferraro, F. R. (1999). Individual differences in information-processing rate and amount: Implications for group differences in response latency. *Psychological Bulletin*, *125*, 777–799.

Garavan, H. (1998). Serial attention within working memory. *Memory and Cognition*, *26*, 263–276.

Hartley, A. A. (2002). *Aging and working memory: Impaired and spared abilities to maintain multiple working memory registers without cost*. Manuscript submitted for publication.

Hartley, A. A., & Little, D. M. (1999). Age-related differences and similarities in dual-task interference. *Journal of Experimental Psychology: General*, *128*, 416–449.

Hartman, M., Dumas, J., & Nielsen, C. (2001). Age differences in updating working memory: Evidence from the delayed-matching-to-sample test. *Aging, Neuropsychology, and Cognition*, *8*, 14–35.

Hasher, L., & Zacks, R. T. (1988). Working memory, comprehension, and aging: A review and a new view. In G. H. Bower (Ed.), *The psychology of learning and motivation* (Vol. 22, pp. 193–225). San Diego, CA: Academic Press.

Hasher, L., Zacks, R. T., & May, C. P. (1999). Inhibitory control, circadian arousal, and age. In D. Gopher & A. Koriat (Eds.), *Attention & performance XVII: Cognitive regulation of performance: Interaction of theory and application* (pp. 653–675). Cambridge, MA: MIT Press.

Hockley, W. E. (1984). Analysis of RT distributions in the study of cognitive processes. *Journal of Experimental Psychology: Learning, Memory, and Cognition, 10*, 598–615.

Kausler, D. H. (1991). *Experimental psychology, cognition, and human aging* (2nd ed.). New York: Springer-Verlag.

Kramer, A. F., Humphrey, D. G., Larish, J. F., Logan, G. D., & Strayer, D. L. (1994). Aging and inhibition: Beyond a unitary view of inhibitory processing in attention. *Psychology and Aging, 9*, 491–512.

Kray, J., Li, K. Z. H., & Lindenberger, U. (2002). Age-related changes in task-switching components: The role of task uncertainty. *Brain and Cognition, 49*, 363–381.

Mayr, U., & Kliegl, R. (1993). Sequential and coordinative complexity: Age-based processing limitations in figural transformations. *Journal of Experimental Psychology: Learning, Memory, and Cognition, 19*, 1297–1320.

Mayr, U., Spieler, D. H., & Kliegl, R. (2001). *Aging and executive control*. Hove, UK: Psychology Press.

McDowd, J. M., & Shaw, R. J. (2000). Aging and attention: A functional prespective. In F. I. M. Craik & T. A. Salthouse (Eds.), *Handbook of aging and cognition* (2nd ed., pp. 221–292). Hillsdale, NJ: Lawrence Erlbaum Associates, Inc.

McElree, B. (2001). Working memory and focal attention. *Journal of Experimental Psychology: Learning, Memory, and Cognition, 27*, 817–835.

McElree, B. M., & Dosher, B. A. (1989). Serial position and set size in short term memory: The time course of recognition. *Journal of Experimental Psychology: General, 118*, 346–373.

Miyake, A., Friedman, N. P., Emerson, M. J., Witzki, A. H., & Howerter, A. (2000). The unity and diversity of executive functions and their contributions to complex "frontal lobe" tasks: A latent variable analysis. *Cognitive Psychology, 41*, 49–100.

Oberauer, K. (2002). Access to information in working memory: Exploring the focus of attention. *Journal of Experimental Psychology: Learning, Memory, and Cognition, 28*, 411–421.

Perfect, T. J., & Maylor, E. A. (2000). Rejecting the dull hypothesis: The relation between method and theory in cognitive aging. In T. J. Perfect & E. A. Maylor (Eds.), *Models of cognitive aging* (pp. 1–18). Oxford: Oxford University Press.

Rubin, D. C., & Wenzel, A. E. (1996). One hundred years of forgetting: A quantitative description of retention. *Psychological Review, 103*, 734–760.

Salthouse, T. A. (1985). *A theory of cognitive aging*. Amsterdam: North-Holland.

Salthouse, T. A. (1991). *Theoretical perspectives on cognitive aging*. Hillsdale, NJ: Lawrence Erlbaum Associates, Inc.

Salthouse, T. A. (1996). The processing-speed theory of adult age differences in cognition. *Psychological Review, 103*, 403–428.

Sternberg, S. (1969). Memory-scanning: Mental processes revealed by reaction-time experiments. *American Scientist, 57*, 421–457.

Sternberg, S. (1998). Discovering mental processing stages: The method of additive factors. In D. Scarborough & S. Sternberg (Eds.), *An invitation to cognitive science: Vol. 4. Methods, models, and conceptual issues* (pp. 703–863). Cambridge, MA: MIT Press.

Sternberg, S. (2001). Separate modifiability, mental modules, and the use of pure and composite measures to reveal them. *Acta Psychologica, 106*, 147–246.

Van der Linden, M., Brédart, S., & Beerten, A. (1994). Age-related differences in updating working memory. *British Journal of Psychology, 85*, 145–152.

Verhaeghen, P., & Cerella, J. (2002). Aging, executive control, and attention: A review of meta-analyses. *Neuroscience and Biobehavioral Reviews, 26*, 849–857.

Verhaeghen, P., & De Meersman, L. (1998a). Aging and negative priming: A meta-analysis. *Psychology and Aging, 13*, 435–444.

Verhaeghen, P., & De Meersman, L. (1998b). Aging and the Stroop effect: A meta-analysis. *Psychology and Aging, 13*, 120–126.

Verhaeghen, P., Kliegl, R., & Mayr, U. (1997). Sequential and coordinative complexity in time–accuracy function for mental arithmetic. *Psychology and Aging, 12*, 555–564.

Verhaeghen, P., & Salthouse, T. A. (1997). Meta-analyses of age–cognition relations in adulthood: Estimates of linear and non-linear age effects and structural models. *Psychological Bulletin*, *122*, 231–249.

Verhaeghen, P., Steitz, D. W., Sliwinski, M. J., & Cerella, J. (2003). Aging and dual-task performance: A meta analysis. *Psychology and Aging*, *18*, 443–460.

Wasylyshyn, C., Verhaeghen, P., & Sliwinski, M. (2003). *Aging and task switching: A meta-analysis*. Manuscript submitted for publication.

PrEview proof published online 7 July 2004

THE QUARTERLY JOURNAL OF EXPERIMENTAL PSYCHOLOGY
2005, 58A (1), 155–168

Ψ Psychology Press
Taylor & Francis Group

Processing speed, executive function, and age differences in remembering and knowing

David Bunce and Anna Macready

Goldsmiths College, University of London, London, UK

A group of young ($n = 52$, $M = 23.27$ years) and old ($n = 52$, $M = 68.62$ years) adults studied two lists of semantically unrelated nouns. For one list a time of 2 s was allowed for encoding, and for the other, 5 s. A recognition test followed where participants classified their responses according to Gardiner's (1988) remember–know procedure. Age differences for remembering and knowing were minimal in the faster 2-s encoding condition. However, in the longer 5-s encoding condition, younger persons produced significantly more remember responses, and older adults a greater number of know responses. This dissociation suggests that in the longer encoding condition, younger adults utilized a greater level of elaborative rehearsal governed by executive processes, whereas older persons employed maintenance rehearsal involving short-term memory. Statistical control procedures, however, found that independent measures of processing speed accounted for age differences in remembering and knowing and that independent measures of executive control had little influence. The findings are discussed in the light of contrasting theoretical accounts of recollective experience in old age.

Tulving's (1985) distinction between autonoetic and noetic forms of consciousness has provided the conceptual basis for a substantial amount of research into episodic memory. Autonoetic consciousness is associated with the type of memory that allows us to intimately recreate and relive subjective experiences in our past. By contrast, noetic consciousness accompanies memories related to the storage of knowledge and facts in the absence of such intimate recollections of their acquisition. This distinction forms the basis of Gardiner's (1988) operational classification that separates recognition memory into remembering and knowing. Gardiner and Richardson-Klavehn (2000) propose that *remembering* involves autonoetic consciousness and relates to personal experiences of the past that recreate previous events and experiences with a clear sense of intimately reliving them. In contrast, *knowing* involves noetic consciousness, and concerns knowledge that is held in a more impersonal way, and does not possess the awareness of reliving events and experiences.

Although an accumulating body of research has investigated age in relation to remembering and knowing, there is good reason for further work in the area. For instance, the proposition that autonoetic and noetic forms of consciousness are supported by differing

Correspondence should be addressed to David Bunce, Department of Psychology, Goldsmiths College, University of London, London, SE14 6NW, UK. Email: d.bunce@gold.ac.uk

http://www.tandf.co.uk/journals/pp/02724987.html   DOI:10.1080/02724980443000197

neural mechanisms (Wheeler, Stuss, & Tulving, 1997) suggests that valuable insights may be gained into ageing processes by investigating remembering and knowing in young and old adults. Additionally, several studies have set out to explain age differences in remembering and knowing by taking into account measures of executive or frontal lobe function (Bunce, 2003; Parkin & Walter, 1992; Perfect & Dasgupta, 1997; Perfect, Williams, & Anderton-Brown, 1995) or processing speed (Loevden, Roennlund, & Nilsson, 2002), or by investigating both types of measure (Clarys, Isingrini, & Gana, 2002). In the present study, we extend this work by investigating age variation in remembering and knowing, having experimentally varied the time allowed for encoding operations. By taking into account independent measures of executive function and processing speed, we seek to shed further light on the mechanisms that underlie recollective experience in old age.

A review of the existing literature suggests that although some studies have found an age-related decrease in remembering (e.g., Bunce, 2003; Loevden et al., 2002; Parkin & Walter, 1992; Perfect & Dasgupta, 1997; Perfect et al., 1995, Exp. 1; Schacter, Koutstaal, Johnson, Gross, & Angell, 1997), others have not (e.g., Mark & Rugg, 1998; Perfect et al., 1995, Exp. 2). One explanation for the minimal age variance found in some studies may stem from the type of processing required during encoding operations. For example, although Perfect and Dasgupta (1997) found an overall age effect for remembering, that effect was minimal when the degree of elaboration at encoding was taken into account; the greater the depth of encoding in older persons, the more age differences in recollective experience were minimized. Similarly, the provision of cognitive or environmental support at encoding, in order to structure or enhance the depth of processing, attenuates age differences relative to conditions where no such support was provided (Loevden et al., 2002). Indeed, cognitive support at encoding was found to be particularly beneficial to remembering in older adults of lower frontal lobe function (Bunce, 2003). Turning to research findings for know responses, again the evidence is inconsistent in that some studies suggest this type of recognition to increase with age (Parkin & Walter, 1992; Perfect et al., 1995), whereas others do not (e.g., Bunce, 2003; Mark & Rugg, 1998; Perfect & Dasgupta, 1997). Here too there is the suggestion that elaboration or structuring at encoding moderates age differences (Perfect et al., 1995), presumably due to the greater depth of encoding that such cognitive operations involve. In sum, it appears that there are inconsistencies in findings relating to age differences in both remembering and knowing. However, there is evidence to suggest that elaboration or structuring of information at encoding may be influential in determining age differences in both types of recognition.

Regarding underlying neural mechanisms, Wheeler et al. (1997) suggest that one of the key roles played by the anterior regions of the frontal cortex is to confer conscious awareness, or autonoetic consciousness, on episodic memory. This facilitates the ability to intimately relive the past that Gardiner and Richardson-Klavehn (2000) refer to. The role of the prefrontal cortex in remembering, or recollective experience, is supported by imaging work showing right dorsolateral activation during recollection of the sociotemporal context of a word's previous occurrence (Henson, Rugg, Shallice, Josephs, & Dolan, 1999). Indeed, it is suggested that prefrontal involvement in encoding operations such as semantic elaboration and organization (both conscious processes) provide inputs to the medial temporal system (Brewer, Zhao, Desmond, Glover, & Gabrieli, 1998; Wagner et al., 1998), an area displaying elevated activation during recollective experience (Eldridge, Knowlton, Furmanski, Bookheimer, & Engel, 2000).

However, the prefrontal cortex undergoes some of the most marked neurological changes with age (Uylings & de Brabander, 2002), and theoretically such changes have been held to account for many of the cognitive deficits exhibited in old age (West, 1996). Given the putative role of the prefrontal cortex in conferring autonoetic consciousness during remembering, the foregoing suggests that age differences in remembering will be accounted for by individual differences in executive or frontal lobe measures. The few studies that have investigated this possibility have produced conflicting results, in that two (Bunce, 2003; Parkin & Walter, 1992) have found evidence that measures of frontal lobe functioning account for age differences in remembering, and others have found weak (Perfect & Dasgupta, 1997) or no evidence (Perfect et al., 1995). The reason for these discrepant findings is not immediately clear, as in all these studies age ranges have been similar, word lists have been used, and there has been considerable overlap in behavioural measures of frontal lobe function. Additional research is required, not least because all of those studies are confirmatory in nature (Parkin & Java, 2000; Perfect, 1997). That is, the explanatory value of executive or frontal lobe measures was not contrasted with measures arising from other theoretical perspectives of cognitive ageing. For instance, Salthouse (e.g., 1991) has argued that general processing speed accounts for much of the age-related variance in memory and other cognitive domains and has produced numerous empirical investigations that support this view (see Salthouse, 1996). In relation to recollective experience, one study found that age differences in remembering were eliminated after controlling for processing speed (Loevden et al., 2002), and another that took both working memory and processing speed into account (Clarys et al., 2002) concluded that the latter construct was more influential in explaining age variance in remembering.

In the present study we gathered further evidence of relations between processing speed, executive function, and age differences in remembering and knowing. In the experiment, participants performed in two conditions where either 2s or 5s were allowed for encoding semantically unrelated words. Previous research (Gardiner, Gawlik, & Richardson-Klavehn, 1994) led us to expect that the longer encoding time would enable a greater level of elaborative rehearsal and structuring of information. Because these cognitive operations require executive processes supported by the neural structures of the prefrontal cortex, a greater level of remembering was expected in this condition. Indeed, Gardiner and colleagues demonstrated that extended encoding time is associated with enhanced recollective experience in younger adults. However, none of the previous studies that have manipulated encoding time in respect to recognition in older adults (e.g., Craik & Rabinowitz, 1985; Wahlin, Backman, & Winblad, 1995) have distinguished between remembering and knowing. Although there is no empirical evidence of whether additional encoding time will enhance older adults' recollective experience, frontal lobe accounts of cognitive ageing (West, 1996) suggest that older persons would be less likely to initiate the elaborative rehearsal and structured encoding strategies that may aid conscious awareness and, therefore, produce fewer remember responses in the longer encoding condition. Regarding age variation in know responses, the absence of any form of cognitive support to guide elaboration and structuring of encoded information in either condition suggests that a greater proportion of know responses would be found in older persons. According to Gardiner et al. (1994), such responding is underpinned by maintenance rehearsal in longer encoding conditions. These predictions were tested in a sample of younger and older adults. In addition, we recorded independent measures of processing speed and executive function. This allowed us to assess how far age differences in remembering and knowing were associated with elaborative processes related to executive control, or the capacity to process information more rapidly.

Method

Participants

A total of 104 persons (49 men) participated in the study, divided into younger ($n = 52$, aged 18 to 36 years) and older ($n = 52$, aged 61 to 78 years) age groups. Younger adults were students of the University of London, and older participants were recruited through advertising and contacts at local church groups and charity organizations. The older participants predominantly came from professional backgrounds, and the two age groups were screened using the National Adult Reading Test (NART) Full Scale IQ (Nelson, 1982). Adults over 65 were screened also for signs of dementia using the Mini-Mental State Examination (MMSE: Folstein, Folstein, & McHugh, 1975). All those taking part in the present study scored 25 or more on that measure. Demographic data for the two age groups are presented in Table 2 (see later).

Materials

Episodic memory task.   Two lists of 12 semantically unrelated concrete nouns were prepared. In one condition, at study, words from one of the lists were presented individually and bimodally (spoken by the experimenter and presented on cards simultaneously) for 2 s each. In the other condition, words from the other list were presented bimodally but for 5 s each. Lists used for the faster and slower encoding conditions and the order in which conditions were administered were counterbalanced within each age group. Participants performed both conditions during a single experimental session.

A recognition test was administered after participants had completed a distracter task (one of either the executive function or processing speed tasks detailed below) lasting approximately four minutes. The 12 words were intermixed with 12 "lure" concrete nouns. Participants circled items they recognized and in doing so classified them as either "remember" or "know" following the procedure described by Gardiner (1988). The 48 words used in the experiment fell within the frequency range of 401 to 792 words per million ($M = 550.35$).

Executive function tasks.   Two measures relating to frontal and executive function were administered. In the FAS Word Fluency Test (Benton, Hamsher, Varney, & Spreen, 1983), participants orally generated as many words as possible beginning with F, A, or S. One minute was allowed for each letter. Names of places or people and multiple words with the same root were disallowed. The total score for the three letters is reported here. The second task was the backward digit-span (BDS) subtest of the Wechsler Adult Intelligence Scale-R (WAIS-R: Wechsler, 1981). Here, participants were required to repeat in reverse order sequences of digits that increased in length from the initial trial of two digits. For each sequence length, two trials were administered, and a score of 1 was awarded for each correct trial. The test terminated if both trials in a particular sequence were incorrect.

Processing speed.   Two measures were used to assess this construct. The first was the digit-symbol substitution subtest of the WAIS. The task involved a sheet of paper upon which a table of paired digits and symbols was displayed. Below the table were rows of paired boxes. In the upper box a digit was displayed, and the participant's task was to fill in the blank lower box with the appropriate symbol from the table. Ninety seconds were allowed for the task, and the final score was the number of correctly completed symbols in that time.

The second task was a PC-administered four-choice reaction time task based upon that of Bunce, Barrowclough, and Morris (1996). Briefly, four black circles appeared psuedorandomly in one of four positions (left, right, above, or below) a central fixation cross on the PC screen. Participants responded by pressing spatially corresponding keyboard keys (S = left upper; C = left lower; L = right upper; M = right lower) with the middle and index fingers of their left and right hands. A total of 20 practice trials were administered, followed by 100 test trials. Speed and accuracy were emphasized in the instructions. Here we present mean reaction time for correct responses.

Procedure

Participants attended the laboratory by appointment. On arrival they completed an informed consent form, and then those aged 65 and over were screened using the MMSE. At this point, several physiological measures were recorded relating to another part of the study. A self-completion questionnaire recording biographical information was administered, followed by the NART. Participants then performed the first of the two recognition conditions (2-s or 5-s encoding), after which processing speed and executive function measures were administered. To finish, participants performed the second recognition condition. Following debriefing, those who were nonstudents were paid £6.50 for participation. Psychology students taking part in the study received course credits required for completing their degree.

Results

Bivariate associations between the main variables in the study and descriptive data for the recognition variables are presented in Tables 1 and 2, respectively. In Table 1 it can be seen that age was significantly associated with higher NART scores but poorer performance on both processing speed measures. The relationships between age and executive function measures were statistically unreliable. Significant negative correlations with remember words in the 5-s condition suggest that older adults were less able to utilize the additional encoding time in this condition. Associations were investigated further through a series of analysis of variance (ANOVA), where condition (2-s and 5-s encoding time) served as the within-subjects factor, and age (young or old) as the between-subjects factor. As preliminary T tests found that the older group recorded significantly higher NART scores ($p < .01$, see Table 2), that variable was entered as a covariate in all of the ANOVAs reported below. In each condition, the numbers of hits and false alarms were calculated for remember and know responses. Although signal detection theory metrics take response bias into account, there are uncertainties concerning their use in relation to know responses (Jacoby, Yonelinas, & Jennings, 1997). Therefore, in order to adjust for possible response bias in the present investigation, we elected to analyse hits adjusted for false alarms (i.e., hits−false alarms).

Remember responses

Hits. Both main effects for age group and condition were statistically unreliable ($ps > .34$). However, the Age × Condition interaction was significant, $F(1, 101) = 4.68$, $\eta^2 = .044$, $p = .033$. Consideration of Table 2 suggests that although the performance of the younger group benefited when more time was allowed for encoding, that was not the case for older individuals. Pairwise comparisons confirmed this impression in that for the younger group, the 5-s condition produced a significantly greater number of hits than did the 2-s condition ($p < .001$), whereas that comparison was nonsignificant in the older group. The

TABLE 1
Bivariate correlation matrix

Variable	1	2	3	4	5	6	7	8	9	10	11	12	13	14	15	16
1. Age group	—															
2. Gender	−.02	—														
3. NART	.35**	−.11	—													
4. Exec func	.06	−.07	.41**	—												
5. FAS	.11	−.08	.41**	.84**	—											
6. BDS	−.13	−.06	.20*	.76**	.30**	—										
7. Speed	−.79***	.08	−.24*	.00	−.05	.21*	—									
8. DSST	−.65***	.19	−.11	.21*	.14	.25*	.84**	—								
9. 4 choice RT	.68***	.06	−.21*	.04	−.02	−.13	−.88***	−.50**	—							
10. R hits 2s	.00	.24*	−.05	−.03	.00	−.03	.14	.12	−.13	—						
11. R hits 5s	−.21*	.13	−.12	.04	.09	.04	.24*	.14	−.30**	.53**	—					
12. Adj R hits 2s	−.03	.23*	−.02	−.01	.02	−.01	.19	.15	−.17	.99***	.52**	—				
13. Adj R hits 5s	−.24*	.13	−.09	.05	.10	.05	.27**	.15	−.33**	.53**	.99***	.53**	—			
14. K hits 2s	−.07	−.22*	.22*	.06	.01	.07	.03	.08	.02	−.66***	−.45***	−.63***	−.43**	—		
15. K hits 5s	.13	−.08	.13	−.06	−.08	−.05	−.12	−.05	.18	−.50**	−.87***	−.47***	−.85***	.53**	—	
16. Adj K hits 2s	−.12	−.25**	.23*	.07	.04	.07	.06	.09	−.02	−.65***	−.44***	−.61***	−.42**	.96**	.52**	—
17. Adj K hits 5s	.06	−.06	.14	−.06	−.07	−.05	−.05	.00	.10	−.34**	−.78***	−.36**	−.75***	.50**	.92**	.52**

Note: NART = National Adult Reading Test; FAS = Verbal fluency; BDS = Backward digit span; DSST = Digit symbol substitution task; R = remember; K = know; Adj = adjusted; Variables 4 and 7 are based upon factor scores.

$*p < .05$; $**p < .01$.

TABLE 2
Means scores for demographic, executive function, processing speed,
and recognition variables for young and old groups

	Encoding time[a]	Young		Old		Overall	
		M	SD	M	SD	M	SD
Demographic							
Age[b]		23.27	4.86	68.62	4.30	45.94	23.24
Women[c]		53.85		51.92		52.89	
NART		107.52	8.20	114.06	9.69	110.79	9.52
Executive function							
Verbal fluency		42.62	10.24	45.04	8.06	43.83	11.42
Backward DS		7.06	1.98	6.58	1.81	6.82	1.90
Processing speed							
Digit symbol		71.42	10.94	52.29	11.38	61.86	14.69
4-CRT[d]		381.01	52.96	503.05	78.31	442.03	90.47
Remember							
Hits	2	5.81	3.33	5.82	3.39	5.82	3.34
	5	7.40	3.26	5.98	3.40	6.69	3.39
False alarms	2	0.12	0.32	0.31	0.61	0.22	0.50
	5	0.04	0.19	0.23	0.51	0.14	0.40
Adjusted hits	2	5.69	3.35	5.51	3.41	5.60	3.37
	5	7.37	3.25	5.75	3.41	6.56	3.41
Know							
Hits	2	3.19	2.50	2.82	2.53	3.01	2.51
	5	2.96	2.74	3.69	3.10	3.33	2.93
False alarms	2	0.37	0.69	0.61	0.77	0.49	0.74
	5	0.33	0.97	0.65	1.66	0.49	1.36
Adjusted hits	2	2.83	2.52	2.22	2.44	2.52	2.49
	5	2.64	3.04	3.04	3.66	2.84	3.36

Note: NART: National Adult Reading Test. DS: Digit span. CRT: Choice reaction time.
[a]In s. [b]In years. [c]In percentages. [d]In ms.

comparison for young and old scores in the 5-s condition was close to conventional levels of statistical reliability ($p = .06$); younger persons produced a greater number of hits. This comparison was nonsignificant in the 2-s condition.

False alarms.   Analysis of false alarms revealed the age main effect to be significant, $F(1, 101) = 18.35$, $\eta^2 = .154$, $p < .001$. Older adults produced a greater number of false alarms than did younger adults (see Table 2). Neither the main effect for condition nor the Age $\times$ Condition interaction was statistically reliable ($ps > .72$).

Adjusted hits.   Both main effects for age and condition were statistically unreliable ($ps >$ .16). However, the two-way interaction between those factors did attain significance, $F(1, 101) = 4.48$, $\eta^2 = .043$, $p = .037$. Again Table 2 suggests that older individuals did not benefit from the additional encoding time in the 5-s encoding condition to the same extent as did younger adults. A pairwise comparison between conditions was significant ($p < .001$) in the younger but not in the older group. Although the comparison between young and old groups in the 5-s condition was statistically reliable ($p = .023$), it was nonsignificant in the 2-s condition.

In sum, the findings suggest that the longer encoding period enabled younger adults to produce a greater number of remember responses. The age difference was minimal in the 2-s encoding condition.

Know responses

Hits.   The main effects for age and condition failed to reach statistical significance ($ps >$ .11). However, the Age × Condition interaction was statistically reliable, $F(1, 101) = 6.46$, $\eta^2 = .060$, $p = .013$. The impression conveyed by Table 2, that older adults produced more hits in the 5-s condition, was confirmed by a pairwise comparison in that group ($p < .01$). None of the other comparisons achieved statistical significance.

False alarms.   In respect to this variable, the main effect for age was significant, $F(1, 101) = 4.78$, $\eta^2 = .045$, $p = .031$. Older adults produced more false alarms. However, neither the condition main effect nor the two-way interaction achieved statistical significance ($ps > .58$).

Adjusted hits.   Although the main effects for age and condition were both nonsignificant ($ps > .31$), the two-way interaction between those factors was statistically reliable, $F(1, 101) = 4.09$, $\eta^2 = .039$, $p = .046$. Table 2 indicates that this was due to a higher number of responses produced by older persons in the 5-s condition. A pairwise comparison between conditions in the older group was significant ($p = .029$), whereas the equivalent comparison in the younger group was nonsignificant. The comparison between young and old in the 2-s condition also achieved statistical significance ($p = .023$).

To summarize, the foregoing analyses indicate that the longer encoding time resulted in a greater number of know responses in older persons. In the younger group, encoding time does not appear to have influenced this type of responding to the same degree.

The mediating role of processing speed and executive function

A major objective of the present research was to evaluate the extent to which either executive function or processing speed accounted for age differences in remembering and knowing where they were found. Before that objective was addressed, however, it was important to confirm statistically that the respective variables factored appropriately. Therefore, the verbal fluency, backward digit span, digit symbol substitution, and choice reaction time (RT) variables were subjected to principal component analysis with varimax rotation. Two components emerged. The first related to processing speed and comprised the digit symbol substitution and choice RT variables (explaining 37.98% of the variance). Executive function

TABLE 3
Principal component analysis rotated factor matrix

	Component	
	Processing speed	*Executive function*
FAS	−.046	**.836**
Backward DS	.206	**.763**
Digit symbol	**.837**	.207
CRT	**−.880**	.037

Note: FAS: Verbal fluency. DS: Digit span. CRT: Choice reaction time.
Factor structures emphasized in bold.

formed the second component (verbal fluency and backward digit span), accounting for 33.10 percent of the variance. The rotated factor matrix is presented in Table 3 with the factor structures emphasized in bold. These results are consistent with the conceptual distinction made between executive function and processing speed.

Hierarchical multiple regression was used to assess the extent to which processing speed or executive function explained the significant Age × Encoding Time interactions relating to remember and know words described earlier. Two models were evaluated. In the first, recognition scores from the 5-s condition were regressed on scores from the 2-s condition at Step 1. It is important to note that the residual from this step represents the benefits to recognition performance associated with the longer encoding condition. At Step 2, NART scores were added for control purposes due to the significant between-group differences in this variable, and at Step 3 age was entered. In Model 2, Steps 1 and 2 were the same as those for Model 1. However, at Step 3 the factor scores for either processing speed or executive function were added, and at Step 4 age was entered. The two crucial elements of this procedure are that in Model 1, age at Step 3 attains statistical significance, whereas in Model 2 age is rendered nonsignificant by the inclusion of the factor scores at Step 3. The results of these analyses are presented in Table 4.

Processing speed.   For remember words, the addition of age in Model 1 significantly accounted for 4% of the residual variance attributable to the longer encoding condition for both hits and adjusted hits. Notably in both analyses, when factors scores for processing speed were taken into account in Model 2, age became nonsignificant. In relation to know words, age significantly added 3% of the variance to hits in Model 1, and this too was rendered statistically unreliable when processing speed was controlled for. With regard to adjusted hits for know words, age failed to attain significance in Model 1.

As the two processing speed measures vary to some degree in the cognitive operations they require (the choice RT task is a relatively pure measure of psychomotor speed, whereas the digit symbol substitution task involves a substantial memory component), it was of interest to assess which of the two variables was most influential in accounting for the age-related variance. Therefore, the regression analyses were repeated, but on this occasion the raw scores for choice RT and digit symbol were added separately at Step 3. In each analysis, beta weights for choice RT were significant, whereas those for digit symbol failed to attain statistical

TABLE 4
Hierarchical multiple regression: The mediating influence of processing
speed on age differences in remembering and knowing

			Model 1			Model 2[a]		
		Step	Beta	R^2	Step	Beta	R^2
Remember	DV = Hits 5 s	1. Hits 2 s	.53	.28***	3. Speed	.16	.02
		2. NART	−.09	.01	4. Age gp	−.20	.01
		3. Age gp	−.21	.04*			
	DV = Adj hits 5 s	1. Adj hits 2 s	.53	.28**	3. Speed	.16	.03
		2. NART	−.08	.01	4. Age gp	−.24	.02
		3. Age gp	−.22	.04**			
Know	DV = Hits 5 s	1. Hits 2 s	.53	.28***	3. Speed	−.14	.02
		2. NART	.01	.00	4. Age gp	.18	.01
		3. Age gp	.19	.03*			
	DV = Adj hits 5 s	1. Adj hits 2 s	.52	.27***			
		2. NART	.02	.00			
		3. Age gp	.14	.02			

Note: Step 1, $df = 1, 102$; Step 2, $df = 1, 101$; Step 3, $df = 1, 100$; Step 4, $df = 1, 99$.
Adj = adjusted; gp = group.
[a]In Model 2, Steps 1 and 2 are as in Model 1.
*$p < .05$; **$p < .02$; ***$p < .01$.

significance. Thus, it appears that psychomotor speed was more influential in accounting for the age-related variance reported in the foregoing analyses.

Executive function. In these analyses, factors scores for executive function were added at Step 3 of Model 2. In all analyses, they failed to account for any of the age-related variance in either remember or know words. Further analyses where the raw scores for verbal fluency and backward digit span were entered separately into the regression equations did not modify these null findings. Therefore, it appears that executive function, as measured by the variables in this experiment, does not account for age differences in the utilization of encoding time, in respect to either remember or know words.

Discussion

This is the first study to investigate age differences in remembering and knowing, having manipulated the time available for encoding operations and having additionally recorded independent measures of executive function and processing speed. Two important findings were obtained. First, although age differences in remembering were minimal in the shorter 2-s condition, the results suggested that younger persons used the longer encoding period (5 s) more effectively and produced significantly more correct remember responses than did older adults. In contrast, however, older persons produced more know responses than younger adults in that longer encoding condition. This dissociation is consistent with the view that younger persons were more able to utilize the longer encoding time to initiate elaborative rehearsal, and this was related to their greater recollective experience. By contrast, the findings suggest that older persons employed maintenance rehearsal, and this was reflected in their elevated know responding. Second, although effect sizes were modest, processing speed but not executive function explained age differences in both remembering and knowing in the longer encoding condition.

Broadly, the findings are consistent with prior research suggesting an age-related decrease in recollective experience (e.g., Bunce, 2003; Parkin & Walter, 1992; Perfect & Dasgupta, 1997; Perfect et al., 1995; Schacter et al., 1997) and confirm that the level of know responding increases with age in the absence of structuring that aids elaboration and organizational strategies at encoding (Perfect et al., 1995). Importantly though, the dissociation in age gradients for remember and know words in the longer encoding condition suggests that the time allowed for encoding was related to age differences in the level of conscious awareness associated with recognition. For younger adults, the results are in line with work (Gardiner et al., 1994) showing that longer encoding time, and the elevated elaborative rehearsal that this allows, increases remember responding. This suggests that executive control processes governing elaborative rehearsal underpinned the observed age differences in remembering. A key question therefore, was whether the factor scores for the executive function measures accounted for the age-related variance in remembering in that longer condition. This would provide further evidence that greater elaborative rehearsal and structuring in the 5-s condition underpinned younger adults' greater recollective experience. The findings of the regression analyses provided little support for this proposal. Executive function factor scores failed to attenuate the age differences in remembering associated with the longer encoding condition. Instead, perceptual processing speed accounted for the age-related variance in both remembering and knowing.

This finding is in agreement with two earlier studies that found processing speed to explain age differences in recollective experience (Clarys et al., 2002; Loevden et al., 2002). However, given the widespread evidence that decline in processing speed is one of the most marked features of cognitive ageing, in the present context it is perhaps not surprising that perceptual speed accounted for age differences in remembering and knowing in the longer encoding condition; given extra time, younger adults are able to process more information, and this is likely to be explained by independent measures of processing speed. The key point, however, is the qualitative dissociation in conscious awareness distinguishing the two age groups. It appears that for younger adults, elaboratively processing more information resulted in a greater level of conscious awareness in recognition. For older adults, it seems that although more information was processed in the longer encoding condition, that processing was shallower and resulted in elevated know responding. This latter finding suggests that older adults used a greater level of maintenance rehearsal—that is, nonassociative rehearsal processes that serve to maintain material in short-term memory (Woodward, Bjork, & Jongeward, 1973).

The lack of association between executive function measures and age differences in remembering was unexpected, particularly given the hypothesized relations between elaborative rehearsal and executive control. Two factors may explain this finding. First, earlier work (Bunce, 2003) has shown that the provision of cognitive support to guide elaboration and structuring attenuates remembering deficits in older adults of lower frontal lobe function.

In the present experiment, cognitive support, or instructions concerning how to encode information, were not provided. It is possible, therefore, that before older adults initiate elaborative rehearsal processes, some form of cue is required (e.g., explicit instructions or some form of cognitive support embedded in the to-be-remembered materials). The absence of both cognitive support and encoding instructions in the present study may account, therefore, for the minimal influence of executive control measures. Second, it is possible that, operationally, the two measures of executive function (FAS test and backward digit span) did not access the executive processes involved in elaborative rehearsal and structuring with sufficient rigour. Had a more extensive range of executive control measures been employed, it is possible that a greater proportion of the age-related variance in remembering would have been accounted for.

It is worth commenting on the finding that the purer measure of speed, the psychomotor task, accounted for age differences in remembering and knowing, whereas the digit symbol substitution task did not. Although commonly used as a measure of perceptual speed, this latter task is not particularly pure. Not only does it contain a substantial memory component but previous research (Piccinin & Rabbitt, 1999) suggests that learning of the symbol–number combinations significantly improves performance. Such learning may involve some of the elaborative and structuring capacities held to underpin recollective experience in the present research. Therefore, the failure of this measure to account for age differences in remembering is noteworthy, as it indicates further the methodological difficulties associated with independent measures and their ability to capture elaborative and structuring processes.

A further possibility that requires consideration is that the psychomotor task responsible for the main mediating effect was tapping a more general factor relating to fluid intelligence. This raises the possibility that fluid intelligence underpinned the findings in respect to processing speed, and, as such, recent research by Duncan and colleagues (Duncan et al., 2000) is informative. They have produced imaging data suggesting selective activation of the lateral frontal cortex during a high-demand fluid intelligence task. Therefore, if our measure was reflecting a higher order general intelligence factor, it is possible that this factor was supported by the neural substrates of the frontal cortex, the brain area held to sustain autonoetic consciousness during remembering.

These possibilities aside, the mixed findings with respect to executive processes in the present study limit any firm conclusions concerning the role of autonoetic consciousness in age differences in recollective experience. On the one hand, following predictions, levels of remembering were elevated in younger adults following the longer encoding time. This is consistent with the view that the hypothesized elevations in elaborative rehearsal in that condition underpinned age differences in remembering. On the other hand, the independent measures of executive function failed to account for those differences. To clarify associations further, it is important that future work employs a more extensive range of executive control measures and includes some manipulation of encoding instructions in study conditions of varying lengths. Moreover, as noted elsewhere (Parkin & Java, 2000; Perfect, 1997), such research should contrast further the competing theoretical accounts of age differences in recollective experience providing the focus for the present study.

Several important conclusions arise from this research. First, our findings suggest that following an experimental manipulation of the time allowed for encoding operations, a dissociation relating to the level of conscious awareness in recognition occurs in younger and older adults. Second, it appears that younger persons were able to utilize the additional encoding time to process more information to a greater depth and, therefore, report a greater level of remembering. By contrast, however, although older adults processed more information, it appears that the level of processing was shallower, and in consequence a greater level of recognition in the absence of conscious awareness resulted. Finally, although executive processes were implicated in age differences in recollective experience, independent measures of perceptual speed explained those differences. Clearly, further work is required that not only evaluates the encoding conditions influencing remembering and knowing in older adults, but also empirically contrasts competing theoretical accounts of the cognitive processes underpinning age differences in recollective experience.

REFERENCES

Benton, A. L., Hamsher, K., Varney, N., & Spreen, O. (1983). *Contributions to neuropsychological assessment*. New York: Oxford University Press.

Brewer, J. B., Zhao, Z., Desmond, J. E., Glover, G. H., & Gabrieli, J. D. E. (1998). Making memories: Brain activity that predicts how well visual experience will be remembered. *Science, 281*, 185–187.

Bunce, D. (2003). Cognitive support at encoding attenuates age differences in recollective experience among adults of lower frontal lobe function. *Neuropsychology, 17*, 353–361.

Bunce, D., Barrowclough, A., & Morris, I. (1996). The moderating influence of physical fitness on age gradients in vigilance and serial choice responding tasks. *Psychology and Aging, 11*, 671–682.

Clarys, D., Isingrini, M., & Gana, K. (2002). Mediators of age-related differences in recollective experience in recognition memory. *Acta Psychologica, 109*, 315–329.

Craik, F. I. M., & Rabinowitz, J. C. (1985). The effects of presentation rate and encoding task on age-related memory deficits. *Journal of Gerontology, 40*, 309–315.

Duncan, J., Seitz, R. J., Kolodny, J., Bor, D., Herzog, H., Ahmed, A., et al. (2000). A neural basis for general intelligence. *Science, 289*, 457–460.

Eldridge, L. L., Knowlton, B. J., Furmanski, C. S., Bookheimer, S. Y., & Engel, S. A. (2000). Remembering episodes: A selective role for the hippocampus during retrieval. *Nature Neuroscience, 3*, 1149–1152.

Folstein, M. F., Folstein, S. E., & McHugh, P. R. (1975). "Mini-mental state": A practical method of grading the cognitive state of patients for the clinician. *Journal of Psychiatric Research, 12*, 189–198.

Gardiner, J. M. (1988). Functional aspects of recollective experience. *Memory and Cognition, 16*, 309–313.

Gardiner, J. M., Gawlik, B., & Richardson-Klavehn, R. (1994). Maintenance rehearsal affects knowing, not remembering; elaborative rehearsal affects remembering, not knowing. *Psychonomic Bulletin & Review, 1*, 107–110.

Gardiner, J. M., & Richardson-Klavehn, A. (2000). Remembering and knowing. In F. I. M. Craik & E. Tulving (Eds.), *The Oxford handbook of memory*. Oxford, UK: Oxford University Press.

Henson, R. N. A., Rugg, M. D., Shallice, T., Josephs, O., & Dolan, R. J. (1999). Recollection and familiarity in recognition memory: An event-related functional magnetic resonance imaging study. *The Journal of Neuroscience, 19*, 3962–3972.

Jacoby, L. L., Yonelinas, A. P., & Jennings, J. (1997). The relation between conscious and unconscious (automatic) influences: A declaration of independence. In J. Cohen & J. W. Schooler (Eds.), *Scientific approaches to consciousness* (pp. 13–47). Mahwah, NJ: Lawrence Erlbaum Associates, Inc.

Loevden, M., Roennlund, M., & Nilsson, L.-G. (2002). Remembering and knowing in adulthood: Effects of enacted encoding and relations to processing speed. *Aging, Neuropsychology, and Cognition, 9*, 184–200.

Mark, R. E., & Rugg, M. D. (1998). Age effects on brain activity associated with episodic memory retrieval: An electrophysiological study. *Brain, 121*, 861–873.

Nelson, H. (1982). *National Adult Reading Test (NART)*. Windsor, UK: Nfer-Nelson.

Parkin, A. J., & Java, R. I. (2000). Determinants of age-related memory loss. In T. J. Perfect & E. A. Maylor (Eds.), *Models of cognitive aging*. Oxford, UK: Oxford University Press.

Parkin, A. J., & Walter, B. M. (1992). Recollective experience, normal aging, and frontal dysfunction. *Psychology and Aging, 7*, 290–298.

Perfect, T. J. (1997). Memory aging as frontal lobe dysfunction. In M. A. Conway (Ed.), *Cognitive models of memory*. Hove, UK: Psychology Press.

Perfect, T. J., & Dasgupta, Z. R. R. (1997). What underlies the deficit in reported recollective experience in old age? *Memory and Cognition, 25*, 849–858.

Perfect, T. J., Williams, R. B., & Anderton-Brown, C. (1995). Age differences in reported recollective experience are due to encoding effects, not response bias. *Memory, 3*, 169–186.

Piccinin, A. M., & Rabbitt, P. M. A. (1999). Contribution of cognitive abilities to performance and improvement on a substitution coding task. *Psychology and Aging, 14*, 539–551.

Salthouse, T. A. (1991). *Theoretical perspectives on cognitive aging*. Hillsdale, NJ: Lawrence Erlbaum Associates, Inc.

Salthouse, T. A. (1996). The processing-speed theory of adult age differences in cognition. *Psychological Review, 103*, 403–428.

Schacter, D. L., Koutstaal, W., Johnson, M. K., Gross, M. S., & Angell, K. E. (1997). False recollection induced by photographs: A comparison of older and younger adults. *Psychology and Aging, 12*, 203–215.

Tulving, E. (1985). Memory and consciousness. *Canadian Psychology, 25*, 1–12.

Uylings, H. B. M., & de Brabander, J. M. (2002). Neural changes in normal human aging and Alzheimer's disease. *Brain and Cognition, 49*, 268–276.

Wagner, A. D., Schacter, D. L., Rotte, M., Koutstaal, W., Maril, A., & Dale, A. M. (1998). Building memories: Remembering and forgetting of verbal experiences as predicted by brain activity. *Science, 281*, 1188–1191.

Wahlin, A., Backman, L., & Winblad, B. (1995). Free recall and recognition of slowly and rapidly presented words in very old age: A community-based study. *Experimental Aging Research, 21*, 251–271.

Wechsler, D. (1981). *WAIS-R manual: Wechsler Adult Intelligence Scale-Revised*. New York: Harcourt Brace Jovanovich.

West, R. J. (1996). An application of prefrontal cortex function theory to cognitive aging. *Psychological Bulletin, 120*, 272–292.

Wheeler, M. A., Stuss, D. T., & Tulving, E. (1997). Toward a theory of episodic memory: The frontal lobes and autonoetic consciousness. *Psychological Bulletin, 121*, 331–354.

Woodward, A. E., Bjork, R. A., & Jongeward, R. H. (1973). Recall and recognition as a function of primary rehearsal. *Journal of Verbal Learning and Verbal Behavior, 12*, 608–617.

PrEview proof published online 6 August 2004

THE QUARTERLY JOURNAL OF EXPERIMENTAL PSYCHOLOGY
2005, 58A (1), 169–190

Psychology Press
Taylor & Francis Group

Contributions of processing ability and knowledge to verbal memory tasks across the adult life-span

Trey Hedden

Stanford University, Stanford, CA, USA

Gary Lautenschlager

University of Georgia, Athens, GA, USA

Denise C. Park

University of Illinois at Urbana-Champaign, Urbana-Champaign, IL, USA

This study investigated the relationships of processing capacity and knowledge to memory measures that varied in retrieval difficulty and reliance on verbal knowledge in an adult life-span sample ($N = 341$). It was hypothesized that processing ability (speed and working memory) would have the strongest relationship to tasks requiring active retrieval and that knowledge (vocabulary ability) would be related to verbal fluency and cued recall, as participants relied upon verbal knowledge to retrieve category items (fluency) or develop associations (cued recall). Measurement and structural equation models were developed for the entire sample and separately for younger (aged 20–54 years, $n = 168$) and older (aged 55–92 years, $n = 173$) subgroups. In accordance with the hypotheses, processing ability was found to be most highly related to free recall, with additional significant relationships to cued recall, verbal fluency, and recognition. Knowledge was found to be significantly related only to verbal fluency and to cued recall. Moreover, knowledge was more important for older than for younger adults in mediating variance in cued recall, suggesting that older adults may use age-related increases in knowledge to partially compensate for processing declines when environmental support is available in memory tasks.

In the study of cognitive ageing, perhaps the most well known finding is that processing ability declines with advancing age even in the absence of pathology (Park, Lautenschlager, Hedden, Davidson, Smith, & Smith, 2002; Rabbitt & Lowe, 2000; Salthouse, 1996). Processing

Correspondence should be addressed to Trey Hedden, Department of Psychology, 434 Jordan Hall, Building 420, Stanford University, Stanford, CA 94305-2130, USA. Email: hedden@psych.stanford.edu

Trey Hedden is supported by an NRSA fellowship from the National Institutes of Health. This research was supported by grant R01-AG06265 from the National Institute on Aging to Denise C. Park. The authors thank Ki Goosens.

http://www.tandf.co.uk/journals/pp/02724987.html   DOI:10.1080/02724980443000179

ability refers to one's capacity for efficiently executing mechanisms of controlled attention that are invoked to perform tasks requiring rapid selection of information, switching among multiple task goals, and actively maintaining multiple representations (e.g., Kane, Bleckley, Conway, & Engle, 2001, Meyer & Kieras, 1997). Common measures of processing ability, such as speed of processing and working memory capacity measures, predict age-related changes and individual differences in fluid intelligence and in long-term memory (Engle, Kane, & Tuholski, 1999a; Engle, Tuholski, Laughlin, & Conway, 1999b; Park et al., 2002; Park et al., 1996; Verhaeghen & Salthouse, 1997). In contrast to the declines in processing abilities, knowledge, as measured by vocabulary ability or semantic knowledge, tends to remain stable across the adult life span or show age-related increases until very late in life (Lindenberger & Baltes, 1997; Park et al., 2002; Salthouse, 1993a; Schaie, 1994, 1996).

Although there are abundant demonstrations of how decreases in measures of processing capacity such as speed and working memory predict performance on a range of higher order tasks that include long-term memory and reasoning, less is known about the relationship of knowledge to such tasks. There is evidence that knowledge may be a more important component of performance in late adulthood compared to earlier adulthood when processing capacity is at its peak. For example, findings indicate that knowledge and expertise in particular domains gained with age aid performance in solving crossword puzzles (Hambrick, Salthouse, & Meinz, 1999), in memory for music (Meinz & Salthouse, 1998), and in playing bridge and chess (Charness & Bosman, 1990). Indeed, older adults are often able to maintain a high level of functioning in familiar tasks of everyday living even while displaying declines in processing ability in laboratory tests (Allaire & Marsiske, 2002; Charness, 2000; Park, 1992; Park & Gutchess, 2000). Nevertheless, increased knowledge and expertise do not always protect against age-related processing declines within a domain of expertise (Meinz & Salthouse, 1998), nor do they slow the rate of decline in general processing abilities (Hambrick et al., 1999). To date, the findings suggest a complex relationship among knowledge, processing capacity, and performance, with knowledge potentially playing an increased role in aiding task performance with advancing age. The interplay between processing ability and knowledge across the lifespan should be most apparent on tasks where both processing capacity and knowledge can be relied upon to support performance.

The environmental support hypothesis proposed by Craik (1983) posited that as self-initiated processing ability declines with age, environmental support from external cues and internal habits plays an increasingly important role in supporting cognitive behaviours. Environmental support is here conceptualized as the prompting of internal processes by external cues. The presence of extensive cues does not itself provide environmental support, but must be accompanied by the successful prompting of task-relevant cognitive processes. We hypothesize that existing verbal knowledge (such as an extensive vocabulary), when prompted by cues contained in a task context, may provide environmental support for older adults and may partially compensate for processing declines on some memory tasks. For older adults, who have impoverished processing ability but a wealth of knowledge, the environmental support available in a memory task may be a particularly important factor in determining success or failure (Craik & Anderson, 1999; Hess, Flannagan, & Tate, 1993; Naveh-Benjamin, Craik, & Ben-Shaul, 2002).

In the present study, we examined the contributions of verbal knowledge and processing abilities (speed and working memory) to a range of commonly used measures of verbal memory: free recall, cued recall, and recognition. These measures, according to Craik and Byrd (1982), vary in the amount of self-initiated processing required to perform them. Verbal free recall tasks, in which a list of individual words is to be recalled, provide few retrieval cues for environmental support, and hence age differences are particularly large on these tasks (Anderson, Craik, & Naveh-Benjamin, 1998b; Craik & Byrd, 1982; Craik, Byrd, & Swanson, 1987; Park, Smith, Dudley, & Lafronza, 1989). Although one might expect that knowledge would assist in developing associations even among unrelated words during the encoding phase of free recall, Craik and Anderson (1999) implicated retrieval, rather than encoding, processes as the primary source of deficits experienced by older adults in remembering contextual associations. The absence of retrieval cues in a free recall task may therefore be particularly detrimental for older adults, who cannot effectively apply their knowledge without external cues and must rely instead on their diminishing processing ability. Suggesting the importance of processing ability to free recall, Park et al. (1996, 2002) reported strong associations between measures of speed and working memory to free recall.

Cued recall tasks, in which associations between paired cues and target words are memorized, also show large age differences (Anderson et al., 1998b; Craik et al., 1987; Park et al., 1989), but provide more of an opportunity for the application of verbal knowledge, particularly when the cues and targets are meaningfully associated with one another (Nelson & McEvoy, 2002). We hypothesized that individuals with large vocabularies may be able to use their superior knowledge to generate more or better associations to connect targets and cues. Thus, we would expect that both processing abilities and verbal knowledge would mediate variance on a cued recall task.

According to Craik and colleagues (Craik & Byrd, 1982; Craik et al., 1987), verbal recognition tasks provide the most environmental support through retrieval cues, as the studied word is provided at retrieval, and a participant need only accept or reject the word as a studied item. In support of this hypothesis, age differences in memory are reduced in cued recall tasks compared to free recall tasks (Anderson et al., 1998b; Craik et al., 1987), and recognition tasks display comparatively small age differences (Anderson et al., 1998b; Kausler, 1994, pp. 249–253; Spencer & Raz, 1995). Despite the small age differences in recognition memory, it seems unlikely that verbal knowledge is the mechanism mitigating age-related declines, as recognition tasks provide little opportunity for the application of verbal knowledge. Typically, all the words presented as targets and lures in a recognition task are known to the participant through extraexperimental knowledge, so that the only distinction among targets and lures is that targets have recently been presented on the study list. Rather than relying on processing ability or verbal knowledge, recognition relies heavily on familiarity processes, in which judgements are based on perceptual fluency or relative activation of items in memory (Anderson, Bothell, Lebiere, & Matessa, 1998a; Johnston, Dark, & Jacoby, 1985; Kausler, 1994, p. 253). These familiarity processes have been found to occur prior to the influences of recollection in recognition tasks (McElree, Dolan, & Jacoby, 1999; Yonelinas & Jacoby, 1994). Furthermore, indices of familiarity in recognition appear to be age invariant, suggesting that familiarity processes may support recognition performance even in the absence of controlled recollection (Jacoby, 1999; Jennings & Jacoby, 1997). In keeping with the work of Jacoby and colleagues and the emphasis on familiarity and fluency (Anderson et al., 1998a; Jennings & Jacoby, 1997; Johnston et al., 1985), we hypothesized that recognition performance would not be strongly related to either processing ability or verbal knowledge.

Besides studying free recall, cued recall, and recognition in the present study, we also examined the relationship of processing ability and verbal knowledge to verbal fluency. In verbal fluency tasks, participants are presented with a letter or a category and are required to retrieve as many words as they can that begin with the letter or that belong to the category. Fluency tasks are commonly used neuropsychological indicators of frontal lobe dysfunction (Bryan & Luszcz, 2000; Lezak, 1995). Fluency measures typically load on the same factors as other executive function tasks and are particularly sensitive to age-related changes in frontal functioning (Glisky, Polster, & Routhieaux, 1995; Glisky, Rubin, & Davidson, 2001). Of interest, individual differences in frontal function, measured in part by fluency, predict which older adults will suffer declines in memory tasks (Davidson & Glisky, 2002; Glisky et al., 2001; Henkel, Johnson, & De Leonardis, 1998; Parkin, Walter, & Hunkin, 1995). Although verbal fluency is not generally considered a memory task, fluency tasks are a type of self-initiated semantic memory task. Performance on a verbal fluency task requires self-initiated retrieval as in free recall, but from semantic rather than episodic memory (Rosen & Engle, 1997). Moreover, fluency tasks share some qualities with cued recall tasks in that the initial cue provided by the experimenter (letter or category name) may provide environmental support. Also, like cued recall, it seems likely that high verbal knowledge would be an important predictor of performance. Although large age differences are typically observed on fluency tasks, one might expect these differences to be limited to processing limitations with ageing, with younger and older adults similarly applying knowledge to aid task performance. Indeed, Salthouse (1993a) found that vocabulary knowledge contributed to production in fluency tasks for both younger and older adults.

In the present study, we used structural equation modelling to investigate the simultaneous relationships of processing ability and verbal knowledge to verbal memory outcome measures that differed in the environmental support provided to participants through retrieval cues. Processing ability was indexed primarily by working memory tasks, but also by measures of speed of processing. Vocabulary was used as a proxy for verbal knowledge. The verbal memory outcomes included free recall, cued recall, fluency, and recognition. We developed models for a lifespan sample and then investigated whether this general model fitted data similarly for older and younger adults.

The initial study design and the reported models were developed to measure specific hypothesis-driven constructs and to investigate theoretically plausible relationships among those constructs. Rather than developing many alternative models for comparison, we instead investigated specific theoretically relevant path strengths within individual models of interest. In developing the models, we relied upon past findings to guide construct development and path specification. Prior reports have found that short-term memory (maintenance of representations) directly contributes to working memory (simultaneous maintenance and manipulation of representations), but does not have direct paths to memory outcomes (Engle et al., 1999b; Park et al., 2002). Although our individual measures of working memory include tasks that use either visuospatial or verbal content, past structural modelling reports have indicated that visuospatial and verbal working memory measures either load on a unitary construct (Engle et al., 1999b) or are so highly related that they should perhaps not be considered as distinct constructs (Park et al., 2002). We therefore include only a single construct of working memory that is perhaps best described as an executive function component of processing ability (Baddeley, 1986, 1996; Engle et al., 1999b).

EXPERIMENT

In testing individual paths from working memory (processing ability) and vocabulary (knowledge), we hypothesized that: (a) greater retrieval demands and less contextual cues, as in free recall, would require greater contributions from working memory and little from vocabulary; (b) as environmental support provided by retrieval cues increases in availability, as in cued recall and verbal fluency, vocabulary will increase in importance; (c) furthermore, vocabulary should be more important to older adults than to younger adults, as the older adults rely on knowledge when they are faced with declines in processing ability; (d) recognition performance would not be well predicted by working memory or by vocabulary, relying instead on familiarity processes.

Method

Participants

Participants were 345 community-dwelling individuals in the Ann Arbor, Michigan area, aged 20 to 92 years. Participants had vision sufficient to be able to read comfortably from a computer screen, had at least a ninth-grade education level, and were able to provide their own transportation to the study site. Other details of the sample are described in Park et al. (2002). Four participants were dropped from the reported analyses due to incomplete data.

Procedure

Participants were tested on three separate days for a total of 7 hours in groups of four or fewer. Tasks were presented either with paper and pencil or using the PsyScope 1.0.2 software package (Cohen, MacWhinney, Flatt, & Provost, 1993) on Apple Power Macintosh 7500 computers with 17-inch Apple colour monitors (Apple Computer, Cupertino, CA). Each participant completed a series of tasks that measured cognition, sensory function, and verbal ability. Task order was invariant across participants. Those tasks relevant to the current report are described below. Details of other tasks and order of task presentation are described in Park et al. (2002). Structural equation analyses were conducted using the LISREL 8.30 software (Jöreskog & Sörbom, 2001).

Description of tasks associated with latent variables

Speed of processing. There were three measures of speed of processing: the digit symbol adapted from the WAIS-III (Wechsler, 1997) and two measures developed by Salthouse and Babcock (1991)— letter comparison and pattern comparison. All were paper-and-pencil tasks.

Digit symbol. Participants were shown nine geometric figures, with each assigned a digit from 1 to 9. The digits were presented in a random order, and participants drew, as quickly as possible, the corresponding geometric figure for each. The dependent measure was the number of items completed in 90 seconds.

Letter comparison. Participants were presented with pairs of letter strings consisting of three, six, or nine letters each. Participants determined whether the two strings were the same or different and responded by writing an S or D on an answer sheet. They were given 30 seconds to complete as many items as possible at each level (three, six, or nine letters). The dependent measure was the sum of the number correct from the three levels.

Pattern comparison. This task was identical to the letter comparison task, except that participants compared pairs of line drawings consisting of three, six, or nine line segments. Again, the dependent measure was the total number of correct responses in the three trials.

Working memory.   There were four working memory tasks. Each task had a processing component, involving a simple decision (e.g., whether three shapes were identical), and a storage component, involving memory for a series of items (e.g., the last word in each sentence in a series). For all tasks, the dependent measure was the total number of trials on which the processing component and the storage component were both correct.

Reading span.   Adapted from the Salthouse and Babcock (1991) version of the task originated by Daneman and Carpenter (1980), participants heard simple sentences read aloud one at a time (e.g., "After dinner, the chef prepared dessert for her guests."). For the processing component, participants answered a question presented on the computer screen after each sentence (e.g., "What did the chef prepare?— A. fish; B. dessert; C. salad") by pressing the appropriate key. For the storage component, participants had to simultaneously remember the last word in each of the sentences. At the end of a sequence of sentences, participants wrote these words on an answer sheet (e.g., "guests"). The number of sentences in a sequence varied from 1 to 6, with three trials given at each of these six levels. The task was discontinued when a participant made an error on the storage component of at least two out of three trials on a level.

Computation span.   Adapted from Salthouse and Babcock (1991), the structure of this task was similar to that of the reading span task. For the processing component, participants heard simple maths problems read aloud, one at a time (e.g., "$5 - 3 =$"). After each problem, three possible solutions were given on the computer screen (e.g., "A. 2, B. 1, C. 9"), and participants pressed the appropriate key to indicate their response. For the storage component, they had to simultaneously remember the last number in each problem (e.g., "3"). At the end of a sequence of problems, participants wrote these numbers on an answer sheet. The number of problems in a sequence ranged from 1 to 6. The number of trials and discontinuation of the task were the same as those in the reading span task.

Line span.   In this task, adapted from Morrell and Park (1993), two types of visuospatial information were displayed simultaneously on a computer screen: (a) three irregular shapes in random locations, and (b) a single line segment (presented horizontally, vertically, or diagonally) in one of 42 possible positions. For the processing component, participants decided whether the three irregular shapes were identical and responded by pressing one of two keys. For the storage component, they had to simultaneously remember the position of the line segment in the display. After a series of these displays, the participants reproduced all of the line segments by drawing them on a grid, in the exact position and orientation in which they had been presented. The number of displays in a sequence varied from one to six, with three trials given at each of these six levels. The task was discontinued when a participant made an error on the storage component of at least two out of three trials on a level.

Letter rotation.   In a task adapted from Shah and Miyake's (1996) spatial span task, participants were shown a series of letters, one at a time on a computer screen. Some letters were presented as mirror images, while others were presented in their normal form. Each letter was also tilted at an angle (45, 90, 135, 180, 225, 270, or 315 degrees from the normal vertical orientation). For the processing component, participants decided whether the letter was normal or mirror-imaged, indicating their decision by pressing one of two keys. For the storage component, they had to simultaneously remember the angle at which the letter was tilted. After a series of these letters, the participants recalled the angles of the letters by marking an answer grid. The number of letters in a series varied from two to five, with five trials given at each of the four levels. The task was discontinued when a participant made an error on the storage component of at least three out of five trials on a level.

Vocabulary.   The three vocabulary tasks were the vocabulary section of the Shipley Institute of Living Scale (Shipley, 1986) and computerized versions of the synonym vocabulary and antonym vocabulary tests developed by Salthouse (1993a). In all tasks, the dependent measure was the total number of correct items.

Vocabulary section of the Shipley Institute of Living Scale.   Forty target words from the Shipley scale (Shipley, 1986) were presented on a computer, one at a time, with four response alternatives.

Participants chose which of the four alternatives had nearly the same meaning as the target word by pressing one of four keys. They were given 10 minutes to complete all 40 items.

Synonym vocabulary.   Participants were presented with 10 words on a computer, one at a time, and indicated which of 5 alternative words had nearly the same meaning as the target word by pressing one of five keys. Participants were given 5 minutes to complete this task.

Antonym vocabulary.   This task was similar to the synonym vocabulary task, except that participants had to decide which of the five alternative words had most nearly the opposite meaning to each target word.

Verbal long-term memory.   For each verbal long-term memory construct, multiple versions of the same task were presented. In the free recall, cued recall, and recognition tasks, participants were instructed to "study each word and try to remember it" during initial presentation of the words to be remembered.

Free recall.   Two versions each consisted of 16 words presented on a computer one at a time for 5 seconds each. After viewing all of the words in a list, participants wrote on an answer sheet as many words as they could recall in any order. Three minutes were given for recall. For the 32 words used in both versions, the Thorndike and Lorge (1944) frequency counts ranged from 120 to 3,133 with mean frequencies for each version of 901 and 904. The dependent measures were the total number of words recalled on each version.

Cued recall.   Two versions each consisted of 16 word pairs presented on a computer. Each word pair consisted of a cue word in lower-case letters and a target word in capital letters, presented one at a time for 5 seconds each. Each cue was a weak associate of its paired target (e.g., dark–CANDLE). After all 16 word pairs in a list had been presented, the cues were presented again, one at a time. Participants wrote on an answer sheet the target originally paired with each cue. Mean frequencies of the targets in the two lists were 908 and 914. The number of words correctly produced was the dependent measure for each version.

Verbal fluency.   Participants completed three forms of this task (Spreen & Benton, 1977). In each form, participants were presented with a letter (F, A, or S) and asked to write as many words beginning with that letter as possible in 90 seconds. Proper nouns, numbers, and repeated words with a different suffix were not counted as correct. Dependent measures were the number of correct words produced on each form.

Recognition.   Two versions each consisted of 48 study words presented on a computer one at a time for 5 seconds each. After all 48 words in a list had been presented, participants were presented with a recognition list consisting of 24 target words and 24 lure words, one word at a time. Participants responded via a key press to indicate whether each word was a target (e.g., on the study list) or a lure. Mean frequencies of the target words were 928 and 902, while mean frequencies of the lure words were 903 and 916. The signal detection measure of d', calculated from the hit rate for targets and the false alarm rate for lures, was the dependent measure for each version.

Results

The analyses were designed to investigate the contributions of processing ability (working memory and speed of processing) and knowledge (vocabulary) to verbal long-term memory tasks (free recall, cued recall, recognition, and verbal fluency) in the entire sample, and then separately in younger adults and older adults. The entire sample was examined first to provide an overall view of developmental changes across the adult life span, and subgroups were compared to assess age differences in early versus late adulthood (Table 1). The analytic procedures included the following steps. First, a measurement, or correlated factors (CF),

TABLE 1
Means and *SDs* for all participants and for subgroups

Task	All participants		Younger		Older		Effect size
	M	SD	M	SD	M	SD	Cohen's d
Letter comparison	35.29	10.61	41.55	9.61	29.21	7.59	1.43
Pattern comparison	49.54	13.11	58.07	10.70	41.27	9.42	1.67
Digit symbol	54.08	16.00	63.89	12.51	44.54	12.98	1.52
Reading span	7.89	3.47	9.61	3.18	6.23	2.88	1.11
Computation span	7.47	4.00	9.35	3.92	5.64	3.15	1.04
Line span	5.46	2.99	6.66	3.04	4.30	2.45	0.85
Letter rotation	8.60	6.27	11.60	5.95	5.68	5.10	1.06
Shipley vocabulary	34.56	3.92	33.83	4.34	35.26	3.32	0.37
Synonym vocabulary	7.51	2.53	7.07	2.68	7.94	2.29	0.35
Antonym vocabulary	6.39	2.59	6.27	2.68	6.51	2.51	0.09
Free recall 1	8.85	2.85	10.13	2.73	7.61	2.38	0.98
Free recall 2	9.28	3.20	10.68	3.28	7.93	2.46	0.95
Cued recall 1	9.95	4.21	11.69	3.43	8.26	4.21	0.89
Cued recall 2	11.09	4.06	12.87	3.29	9.36	4.00	0.96
Verbal fluency F	15.22	4.49	16.86	4.61	13.64	3.75	0.77
Verbal fluency A	15.25	4.86	16.87	4.96	13.68	4.21	0.69
Verbal fluency S	19.38	5.78	21.86	5.69	16.97	4.80	0.93
Recognition 1	2.29	1.06	2.50	1.06	2.09	1.01	0.40
Recognition 2	2.37	1.14	2.71	1.19	2.03	0.98	0.62
Age	55.25	19.79	37.78	10.11	72.21	9.35	3.54

model was constructed to assess the relationships between individual tasks and their associated latent constructs in the entire sample ($N = 341$) (Table 2). Second, separate CF models were developed for younger (aged 20–54 years, $n = 168$) and older (aged 55–92 years, $n = 173$) subgroups to address the possibility that the two age groups differed at the level of observed relationships between tasks and constructs. Third, a confirmatory structural equation (SE) model using the latent constructs developed in the CF models was estimated. This SE model provided an estimate of the contributions of process and knowledge to each verbal memory construct. Finally, separate SE models were estimated for the younger and older subgroups and used to directly compare the contributions of process and knowledge to verbal memory in each age group.

Correlated factor models

The first step, the development of a CF model, measured whether the indicators hypothesized to form conceptual latent constructs (e.g., letter comparison, pattern comparison, and digit symbol are hypothesized to be indicators of the latent construct of speed of processing) actually shared sufficient variance to form latent constructs. The CF model used in this study included seven latent constructs: speed of processing, working memory, vocabulary, free recall, cued recall, verbal fluency, and recognition. A total of 19 dependent measures were used as indicators of these constructs. Although age had only a single indicator and could be viewed as an exogenous variable, it was included in the CF model to allow a direct comparison with

TABLE 2
Correlations among tasks for all participants

Task	1	2	3	4	5	6	7	8	9	10	11	12	13	14	15	16	17	18	19	20
1. Letter comparison	1.0																			
2. Pattern comparison	.83	1.0																		
3. Digit symbol	.75	.76	1.0																	
4. Reading span	.59	.55	.58	1.0																
5. Computation span	.56	.54	.51	.62	1.0															
6. Line span	.54	.56	.50	.55	.52	1.0														
7. Letter rotation	.53	.54	.54	.62	.55	.64	1.0													
8. Shipley vocabulary	.09	-.01	.03	.19	.21	.15	.18	1.0												
9. Synonym vocabulary	.09	-.05	.01	.17	.15	.10	.12	.75	1.0											
10. Antonym vocabulary	.20	.12	.14	.29	.32	.21	.23	.66	.71	1.0										
11. Free recall 1	.52	.50	.55	.55	.47	.44	.48	.11	.12	.20	1.0									
12. Free recall 2	.55	.54	.58	.52	.42	.47	.53	.15	.16	.25	.69	1.0								
13. Cued recall 1	.54	.48	.53	.49	.46	.48	.49	.25	.26	.36	.56	.57	1.0							
14. Cued recall 2	.53	.50	.56	.50	.46	.46	.51	.21	.32	.31	.58	.61	.76	1.0						
15. Verbal fluency F	.53	.47	.46	.48	.47	.38	.39	.28	.32	.34	.43	.47	.46	.44	1.0					
16. Verbal fluency A	.50	.45	.44	.48	.49	.37	.39	.38	.39	.47	.45	.48	.50	.44	.75	1.0				
17. Verbal fluency S	.58	.55	.55	.54	.51	.41	.46	.22	.24	.36	.51	.54	.51	.50	.75	.76	1.0			
18. Recognition 1	.21	.25	.27	.23	.23	.23	.28	.11	.11	.17	.44	.40	.46	.40	.26	.28	.32	1.0		
19. Recognition 2	.31	.35	.39	.29	.30	.32	.34	.07	.10	.17	.50	.51	.53	.54	.34	.31	.41	.61	1.0	
20. Age	-.66	-.75	-.70	-.56	-.55	-.50	-.57	.22	.23	.07	-.49	-.49	-.45	-.49	-.36	-.32	-.44	-.22	-.34	1.0

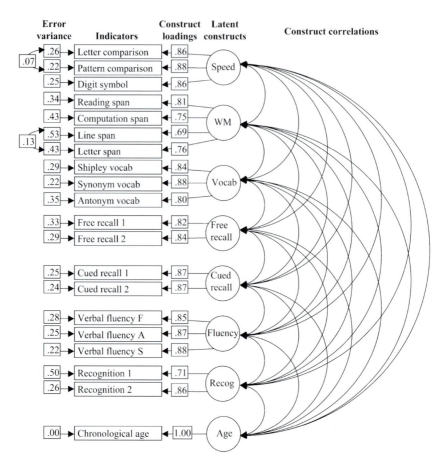

Figure 1. Measurement model for all participants. All values are from the completely standardized solution. Correlations among constructs are given in Table 3. Speed = speed of processing; WM = working memory; Vocab = vocabulary; Fluency = verbal fluency; Recog = recognition memory.

the later structural models. The CF model specifying the relationships among indicators and latent constructs for all participants is depicted in Figure 1. Note that this model yields information about the correlations among the latent constructs (see Table 3), but does not specify the directionality or hierarchy of relationships among the constructs (as do the structural equation models described later). The overall goodness of fit of the model was acceptable, suggesting that the hypothesized relationships between indicators and constructs were statistically confirmed. Although no single criterion for assessing goodness of fit has been established, a model considered to have acceptable fit would have several characteristics:

1. Perhaps the most likely statistic to become a standard measure of model fit is the root mean square error of approximation (RMSEA), an estimate of the amount of error in the

TABLE 3
Correlations between latent constructs in measurement models

Participants	Construct	1	2	3	4	5	6	7
All	1. Speed	–						
	2. Working memory	.82	–					
	3. Vocabulary	.07	.29	–				
	4. Free recall	.75	.77	.22	–			
	5. Cued recall	.69	.73	.35	.80	–		
	6. Recognition	.45	.46	.16	.71	.71	–	
	7. Verbal fluency	.66	.70	.44	.67	.63	.47	–
	8. Age	−.81	−.72	.22	−.59	−.54	−.37	−.43
Young[a]	1. Speed	–						
	2. Working memory	.65	–					
	3. Vocabulary	.32	.56	–				
	4. Free recall	.64	.63	.44	–			
	5. Cued recall	.69	.63	.51	.80	–		
	6. Recognition	.33	.29	.16	.66	.66	–	
	7. Verbal fluency	.60	.66	.62	.57	.59	.32	–
	8. Age	−.44	−.39	.23	−.24	−.27	−.15	−.05
Old[b]	1. Speed	–						
	2. Working memory	.79	–					
	3. Vocabulary	.25	.43	–				
	4. Free recall	.63	.73	.28	–			
	5. Cued recall	.48	.65	.53	.70	–		
	6. Recognition	.32	.44	.32	.66	.67	–	
	7. Verbal fluency	.55	.52	.52	.58	.51	.48	–
	8. Age	−.69	−.62	.04	−.40	−.28	−.21	−.22

[a]Aged 20–54 years. [b]Aged 55–89 years.

model. RMSEA should be less than .08 for acceptable fit and less than .05 to be considered an excellent fit (see Browne & Cudeck, 1993, p. 144; Loehlin, 1998, pp. 76–78).

2. The non-normed index (NNFI) and comparative fit index (CFI) should be greater than .90 for acceptable fit and greater than .95 for close fit (Bentler & Bonett, 1980).

3. Some researchers have suggested that an indication of good fit occurs when the χ^2 value is no greater than twice the degrees of freedom (Bollen, 1989, p. 278). Although ideally a model will have a nonsignificant χ^2 value, this metric tends to have excessive power at larger sample sizes, and even a model with excellent fit will possess a significant χ^2 value (Tanaka, 1993).

The CF model provides an upper limit on the best possible fit for its corresponding SE models. Goodness of fit index (GFI) statistics are reported in Table 4. Although the x2 value was significant, the model meets all three of the above criteria and was accepted as a model of good fit for the entire sample.

For the second step in the analyses, we were interested in determining whether the CF model presented in Figure 1 for the entire sample differed in fit for younger adults

TABLE 4
Fit statistics of measurement and structural models

Model	Participants	N	χ^2	df	p	GFI	NNFI	CFI	RMSEA	χ^2/df
Correlated factors	All	341	210.29	141	<.001	.94	.98	.99	.038	1.49
	Younger[a]	168	152.10	141	.25	.92	.99	.99	.015	1.08
	Older[b]	173	189.52	141	<.005	.90	.96	.97	.044	1.34
Structural models	All	341	386.73	157	<.001	.89	.94	.95	.070	2.46
	Younger[a]	168	275.05	157	<.001	.85	.92	.94	.073	1.75
	Older[b]	173	260.67	157	<.001	.87	.93	.94	.063	1.66

Note: GFI = goodness of fit index; NNFI = non-normed fit index; CFI = comparative fit index; RMSEA = root mean square error of approximation.
[a]Aged 20–54 years. [b]Aged 55–89 years.

compared to older adults. Prior studies have reported group differences in relationships between indicators and the constructs they measure for young adults compared to older adults and in relationships among constructs, although the pattern of loadings and constructs has generally been found to be age invariant (Babcock, Laguna, & Roesch, 1997; Hertzog, 1987; Nyberg et al., 2003). In order to address this issue, we directly compared the CF models for a younger and an older subgroup of participants. The sample was split at age 55 years, so that there were 168 participants aged 20–54 years, and 173 aged 55–89 years. Both age groups displayed acceptable fit with goodness of fit indices for the individual subgroup models shown in Table 4. To assess whether there were differences in fit between the age groups, we performed a series of successively restrictive tests. This sequence (adapted from Jöreskog, 1971) begins by examining the relationship of constructs to their indicators, followed by an examination of the amount of variance not accounted for by the constructs and an examination of the relationships among constructs. The first three comparisons provide an increasingly restrictive estimation of how similarly the constructs account for task variance in each group, while the fourth comparison estimates the similarity of construct correlations. We first compared the CF models for qualitative (or configural) equivalence, constraining only the number of latent constructs and the pattern of loadings from indicators to constructs to be equal between the groups. This comparative model (H1 in Table 5) provides acceptable fit statistics, indicating that the general pattern of constructs and their indicators was similar among younger and older adults. The second comparison constrained the loadings of indicators to constructs to be invariant between the groups, testing quantitative (or metric) fit (H2 in Table 5). This comparison, although providing acceptable fit, had a significantly poorer fit than the prior comparison (based on $\Delta\chi^2$). To determine the source of this difference, each loading from an indicator to its construct was independently constrained to be equal between the groups. Only one loading, that from the second recognition task to the recognition construct, showed a significant group difference, $\Delta\chi^2$ $(1, N = 341) = 7.65$, $p = .006$, at the Bonferroni-corrected level when accounting for the mean correlation among tasks ($r = .41$, $\alpha = .01$). This loading was larger in the younger than in the older subgroup. A third comparison added the constraint that residuals for the indicators (error variance not accounted for by the constructs) were invariant between the

TABLE 5
Equality of measurement models for younger and older subgroups

Hypothesis	χ^2	df	$\Delta\chi^2$	Δdf	p	GFI	NNFI	CFI	RMSEA	χ^2/df
H1: Equal factor patterns	341.62	282	–	–	–	.90	.98	.98	.033	1.21
H2: Invariant factor loadings	363.20	294	21.58	12	.04	.90	.97	.98	.033	1.24
H3: Invariant residuals	428.18	315	64.98	21	<.001	.88	.96	.97	.042	1.36
H4: Equal factor covariation	518.01	351	89.83	36	<.001	.86	.95	.95	.048	1.48

Note: Each subsequent test adds a constraint to the immediately prior model, and the $\Delta\chi^2$ is tested against that prior model.

groups (H3 in Table 5). This comparison produced a significant change in χ^2 when compared to the prior model (H2). As above, each residual was independently constrained to be equal between the groups. Three residuals—those for the letter comparison task, the pattern comparison task, and the line span task—showed a significant group difference, smallest $\Delta\chi^2 (1, N = 341) = 7.37, p = .007$, at the Bonferroni-corrected level ($r = .41, \alpha = .01$). In all three cases, the residual variance was larger in the younger subgroup than in the older subgroup. A fourth comparison added to the prior model the constraint that the variance–covariance matrix among constructs be equivalent between the age groups (H4 in Table 5). This comparison also had a significantly poorer fit than the prior model (H3). Again, each variance and covariance was independently constrained to be equal between the groups. The variance of the vocabulary construct showed a significant group difference with greater variance in the younger group, $\Delta\chi^2 (1, N = 341) = 8.13, p = .004$, at the Bonferroni-corrected level ($r = .55, \alpha = .01$), as did covariances involving the vocabulary and fluency constructs.[1] Hence, the two age groups appear to have models of similar configural form, while differences in metric properties were relatively limited. When metric differences did occur, they were due to larger variance or covariance values in the younger than in the older subgroup.

Structural equation models

For the third step in the analyses, we used the CF models developed in the first two steps as the basis for structural equation models that allowed us to specify relationships among constructs in the entire sample and in the two subgroups. Because we observed some differences in covariation among constructs for the young adult compared to the older adult CF models, we expected differences in structural equation model fit between the two subgroups.

---

[1]Significantly different covariances were between fluency and working memory, $\Delta\chi^2 (1, N = 341) = 7.29$, $p = .007$, and between vocabulary and fluency, $\Delta\chi^2 (1, N = 341) = 6.97, p = .008$. In both cases, the covariance was greater for the younger than for the older adults.

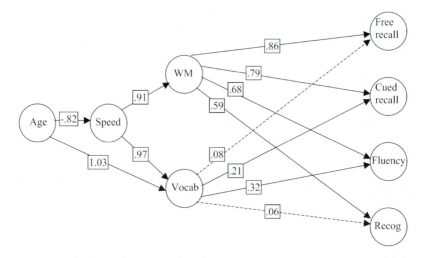

Figure 2. Structural model for all participants. Path values are standardized coefficients. Nonsignificant paths ($p > .05$) are indicated by dashed lines. Age = chronological age; Speed = speed of processing; WM = working memory; Vocab = vocabulary; Fluency = verbal fluency; Recog = recognition memory.

Structural models were developed in which speed of processing, working memory, and vocabulary were used as mediators of age-related variance in the verbal memory constructs. Our primary interest was in the relative strength of paths from processing ability (as indexed by working memory) and knowledge (indexed by vocabulary) to each of the verbal memory constructs. We expected that for free recall, the most process-intensive of the memory constructs, knowledge would have a relatively small contribution, while processing ability would play a large role. For cued recall and fluency, we expected that both processing and knowledge would have a significant contribution, as these memory measures provide support for or even necessitate the use of knowledge in task performance. For recognition, we expected that the roles of processing and knowledge would be relatively small, as recognition largely relies upon familiarity processes (Jennings & Jacoby, 1997; Kausler, 1994, p. 253).

The structural equation model for the entire sample is depicted in Figure 2, and overall fit statistics are reported in Table 4. As expected, age had a direct negative relationship to speed of processing, but a direct positive relationship to vocabulary.[2]

The model generally indicates that age-related variance was mediated by speed of processing, which in turn was mediated by working memory. Of primary interest, all four

---

[2]The positive relationship of age to vocabulary was in part due to the presence of a path from speed to vocabulary, which has a strongly positive value. Removing the path from speed to vocabulary greatly reduces the fit of the model, $\Delta\chi^2$ (1, $N = 341$) = 74.02, $p < .001$, but does not significantly alter any of the path values from vocabulary to the memory measures. This path suggests a strong relationship between speed and vocabulary, which may be expected due to the substantial relationships reported between speed and intelligence measures (e.g., Salthouse, 1992). However, including this path also uncovers a substantial relationship between age and vocabulary, and it suggests that ageing is associated with two counteracting processes that affect vocabulary ability—lowered speed of processing tends to reduce access to vocabulary, while increased experience tends to increase vocabulary knowledge.

paths from working memory to the verbal memory constructs were significant. However, these path values did differ from one another, as constraining them to be equal resulted in a significant decrease in model fit, $\Delta\chi^2$ (3, $N = 341$) $= 351.83$, $p > .001$. As expected, working memory had the largest relationship to free recall and the smallest relationship to recognition, supporting the hypothesis that as environmental support provided by retrieval cues in a task increases, reliance upon processing ability decreases. Of the paths from vocabulary to the verbal memory constructs, only the paths to cued recall and to fluency were significant. These two path values did differ significantly from one another, $\Delta\chi^2$ (1, $N = 341$) $= 4.51$, $p = .03$, with the path from vocabulary to fluency being larger than that to cued recall. Fluency tasks appear to necessitate the use of knowledge, while cued recall provides an opportunity for its use. In general, these results support the hypothesis that knowledge contributes to task performance through the environmental support invoked by the presence of retrieval cues.

We should note that direct paths from age to working memory and to the verbal memory constructs were not indicated by an analysis of the modification indices and expected path changes (largest expected change of .02). Prior studies have also found age-related variance in memory outcomes to be directly mediated only by speed of processing (Park et al., 1996; Park et al., 2002; Salthouse, 1993b). The influence of speed on the verbal memory measures was entirely mediated by working memory and vocabulary, as adding direct paths from speed to the four verbal memory constructs resulted in negative path values that did not significantly differ from 0 (largest $t = -0.66$, $p = .50$). This result confirms prior findings that the relationship of speed to memory operates through working memory (Park et al., 1996; Park et al., 2002).

We next developed identical structural models for the younger and older subgroups, displayed in Figures 3a and 3b, respectively. Goodness of fit indicators for the two separate models are reported in Table 4, with each model having acceptable fit. Each group shows a similar overall pattern to that seen in analyses of the entire sample, with the exception that the younger adults displayed a nonsignificant path value from vocabulary to cued recall ($t = 1.91$, $p = .06$), whereas the path was significant in the model for older adults ($t = 4.42$, $p < .001$). In addition, the path from vocabulary to recognition was significant only in the model for older adults ($t = 2.04$, $p = .04$). When we directly compared the two structural models to one another with all specified parameters free to vary in each group, this comparison had acceptable fit, $\chi^2(314, N = 341) = 535.71$, $p < .001$, GFI $= .87$, NNFI $= .92$, CFI $= .94$, RMSEA $= .068$, $\chi^2/df = 1.71$, indicating that the two groups had similar overall patterns of relationships among constructs. Using this model as a reference, we next made direct metric comparisons between the age groups among individual path values of interest. Based upon the hypothesis that age would affect the relationship between knowledge and verbal memory but not between process and memory, we assessed the equality between the groups of each path from working memory to the verbal memory constructs and of each path from vocabulary to the verbal memory constructs, for a total of eight individual tests. The only path to significantly differ between the younger and older subgroup was the path from vocabulary to cued recall, $\Delta\chi^2$ (1, $N = 341$) $= 8.66$, $p = .003$. This difference was significant at the Bonferroni-corrected level, both when the mean correlation among the verbal memory constructs was considered ($r = .60$, $\alpha = .02$) and when the correlation was not considered ($\alpha = .006$). All other path values were equivalent among the groups, as constraining

a)

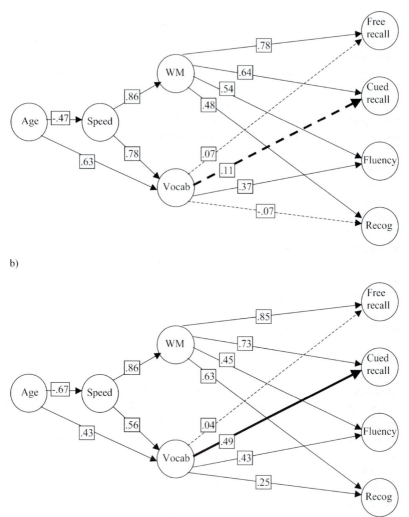

Figure 3.   (a) Structural model for younger (age 20–54 years) participants. (b) Structural model for older (age 55–89 years) participants. Path values are common metric standardized coefficients. Nonsignificant paths ($p > .05$) are indicated by dashed lines. Note that only the path value from vocabulary to cued recall (bold line) significantly differed among the age groups. Age = chronological age; Speed = speed of processing; WM = working memory; Vocab = vocabulary; Fluency = verbal fluency; Recog = recognition memory.

all paths except vocabulary to cued recall did not result in a significant change in model fit, $\Delta\chi^2$ (11, $N = 341$) = 15.72, $p = .15$. Although the path from vocabulary to recognition had a significant value in the older subgroup but not in the younger subgroup, constraining this path to be equal between the groups did not result in a significant change at the Bonferroni-corrected level, $\Delta\chi^2$ (1, $N = 341$) = 4.76, $p = .03$.

Discussion

This study assessed how processing ability and verbal knowledge contributed to a range of verbal memory tasks, and how those contributions differ across the adult life span. Structural equation models demonstrated that processing ability, as measured by speed and working memory, contributed most to verbal memory when environmental support prompted by retrieval cues was least available (as in free recall) and contributed least when such support was most available (as in recognition). These results confirm predictions of the environmental support hypothesis (Anderson et al., 1998b; Craik, 1983) in that greater processing ability is required for free recall than for recognition (see also Park et al., 1996). Despite age-related decreases in processing ability, working memory contributed similarly to memory performance for younger and older adults, suggesting that environmental support is an important variable in predicting memory performance across the adult life span. When processing ability is most invoked, and environmental support from cues is least available, as in free recall, observed age differences in memory tend to be largest (see effect sizes in Table 1). In recognition, where processing ability is less invoked and environmental support from cues is most available, age differences in memory are smallest (see Table 1). In contrast, knowledge, as measured by vocabulary ability, contributed only to the verbal memory tasks of cued recall and verbal fluency. Of particular interest was the finding that age-related differences in these relationships were observed. Younger adults relied solely upon processing ability in cued recall tasks whereas older adults invoked both knowledge and processing ability in cued recall. These results indicate that verbal knowledge operates jointly with processing ability to support performance on some memory tasks where knowledge can play a role, and that older adults are more likely than younger adults to take advantage of the application of knowledge in such tasks.

The findings emphasize the importance of processing ability for long-term memory function across the lifespan, as reported by Park et al. (1996, 2002). Although age operated directly through speed, speed had no direct paths to the memory measures. The influence of processing ability on memory was therefore indexed by working memory, which had significant direct paths to all measures of verbal memory in analyses of the entire sample and in analyses of the two age subgroups. In all groups, working memory had the strongest path to free recall, suggesting that processing ability is most important to performance when environmental support provided by retrieval cues is absent. In contrast, vocabulary was observed to have a significant direct path only to fluency in all groups, suggesting that verbal knowledge is used to support memory when appropriate semantic retrieval cues are provided as a form of environmental support. Verbal fluency is a semantic rather than episodic memory task, as the processing requirements are not tied to an encoded event. Rather, participants must use a combination of processing ability and extraexperimental knowledge to retrieve semantically or orthographically related items from memory. Hence, both younger and older adults exhibited a relationship between knowledge and memory in fluency tasks (see Salthouse, 1993a, for a similar finding).

Vocabulary was positively related to speed of processing, indicating that age-related declines in speed and increases in experience have counteracting influences on vocabulary ability. This may, in part, explain the curvilinear trajectory of vocabulary ability across the adult life span, with gains throughout most of life followed by late-life declines

(Park et al., 2002; Schaie, 1996). Such a curvilinear trajectory later in life accounts for the lack of a correlation between age and vocabulary in the older subgroup (see Table 3), although there is still a substantial path from age to vocabulary when the influence of speed is taken into account (see Figure 3b). This pattern also helps explain why speed is positively correlated with vocabulary in both age subgroups, but has a small correlation to vocabulary in the combined sample. When the subgroups are combined, the influence of age on vocabulary becomes greater than that of speed (see Table 3), although the path from speed to vocabulary remains substantial when accounting for age (see Figure 2).

Within the two age subgroups, the paths from age to vocabulary were positive and equivalent. However, vocabulary was related to cued recall performance only in the older subgroup. Vocabulary was also significantly related to recognition in the older subgroup only, although this relationship did not differ from the nonsignificant path exhibited in the younger subgroup and should therefore be interpreted cautiously. These results suggest that as individuals age there is a shift in cognitive emphasis from reliance upon processing ability to the use of increasing knowledge in performing memory tasks where environmental support is available to facilitate its application. This pattern of findings suggests that not only do older adults exhibit poorer levels of absolute memory performance than do young adults, but that the qualitative nature of their memory processes may differ from younger adults. These results are in agreement with prior research indicating that older adults invoke accumulated knowledge in support of task performance. Older adults perform well on measures of wisdom (Baltes & Staudinger, 2000; Baltes, Staudinger, Maercker, & Smith, 1995), but also rely upon knowledge of stereotypes in making memory judgements (Mather, Johnson, & De Leonardis, 1999). Social knowledge can be used by older adults to aid in making impression judgments (Hess & Auman, 2001) and to assist in making source memory judgments (Rahhal, May, & Hasher, 2002).

The present results are relevant to recent debates in the literature on the cognitive neuroscience of ageing regarding neural compensation and strategic shifts with advancing age (e.g., Meyer, Glass, Mueller, Seymour, & Kieras, 2001; Reuter-Lorenz, 2002). Age-related increases in knowledge, such as vocabulary ability, may allow older adults to institute strategies not readily available to younger adults with a less established knowledge base. Such strategic shifts could, in principle, account for compensation in behavioural performance (Charness & Bosman, 1990; Rogers, Hertzog, & Fisk, 2000) and for neural activation patterns unique to older adults (Cabeza, 2002; Reuter-Lorenz, 2002). Alternatively, such knowledge may be automatically activated by older adults in situations when a task cues representations of relevant knowledge (Craik & Anderson, 1999; Park & Gutchess, 2000). It may be possible to resolve the strategic differences with age versus automatic activation argument by studying contrasts between situations where automatically activated knowledge would detract from or facilitate performance. A complementary approach would be to train older adults in the use of strategies that invoke task-relevant knowledge.

Recognition memory was relatively poorly explained by the constructs in the models. Indeed, only 36% of the variance in recognition was accounted for among all participants, in contrast to 62% for fluency, 70% for cued recall, and 75% for free recall. Recognition had the weakest relationship to working memory and no significant relationship to vocabulary. Even in the older subgroup, where recognition was significantly related to vocabulary, this relationship was quite weak. The latter results were observed despite the fact that recognition provides extensive retrieval cues (Craik, 1983); indeed, it could be said to supply maximal cueing, as the item to be retrieved is itself provided as a cue. However, it may be difficult to effectively apply knowledge in recognition tasks because all items are known. Hence, knowledge may not help to discriminate items that were seen earlier in the experimental setting from items not seen. In this sense, recognition is a source or context memory task that can be solved on the basis of familiarity due to recent presentation (Anderson et al., 1998a; Kausler, 1994, p. 253).

Also noteworthy is the finding that the older subgroup did not display a pattern of larger correlations among constructs than did the younger subgroup (see Table 3). Indeed, only three correlations among the seven latent constructs differed significantly between the younger and older adults. These were the correlation between speed and working memory ($z = -2.71$, $p = .007$), which was larger in the older adults, and the correlations between speed and cued recall ($z = 2.97$, $p = .003$) and between working memory and verbal fluency ($z = 1.98$, $p = .048$), which were both larger in the younger adults. This pattern of findings fails to support the hypothesis of dedifferentiation, which holds that cognitive abilities become more related with advancing age, possibly due to common neurobiological processes affecting multiple cognitive systems (Anstey, Hofer, & Luszcz, 2003; Balinsky, 1941). Other recent studies have also found no evidence of dedifferentiation with advancing age (Anstey et al., 2003; Park et al., 2002). The current findings are consistent with an interpretation in which cognitive processes remain distinct into advanced age, yet are used differentially by younger and older adults as task conditions change.

In conclusion, adult age-related differences were observed in the contributions between processing ability and knowledge to performance on verbal memory tasks. Although both younger and older adults displayed similar relationships between processing ability and memory, the influence of knowledge increased with adult ageing. Processing ability was most highly related to memory when environmental support was limited, as in free recall performance, and was least related to memory in recognition performance, providing evidence for the environmental support hypothesis (Craik, 1983). Knowledge, in turn, contributed to memory when cues facilitated its use, as in cued recall and verbal fluency. Furthermore, older adults displayed a greater relationship between knowledge and cued recall performance than did younger adults, whereas both age groups applied knowledge to verbal fluency performance. This suggests that when a memory task allows for, but does not necessitate, the use of knowledge, older adults can successfully support memory performance through the increased verbal abilities that often accompany ageing.

REFERENCES

Allaire, J. C., & Marsiske, M. (2002). Well- and ill-defined measures of everyday cognition: Relationship to older adults' intellectual ability and functional status. *Psychology and Aging, 17,* 101–115.

Anderson, J. R., Bothell, D., Lebiere, C., & Matessa, M. (1998a). An integrated theory of list memory. *Journal of Memory and Language, 38,* 341–380.

Anderson, N. D., Craik, F. I. M., & Naveh-Benjamin, M. (1998b). The attentional demands of encoding and retrieval in younger and older adults: I. Evidence from divided attention costs. *Psychology and Aging, 13,* 405–423.

Anstey, K. J., Hofer, S. M., & Luszcz, M. A. (2003). Cross-sectional and longitudinal patterns of dedifferentiation in late-life cognitive and sensory function: The effects of age, ability, attrition, and occasion of measurement. *Journal of Experimental Psychology: General, 132,* 470–487.

Babcock, R. L., Laguna, K. D., & Roesch, S. C. (1997). A comparison of the factor structure of processing speed for younger and older adults: Testing the assumption of measurement equivalence across age groups. *Psychology and Aging*, *12*, 268–276.

Baddeley, A. D. (1986). *Working memory*. New York: Oxford University Press.

Baddeley, A. D. (1996). The concept of working memory. In S. E. Gathercole (Ed.), *Models of short-term memory* (pp. 1–27). Hove, UK: Psychology Press.

Balinsky, B. (1941). An analysis of the mental factors of various age groups from nine to sixty. *Genetic Psychology Monographs*, *23*, 191–234.

Baltes, P. B., & Staudinger, U. M. (2000). Wisdom: A metaheuristic (pragmatic) to orchestrate mind and virtue toward excellence. *American Psychologist*, *55*, 122–136.

Baltes, P. B., Staudinger, U. M., Maercker, A., & Smith, J. (1995). People nominated as wise: A comparative study of wisdom-related knowledge. *Psychology and Aging*, *10*, 155–166.

Bentler, P. M., & Bonett, D. G. (1980). Significance tests and goodness-of-fit in the analysis of covariance structures. *Psychological Bulletin*, *88*, 588–600.

Bollen, K. A. (1989). *Structural equations with latent variables*. New York: John Wiley & Sons.

Browne, M. W., & Cudeck, R. (1993). Alternative ways of assessing model fit. In K. A. Bollen & J. S. Long (Eds.), *Testing structural equation models* (pp. 136–162). Newbury Park, CA: Sage.

Bryan, J., & Luszcz, M. A. (2000). Measurement of executive function: Consideration for detecting adult age differences. *Journal of Clinical and Experimental Neuropsychology*, *22*, 40–55.

Cabeza, R. (2002). Hemispheric asymmetry reduction in older adults: The HAROLD model. *Psychology and Aging*, *17*, 85–100.

Charness, N. (2000). Can aquired knowledge compensate for age-related declines in cognitive efficiency? In S. H. Qualls & N. Abeles (Eds.), *Psychology and the aging revolution: How we adapt to longer life* (pp. 99–117). Washington, DC: American Psychological Association.

Charness, N., & Bosman, E. A. (1990). Expertise and aging: Life in the lab. In T. M. Hess (Ed.), *Aging and cognition: Knowledge organization and utilization* (pp. 343–385). Oxford: North-Holland.

Cohen, J. D., MacWhinney, B., Flatt, M., & Provost, J. (1993). PsyScope: A new graphic interactive environment for designing psychology experiments. *Behavioral Research Methods, Instruments, and Computers*, *25*, 257–271.

Craik, F. I. M. (1983). On the transfer of information from temporary to permanent memory. *Philosophical Transactions of the Royal Society of London*, *B302*, 341–359.

Craik, F. I. M., & Anderson, N. D. (1999). Applying cognitive research to problems of aging. In D. Gopher & A. Koriat (Eds.), *Attention and performance XVII: Cognitive regulation of performance: Interaction of theory and application* (pp. 583–615). Cambridge, MA: The MIT Press.

Craik, F. I. M., & Byrd, M. (1982). Aging and cognitive deficits: The role of attentional resources. In F. I. M. Craik & S. Trehub (Eds.), *Aging and cognitive processes* (pp. 191–211). New York: Plenum.

Craik, F. I. M., Byrd, M., & Swanson, J. M. (1987). Patterns of memory loss in three elderly samples. *Psychology and Aging*, *2*, 79–86.

Davidson, P. S. R., & Glisky, E. L. (2002). Neuropsychological correlates of recollection and familiarity in normal aging. *Cognitive, Affective, and Behavioral Neuroscience*, *2*, 174–186.

Daneman, M., & Carpenter, P. A. (1980). Individual differences in working memory and reading. *Journal of Verbal Learning & Verbal Behavior*, *19*, 450–466.

Engle, R. W., Kane, M. J., & Tuholski, S. W. (1999a). Individual differences in working memory capacity and what they tell us about controlled attention, general fluid intelligence and functions of the prefrontal cortex. In A. Miyake & P. Shah (Eds.), *Models of working memory* (pp. 102–134). Cambridge: Cambridge University Press.

Engle, R. W., Tuholski, S. W., Laughlin, J. E., & Conway, A. R. A. (1999b). Working memory, short-term memory, and general fluid intelligence: A latent-variable approach. *Journal of Experimental Psychology: General*, *128*, 309–331.

Glisky, E. L., Polster, M. R., & Routhieaux, B. C. (1995). Double dissociation between item and source memory. *Neuropsychology*, *9*, 229–235.

Glisky, E. L., Rubin, S. R., & Davidson, P. S. R. (2001). Source memory in older adults: An encoding or retrieval problem? *Journal of Experimental Psychology: Learning, Memory, and Cognition*, *27*, 1131–1146.

Hambrick, D. Z., Salthouse, T. A., & Meinz, E. J. (1999). Predictors of crossword puzzle proficiency and moderators of age–cognition relations. *Journal of Experimental Psychology: General*, *128*, 131–164.

Henkel, L. A., Johnson, M. K., & De Leonardis, D. M. (1998). Aging and source monitoring: Cognitive processes and neuropsychological correlates. *Journal of Experimental Psychology: General*, *127*, 251–268.

Hertzog, C. (1987). Applications of structural equation models in gerontological research. In K. W. Schaie (Ed.), *Annual review of gerontology and geriatrics* (Vol. 7, pp. 265–293). New York: Springer.

Hess, T. M., & Auman, C. (2001). Aging and social expertise: The impact of trait-diagnostic information on impressions of others. *Psychology and Aging, 16,* 497–510.

Hess, T. M., Flannagan, D. A., & Tate, C. S. (1993). Aging and memory for schematically vs taxonomically organized verbal materials. *Journal of Gerontology: Psychological Sciences, 48,* 37–44.

Jacoby, L. L. (1999). Ironic effects of repetition: Measuring age-related differences in memory. *Journal of Experimental Psychology: Learning, Memory, and Cognition, 25,* 3–22.

Jennings, J. M., & Jacoby, L. L. (1997). An opposition procedure for detecting age-related deficits in recollection: Telling effects of repetition. *Psychology and Aging, 12,* 352–361.

Johnston, W. A., Dark, V. J., & Jacoby, L. L. (1985). Perceptual fluency and recognition judgments. *Journal of Experimental Psychology: Learning, Memory, and Cognition, 11,* 3–11.

Jöreskog, K. G. (1971). Simultaneous factor analysis in several populations. *Psychometrika, 36,* 409–426.

Jöreskog, K. G., & Sörbom, D. (2001). LISREL 8 (Version 8.30) [Computer software]. Chicago: Scientific Software International.

Kane, M. J., Bleckley, M. K., Conway, A. R., & Engle, R. W. (2001). A controlled-attention view of working memory capacity. *Journal of Experimental Psychology: General, 130,* 169–183.

Kausler, D. H. (1994). *Learning and memory in normal aging.* San Diego, CA: Academic Press.

Lezak, M. D. (1995). *Neuropsychological assessment* (3rd ed.). New York: Oxford University Press.

Lindenberger, U., & Baltes, P. B. (1997). Intellectual functioning in old and very old age: Cross-sectional results from the Berlin Aging Study. *Psychology and Aging, 12,* 410–432.

Loehlin, J. C. (1998). *Latent variable models* (3rd ed.). Mahwah, NJ: Lawrence Erlbaum Associates, Inc.

Mather, M., Johnson, M. K., & De Leonardis, D. M. (1999). Stereotype reliance in source monitoring: Age differences and neuropsychological test correlates. *Cognitive Neuropsychology, 16,* 437–458.

McElree, B., Dolan, P. O., & Jacoby, L. L. (1999). Isolating the contributions of familiarity and source information to item recognition: A time course analysis. *Journal of Experimental Psychology: Learning, Memory, and Cognition, 25,* 563–582.

Meinz, E. J., & Salthouse, T. A. (1998). The effects of age and experience on memory for visually presented music. *Journal of Gerontology: Psychological Sciences, 53,* 60–69.

Meyer, D. E., Glass, J. M., Mueller, S. T., Seymour, T. L., & Kieras, D. E. (2001). Executive-process interactive control: A unified computational theory for answering 20 questions (and more) about cognitive aging. *European Journal of Cognitive Psychology, 13,* 123–164.

Meyer, D. E., & Kieras, D. E. (1997). A computational theory of executive cognitive processes and multiple-task performance: Part 1. Basic mechanisms. *Psychological Review, 104,* 3–65.

Morrell, R. W., & Park, D. C. (1993). The effects of age, illustrations, and task variables on the performance of procedural assembly tasks. *Psychology and Aging, 8,* 389–399.

Naveh-Benjamin, M., Craik, F. I. M., & Ben-Shaul, L. (2002). Age-related differences in cued recall: Effects of support at encoding and retrieval. *Aging, Neuropsychology, & Cognition, 9,* 276–287.

Nelson, D. L., & McEvoy, C. L. (2002). How can the same type of prior knowledge both help and hinder recall? *Journal of Memory and Language, 46,* 652–663.

Nyberg, L., Maitland, S. B., Rönnlund, M., Bäckman, L., Dixon, R. A., Wahlin, A., & Nilsson, L.-G. (2003). Selective adult age differences in an age-invariant multifactor model of declarative memory. *Psychology and Aging, 18,* 149–160.

Park, D. C. (1992). Applied cognitive aging research. In F. I. M. Craik & T. A. Salthouse (Eds.), *The handbook of aging and cognition* (pp. 449–493). Hillsdale, NJ: Lawrence Erlbaum Associates, Inc.

Park, D. C., & Gutchess, A. H. (2000). Cognitive aging and every day life. In D. C. Park & N. Schwarz (Eds.), *Cognitive aging: A primer* (pp. 217–232). Philadelphia, PA: Psychology Press.

Park, D. C., Lautenschlager, G., Hedden, T., Davidson, N. S., Smith, A. D., & Smith, P. K. (2002). Models of visuo-spatial and verbal memory across the adult life span. *Psychology and Aging, 17,* 299–320.

Park, D. C., Smith, A. D., Dudley, W. N., & Lafronza, V. N. (1989). Effects of age and a divided attention task presented during encoding and retrieval on memory. *Journal of Experimental Psychology: Learning, Memory, and Cognition, 15,* 1185–1191.

Park, D. C., Smith, A. D., Lautenschlager, G., Earles, J. L., Frieske, D., Zwahr, M., & Gaines, C. L. (1996). Mediators of long-term memory performance across the adult life span. *Psychology and Aging, 11,* 621–637.

Parkin, A. J., Walter, B. M., & Hunkin, N. (1995). Relationships between normal aging, frontal lobe function, and memory for temporal and spatial information. *Neuropsychology, 9,* 304–312.

Rabbitt, P., & Lowe, C. (2000). Patterns of cognitive ageing. *Psychological Research, 63,* 308–316.

Rahhal, T. A., May, C. P., & Hasher, L. (2002). Truth and character: Sources that older adults can remember. *Psychological Science, 13,* 101–105.

Reuter-Lorenz, P. A. (2002). New visions of the aging mind and brain. *Trends in Cognitive Sciences, 6,* 394–400.

Rogers, W. A., Hertzog, C., & Fisk, A. D. (2000). An individual differences analysis of ability and strategy influences: Age-related differences in associative learning. *Journal of Experimental Psychology: Learning, Memory, and Cognition, 26,* 359–394.

Rosen, V. M., & Engle, R. W. (1997). The role of working memory capacity in retrieval. *Journal of Experimental Psychology: General, 126,* 211–227.

Salthouse, T. A. (1992). Influence of processing speed on adult age differences in working memory. *Acta Psychologica, 79,* 155–170.

Salthouse, T. A. (1993a). Speed and knowledge as determinants of adult age differences in verbal tasks. *Journal of Gerontology: Psychological Sciences, 48,* 29–36.

Salthouse, T. A. (1993b). Speed mediation of adult age differences in cognition. *Developmental Psychology, 29,* 722–738.

Salthouse, T. A. (1996). The processing-speed theory of adult age differences in cognition. *Psychological Review, 103,* 403–428.

Salthouse, T. A., & Babcock, R. L. (1991). Decomposing adult age differences in working memory. *Developmental Psychology, 27,* 763–776.

Schaie, K. W. (1994). The course of adult intellectual development. *American Psychologist, 49,* 304–313.

Schaie, K. W. (1996). *Intellectual development in adulthood: The Seattle Longitudinal Study.* New York: Cambridge University Press.

Shah, P., & Miyake, A. (1996). The separability of working memory resources for spatial thinking and language processing: An individual differences approach. *Journal of Experimental Psychology: General, 125,* 4–27.

Shipley, W. C. (1986). *Shipley Institute of Living Scale.* Los Angeles, CA: Western Psychological Services.

Spencer, W. D., & Raz, N. (1995). Differential effect of aging on memory for content and context: A meta-analysis. *Psychology and Aging, 10,* 527–539.

Spreen, O., & Benton, A. L. (1977). *Neurosensory Center Comprehensive Examination for Aphasia* (NCCEA) (Rev. ed.). Victoria, BC: University of Victoria Neuropsychology Laboratory.

Tanaka, J. S. (1993). Multifaceted conceptions of fit in structural equation models. In K. A. Bollen & J. S. Long (Eds.), *Testing structural equation models* (pp. 10–39). Newbury Park, CA: Sage.

Thorndike, E. L., & Lorge, I. (1944). *The teacher's word book of 30,000 words.* New York: Teachers College, Columbia University.

Verhaeghen, P., & Salthouse, T. A. (1997). Meta-analyses of age–cognition relations in adulthood: Estimates of linear and nonlinear age effects and structural models. *Psychological Bulletin, 122,* 231–249.

Wechsler, D. (1997). *Wechsler Adult Intelligence Scale* (3rd ed.). San Antonio, TX: Psychological Corporation.

Yonelinas, A. P., & Jacoby, L. L. (1994). Dissociations of processes in recognition memory: Effects of interference and of response speed. *Canadian Journal of Experimental Psychology, 48,* 516–534.

PrEview proof published online 7 July 2004

Subject index